HIGH PRAISE FOR VICT...
BESTSELLING 1...
OF HIS MOTHER...

RAIN OF GOLD

"A BIG BOOK . . . A STORY THAT DESERVES
TO BE TOLD . . . EXTREMELY MOVING . . .
A COMPELLING NARRATIVE."
—*The Washington Post Book World*

"A TRIUMPH . . . *RAIN OF GOLD* IS ONE OF
THE BEST—and the most American—books of this
or any other year." —*USA Today*

"A GRAND AND VIVID HISTORY . . . The
characters are keenly drawn . . . often I felt like a
family member watching from a corner stool."
—*The New York Times*

"A MAJOR WORK . . . affirms life in all its tragic
and comic dimensions." —*San Diego Tribune*

"VILLASEÑOR IS A BORN STORYTELLER . . .
an inspirational epic full of wild adventure,
bootlegging, young love, miracles, tragedies, murder
and triumph over cultural barriers."
—*Publishers Weekly*

"A MULTIFACETED BRILLIANT STORY OF
TRIUMPH . . . an astounding tale of a family
odyssey from pre-revolutionary Mexico to the barrios
of Carlsbad, California." —*The Denver Post*

OTHER WORKS BY
VICTOR VILLASEÑOR

FICTION
Macho!

NONFICTION
Jury: The People vs. Juan Corona
Rain of Gold
Walking Stars
Snow Goose: Global Thanksgiving

SCREENPLAYS
The Ballad of Gregorio Cortez

WILD STEPS OF HEAVEN

VICTOR VILLASEÑOR

Delta
Trade Paperbacks

A Delta Book
Published by
Dell Publishing
a division of
Bantam Doubleday Dell Publishing Group, Inc.
1540 Broadway
New York, New York 10036

The trademark Delta® is registered in the U.S. Patent and Trademark Office and in other countries.

ISBN 0-385-31569-4

Reprinted by arrangement with Delacorte Press

Manufactured in the United States of America
Published simultaneously in Canada

March 1997

10 9 8 7 6 5

BVG

This second volume of my family's ongoing story is dedicated to Barbara and our two sons, David and Joseph. The background sounds of *la familia* as I'm busy writing is the most beautiful and reassuring music I can possibly ever want to hear. Let's keep reaching for the stars, little *familia*. Love you always. Your sounds . . . are what feed *mi corazón* and, yes, my very soul.

PREFACE

Originally, in 1975, when I first started interviewing *mi papá* and *mi mamá,* so I could write our family's story, it was always my intent to start with my father's people first, because my father was older than my mother, so naturally his story came first. But then my father's story alone grew into four hundred pages, and was so wild and huge and, well, incredible, that it overpowered the story of my mother's people. And, also, at that time, I just didn't have the writing tools or enough faith in God to bring off my father's story.

You see, my mother's family were basically good, honest, hardworking people who had their shortcomings and hardships like all other people. But on the other hand, the story of my father's people was filled with so much rage and violence and yet this incredible faith in God that I just knew that if I could get my father's stories right, they could affect our entire human predicament. For the story of my father's *familia* was the story of all Mexico, and the story of Mexico was the story of the last five hundred years of European dominance all over our globe.

I polished the four hundred pages of my father's people for years, but I just kept getting consumed by the fire of my father's story: my grandmother—a small, wise, beautiful Indian woman

—coming from the heart-center of the earth; and my grandfather—a tall, handsome European of Spanish royal blood—coming with all the arrogance of his world-conquering culture.

These, then, are the pages that had been originally intended to kick off the three volumes of *Rain of Gold.* And, I'll tell you, these pages have forced me to the limits of my understanding of what it is to be human. For not only were my grandparents at love and at war with each other culturally and personally, but they were also from a region of Mexico where the earth itself is red, and the people from the area of Los Altos de Jalisco pride themselves in being rough and tough. This region is where tequila was first invented, and supposedly the *mariachis* come from here, too. People from this area of Mexico like to think of themselves as being great horsemen, wild, and they have a certain cockiness, thinking that the earth is still young and the stars above speak to them.

And yet, even though I knew all of this, some of the stories that my father told me about his people were still so violent and crazy that at times it was difficult for me to believe *mi papá* or to comprehend the world he came from.

Take, for instance, the story that my father told me about my grandfather, Don Juan Villaseñor, coming home drunk one night on horseback. My grandfather stopped by a little inn to have one more drink *para el estribo,* for the stirrup, before going home. But the man who owned the inn was a good friend of his, so he refused to serve my grandfather, telling him that he was already too drunk and he might fall off his horse and get hurt going up the mountain.

"Well, your grandfather became so enraged," my father said to me, laughing *con gusto,* "that he drew his gun and took a few shots at his friend, missing him, then he roped a hay wagon, set it on fire, and ran it into the man's house, burning it to the ground."

Hearing this story, I was shocked and said, "But, Papa, how can you tell me this story with such *gusto?* This is awful!"

"So," said my father, still grinning, "life can be awful. So what?"

"But, Papa," I said, "to burn a man's house down because he sees you're drunk and tries to help you so you don't get hurt, is crazy."

"Bull!" said my father, laughing. "What was crazy was for that man to try to talk sense to a wild man who's drunk and armed! That stupid innkeeper should have just served my father his drink and had enough faith in God to let life be life! For as my mother always said, 'Each one of us has his own destiny to live, and it isn't for little, scared nobodies to interfere with the grand plans of the Almighty!' "

And so here you have it, my father's story, filled with love and fire, rage and hate, and yet the profound understanding that everything is all right, if only we have enough faith in the eternal goodness of God and life, *la vida.*

VICTOR E. VILLASEÑOR
Rancho Villaseñor
Oceanside, CA

ONE

GRANDFATHER

(A TIME OF MALE CONSCIOUSNESS
that began about 26,000 B.C., 20,000 years
after language started. A time of mindful
creation, of volcanic-like birthing; a time of
bursting forth from the female womb of
dream-like possibilities with the deliberate,
measured male intent of becoming.)

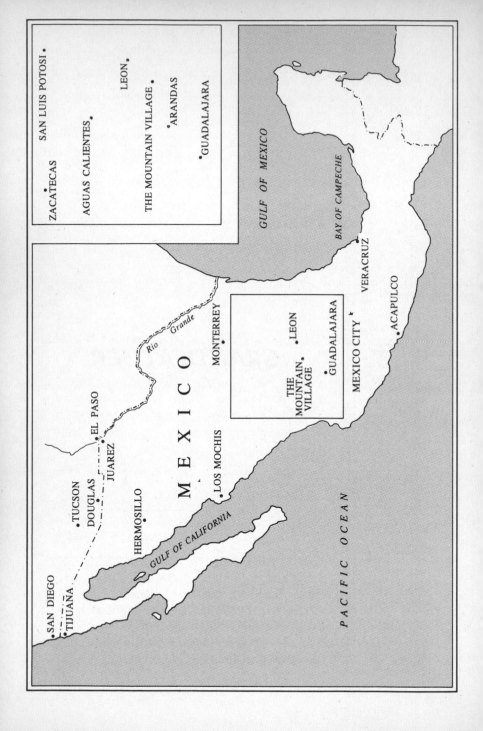

Way back, in the beginning, when men and women still danced to the wild steps of heaven, there lived a great serpent right over there by that *barranca,* just beyond that little canyon. The serpent had already eaten several small children, a couple of baby pigs, and terrified innumerable grown men and women; and so, for months now, the whole village lived in constant terror.

The serpent was huge, could stand up as tall as a man on horseback, and was so heavy of body that it was said that when she threw herself at a human being, she would crush the person, rendering him or her senseless with just one mighty blow. Oh, *la gente* of the village just didn't know what to do. They were scared to death to go outside at night or even afraid to fall asleep in their homes because, who knew, maybe the great serpent would come to their very house and crush it while they slept and would eat them all alive.

People began to wear necklaces of garlic, and hot chili pep-

pers about their waists. The garlic was to ward off the evil spirits
and the hot peppers were in case the serpent caught you and ate
you. Then, hopefully, her asshole would burn so badly as she
crapped you out thirty-seven days later, that she'd never eat
another Mexican again as long as she lived because she'd figure
they were all too hot.

Oh, it was truly awful. Only a handful of people had actually
seen the serpent so far and yet she was already the biggest living
reality of all the people of the entire region. Some began to
equate the serpent to the Devil himself. Others said it was the
end of the world, and Judgment Day was close at hand. But still
others, with a little more room for humor in their old souls, said
that maybe the serpent was a sign from God, announcing the
return to the Garden of Eden. And this time, different than the
last, the fate of man and woman wouldn't be done by a sneaky
little male snake with an apple, but by a big *macho* female snake,
a toda madre, from Los Altos de Jalisco. Then, once and for all,
the whole world would know the obvious truth, which was that
the true *paraíso* of the earth had always been in *Méjico,* now and
forever!

And so one day here came Grandfather on horseback, nursing the biggest *cruda,* a mean-raw-hangover, that he'd ever had
in all his life. He was having trouble staying on his horse, and
every few miles he'd have to stop and lean over to vomit. His
name was Juan Jesus Villaseñor, and the week before, he'd
taken a herd of cattle down to the lowlands with his four older
sons, Alejo, Teodoro, Jesus and Jose, to the railhead and sold
them for a damn good price. Then, to celebrate the fine deal
he'd made, Grandfather took the three older boys, Alejo, Jesus,
and Teodoro, on a wild drinking *parranda* all through the city of
Leon, which lasted three days and nights. Jose, the youngest
and looking too Indian to really be a good drinking man in
Grandfather's opinion, was given the money to hold for them
and told to behave himself and to guard the money with his life.
He was also to keep a sharp eye out on them, so that when Jose

got older he'd know what not to do as they drank themselves into glorious, blissful oblivion.

Don Juan also gave little Jose his Colt .45, the one that he'd brought back from Albuquerque when he'd gone up to the United States on business a few years back. Oh, that had also been a fine Christian celebration, taking Grandfather from El Paso, Texas, to Las Cruces, New Mexico, and then on to Albuquerque and Santa Fe, where he'd settled in for a final week.

Giving his .45 to the boy, Don Juan said, "You are my little *indio*, my little dark, wonderful son, and if anything happens to me or your brothers, then you race back to our beloved mountains as fast as you can and give that money to your mother, the love of my life, and you keep that .45 for yourself and grow up to be a man. Understand? You're a little man now, and with this gun no man can walk on your shadow, pretending to be superior just because he's bigger or older." He embraced little Jose in a big *abrazo*, kissing him before going off to get drunk with his three older, fair-headed sons.

But now, several days later, Juan Villaseñor rode alone. After the big *parranda*, he'd sent all four of his sons on ahead, because there were certain things that a man had to do alone when he went into town, and it was best that none of his sons knew about these matters until they were much older and married with children themselves. Because, in Don Juan's opinion, a married man with children had to sometimes be the loneliest man on earth, and so it was best for the young people to never realize this awful truth of life until they were married, had children and it was too damn late for them to back out of normal life.

"Yes, this is definitely one of the biggest secrets of life," said Juan to himself, stopping to throw up once more. "And ignorance, only complete ignorance, can get a man through the whole catastrophe!"

Juan wondered why it was that he was always so brilliant, so lucid of mind, when he was drunk or nursing a *cruda* but then, when he sobered up, it all just disappeared. And at that moment, at the very instant when he was leaning over vomiting his guts out, was when he suddenly felt a presence coming at him with all the evil powers of hell itself.

Juan glanced up and his tired, weary horse glanced up, too; and there, no more than twenty feet away from them, came the biggest, meanest-looking snake in all the world. It stood eight feet tall, at least, and it was flying, dodging, darting, hissing, as it came, and had an upper body so huge that Don Juan thought its head alone outweighed a newborn calf.

"Oh, Lord God!" screamed Juan, spinning his horse about and bolting off in a run. "What have You done, dear God? Sent me the Devil himself?" But then, feeling the blood come racing to his liquor-soaked brain, Juan slid his horse to a stop and gripped his forehead. "I'm too sick to run," he said. "Oh, Lord God, what a time to test me! Jesus!"

He turned his horse back around. Seeing the snake still coming at them, the big black gelding went wild with fear, twisting and rearing and trying to run away. Don Juan's head jerked and bounced in awful pain. He closed his eyes, trying to clear his head, but his eyes were watering too much and he felt terrible. Then, reopening his eyes, he couldn't believe it; now the serpent didn't just have one huge head, but two big giant heads and three pair of eyes as the monster came in to devour him and his horse.

But Juan didn't care. He was too sick to run, and his tequila-soaked brain was throbbing all through his head. "Hell, I come from kings!" he said. "From a thousand years of the greatest horsemen the earth has ever produced, and no no-good, giant, two-headed son-of-a-bitch serpent-snake is going to ruin my tequila-drunk! I don't care if you are the Devil himself; I'm a Villaseñor, and no Villaseñor has ever run in fear since the days we served the kings of Spain! Here I come, you two-headed, six-eyed ugly monster!" And Juan went to draw his Colt .45 and charge the snake head-on, firing as he came, but when he went for his gun, he found that it wasn't there. Suddenly, sobering up, he remembered that he'd given the gun to his little son Jose, along with all the money.

And here came the monstrous snake—eight feet tall and dodging, darting, flying over the brush and rocks. Pushing back his great *sombrero,* Don Juan let out a second scream, *"¡Aquí viene un charro de* Los Altos de Jalisco, *cabrón! ¡Borracho y con hambre!"* Here comes a Mexican cowboy from the highlands of Jalisco, you bastard—drunk and starving! And Juan Jesus now put the spurs to his great gelding, charging the mighty serpent.

All this time, from a distant hilltop, little Jose Maria Villa-señor, ten years old and riding a little buckskin mare, helplessly watched his father. When their father had told the four boys to go on home ahead of him, the three older boys had all known what this was about, and so they'd told Jose to obey their father's words and go on home. But they themselves, on the other hand, were already grown men, too, and so they'd taken off across the city of Leon, Guanajuato, to another whorehouse. Being left alone, Jose hadn't known what to do. He had all the money and his father's Colt .45 and so, finally, with much fear and apprehension, he'd headed for home, talking to no one and being very careful with the saddlebags full of gold coins.

Getting to the foothills, where he felt safe because from here on he knew every inch of the countryside, Jose made camp, pastured his little mare, and waited for his father and brothers. His father was the first one to show up two days later, and he was so drunk and singing so terribly off-key that Jose decided to trail him and not present himself and embarrass him.

But now Jose realized that he'd made a horrible mistake, for there was his father on the opposite hillside in mortal combat with the biggest, meanest-looking snake the earth had ever produced, and he was totally unarmed. Jose watched in complete terror as his father now charged the monstrous snake, hitting it with the gelding's chest. The horse was terrified and began to buck, trying to throw his crazy rider and get away from the

monster. But Don Juan was one of the greatest horsemen of all
the land, and he stayed with that bucking horse like a bear on
honey.

The snake was up again and slashing out at Juan Jesus, trying
to knock him off his horse so it could devour him alive. Juan
rode the bucking horse into a thicket and reached up, tearing a
broken limb off a tree. Jose couldn't believe what his eyes saw
next. For, instead of using the stout limb on his horse and
racing away toward home, his father—a huge, six-foot red-
headed man of pure Spanish blood—now pulled in his big black
gelding, whirled the horse around and around in a spinning
fury, completely confusing the animal's frightened brain, and
then he bolted the well-trained gelding right at the monstrous
dragon, shoving the limb into the snake's mouth as he raced by
con un grito de gusto! For what could be greater here on earth
than for a good Christian to be in mortal combat with the Devil
himself?

The serpent gagged, momentarily losing all power. Now Jose
watched his father spin his horse around and around again,
unleash his long *reata*, and come racing by, rope swinging,
whirling, and he lassoed the huge-headed monster, jerking him
to the ground with all the power of his thousand-pound gelding.
The snake began to thrash and scream, hiss and leap, roll and
spin, trying to get free and kill this crazy man who'd dare fight
him. But Juan had already dallied his *reata* about his saddle
horn, and the wooden horn was smoking fire as he dragged and
fished and pulled and jerked the mighty snake through the
brush and boulders.

Jose was transfixed. Never in his wildest dreams had he ever
imagined such bravery, such horsemanship! Why, his father
was, indeed, a god who'd come down from the heavens to show
all humankind what a real *charro*-cowboy could do, even on his
worst day. Jose felt his whole body turn cold as ice, realizing
that in his veins ran the blood of such a mighty god.

Jose now followed behind his father, too much in awe to get

any closer, as Juan Jesus dragged the still-thrashing monster all the way to their village. There the people came out of their homes, trembling in cold fear, and they made the sign of the cross over themselves again and again, giving witness to the terrible snake that had been holding them all in evil hostage.

A couple of the strongest woodsmen came out with their axes and chopped the head off the monstrous snake; yet it was said that it was a full two days before the snake's eyes closed and the great long body stopped jerking. On the third day, the priest came and gave blessing to the community, and people came from as far away as three towns just to feast their eyes on the serpent's great head and long, heavy body. The world had been saved once more, the priest said. The Devil had lost. Once again, God had given a good Christian the power to overcome the fears of darkness.

A barrel of the finest tequila was donated by the local tequila makers, and a great celebration began. Don Juan Jesus was the hero of the day, and every man, woman, and child came to give him honor. Don Juan had one of his finest steers slaughtered, and everyone ate for days. By the time Alejo, Jesus, and Teodoro rode up, their father was, indeed, being called the savior *de Los Altos*. But the three boys had a hard time comprehending the incredible truth of what had really come to pass.

And Jose never told anyone—not even his own father—that he had given witness to the whole thing. For how could he? To talk about it would mean that a human being could speak the tongue of the gods. And Jose could no more figure out how to put into words all these emotions that he was feeling for his beloved father, than he could fly with the angels. Why, in his mind, he'd seen God Himself, the Ruler of the universe, come down upon the earth that day and take on the form of a *charro* through the body of his father, Don Juan Villaseñor, as he'd fought the battle of all battles against the Devil himself.

And so Jose kept silent—loving, adoring his father from afar; this man, this god, this hero of his entire known-world.

1

And so, just before the Mexican Revolution of 1910 burst forth all over Mexico, it was a time of gods, a time of serpents, and, yes, a time of love.

It was said that the day her cruel and ambitious husband died, the angels of love came down from heaven to visit her. For no other explanation could be given for the extraordinary beauty that came to the young widow overnight.

For years, Mariposa had been married to the honest, hard-working Camacho, who had great, strong arms and three sturdy burros. He was the local coal-maker and he cut down old trees and built tepee-like piles of wood, covering them with long green timbers and mud, then set a small fire at the bottom of each pile to smoke-dry the wood for days, non-stop, until it was coal-like.

He was young and ambitious and worked long, hard hours and yet each night he still had plenty of power to mount his young wife again and again and try to put her with child. Besides having a good business going, Camacho envisioned himself having many sons and building up a coal-wood business that would stretch all the way to Guadalajara, a huge city three days away by horseback, where lots and lots of good people needed hard, coal-like wood for smokeless cooking. But fate was difficult with Camacho, and no matter how often he mounted his good young wife, no child would fill her belly.

Camacho began to drink and yell a lot at night and blame Mariposa for his misfortune. He began to envision that people were laughing at him behind his back, and so he'd get into fights and bloody many people's faces. The years passed, and Mariposa became pale, withdrawn, and more plain than ever. Finally, it was said that she even began to go to church every day, along with the old women and lost widows.

Then as fate would have it, six months to the day before the Father Sun gave birth to a Baby Shooting Sun with His Long Tail on the 17th of January, 1910, Camacho chopped open his left leg, up high in his crotch right next to his organ, with a new double-bladed ax from the United States, and he bled to death on the spot.

Hearing about her poor husband's death that evening, it was said that Mariposa got all dressed in black to go to the church to mourn over Camacho's body, where it had been brought in to rest by other woodsmen. But, going out her door, she realized that she wasn't crying like a good wife was supposed to do. So Mariposa went back inside her home and took ten large onions out of the straw basket and began to cut them up so that her eyes would cry. But no matter how much she cut, her eyes would not cry. She then poured out the whole basket of onions and worked for well over an hour, cutting and cutting, chopping and chopping, until finally her eyes began to weep. She looked at herself in the mirror before she went out, and she felt proud of how red and all weepy her eyes were. Still, there was nothing she could do to stop the song of joy that kept leaping out of her throat and filling the room with sound, for she was as happy as a bird after a long, cold storm, singing from the treetops.

Finally, Mariposa felt she was ready, and she put on a long

black shawl over her head and went to the church and cried and cried over her husband's dead body. For, truly, she had loved Camacho very much until the day that they married and he'd taken her off to the fine house that he'd built for them and begun to mount her like a tree that he was chopping down with one of his sharp axes. Not once—not one single time—in all the years that they'd been married had he ever touched her with a slow, gentle hand and asked her what it was that she wanted or what she was thinking or what dreams had she had that day while he was gone for the day in the woods. No, his mind was always filled with his business, his worth, and their house and their children-to-be and the great future that they were sure to have someday.

Most of the men and women who came that evening to the church to mourn the good, honest, hardworking coal-maker's death were very impressed with how freely Mariposa wept over her husband's dead body. But a couple of the wiser, older housewives were not. For they could smell the onions on the young widow's clothes, and they well knew the secret remedies that good women had been using since the beginning of time in order to survive in this world of men's foolish pretenses. And, also, as Doña Margarita Villaseñor and a few older women would later say, "even as early as that evening, many of us women could already see that no matter how much the poor young woman wept and dried her red, swollen eyes, the song of love's wondrous freedom was being born within her very soul."

At the funeral the next day, the men began to flock to the young widow like bees to a budding flower. Overnight, this plain-looking woman had blossomed into a beauty. And often it had been seen that many a woman becomes stronger and happier once an abusive husband has passed away, but never had anyone witnessed such a miracle of transformation as this. For Mariposa was now no ordinary woman; no, she was an absolute angel who could move hearts by simply doing the most ordinary of chores. Like now, when she went down to the plaza to draw water from the well; this was no small daily task. No, it was a wondrous dance of movement and posture, and the song that sprang from her heart as she worked was so beautiful that it drove men wild. Oh, within a month the fame of her beauty grew so great that it spread to towns two days away by horseback, and suitors began to present themselves to Mariposa by the dozens. But the poor, crazy fools never realized that what the good widow really wanted more than anything else in all the world was simply the freedom to sing and play by herself at the game of living life, *la vida*.

But then, in the third month of her new life, Mariposa found that even though she loved doing everything for herself, she couldn't. And so she asked the women whom she saw at church each day if they knew of some man who could help her around the house with her firewood and other things and, yet, would also have the respectful decency to keep his distance.

Instantly, Doña Margarita Villaseñor asked the young widow to walk her home, and on the pathway leading away from the holy church, Doña Margarita confided in the young woman that, yes, she knew of such a man.

"My son Jose," said Doña Margarita.

"Oh, the one who lives with—" The young widow stopped her words.

But Doña Margarita was not offended and she completed the young widow's sentence. "Yes, the one who lives with the animals."

"Well, fine," said the young woman, not quite knowing what else to say. "I've never spoken to him, but I have seen him around. Please ask Jose to stop by and I'll speak with him."

"It is done," said Doña Margarita.

Walking home alone, Mariposa wondered about this young man, Jose Maria Villaseñor. The story went that Jose lived with the animals because, years ago, when he'd still only been a child of twelve, his father, the big, handsome, red-headed Juan Villaseñor, had banished him from his home. And this banishment had happened the day that Don Juan had come home with a great new stallion that he'd purchased from a ranch in Guadalajara that was well known for having the finest horses in all the Americas.

Getting home that day, Don Juan Villaseñor tied the four-white-stockinged stallion up outside of the *ramada* of his home and went inside to tell his family. For years, Don Juan had been saving up enough money to buy this horse, and now he wanted all his loved ones to hurry out and see the fine animal that he'd purchased. Because with this great stallion they, the Villaseñors, would now have some of the finest horses of all the region—horses so good that men would come from as far away as Zacatecas, Sonora, Texas, Arizona, and New Mexico to purchase yearlings.

"Hurry!" shouted Don Juan, entering the house. *"Pronto!* Come out and see the wonderful horse I managed to buy! He's a dream! Not just beautiful, but so intelligent and fast and curious about everything new that he'd see on the trail as I rode him home through the mountains, that I still can't quite figure him out yet. Hurry! Come on, everyone! *Pronto! Pronto!"*

Don Juan was so excited, just bubbling with joy, that everyone rushed outside immediately—Doña Margarita, thirteen of their children, and half a dozen cousins. But what they saw when they got outside wasn't just the stallion, but little Juan as well, the youngest Villaseñor, who hadn't learned how to walk yet, and Juan was hugging the great horse's hind leg.

Everyone froze in terrible fear, realizing that just one move, one kick, and the stallion was sure to kill little Juan. But little Juan had no fear, and he was laughing and pulling at the horse's hind white stocking, jerking and pulling at it with all the joy in the world. No one knew what to do. The great horse was standing perfectly still, ears back, trying to figure out what was being done to him, but he was trembling with anticipation and ready to explode.

Don Juan drew his Colt .45. "Move back," he said to everyone. "I'm going to have to shoot Four White Stockings to save the child!"

Don Juan took aim and the people began to make the sign of the cross over themselves. But then, before Don Juan could shoot the horse between the eyes, the boy—Jose—stepped forward.

"No, Papa, please!" he said. "If you shoot, then the horse is sure to kill Juanito. Let me talk to him. I talk horse; you know that."

"No," said Don Juan, "keep back, Jose. You don't know this stallion. I, who've ridden him for three days, am still baffled by him."

"Papa," insisted Jose, "if he's as intelligent as you say, then he'll know I mean him no harm. And remember, a dying horse can still kick."

And saying this, Jose quickly approached the great horse with all the confidence of young David approaching Goliath. Don Juan saw and lowered his revolver. Everyone stood perfectly still, not even breathing, they were so frightened. Inch by inch, Jose moved closer to the huge, well-fed, well-muscled stallion— a beautiful red sorrel with a coat as smooth and shiny as the finest silk.

"Ooooooo, boy. Ooooooo, boy," purrrrred Jose softly, gently, as he crept closer, step by step, looking the great animal in the eyes, never once taking his eyes off of the stallion's, even for a split second.

And the great horse flipped one ear toward Jose, keeping the other ear pinpointed on Juanito, who kept laughing and pulling and jerking on his hind leg. As Jose got closer and closer, the huge horse began to tremble less and less, to not heave in big-belly-jerking breaths anymore, but to calm himself and breathe more regularly as he watched this remarkable little skinny boy approach him.

Then Jose was close, and Four White Stockings flipped both of his ears directly at him, rolling his great dark blue eyes at the boy as he now held, ready to explode, to leap and kick and fight for his freedom if anyone or anything so much as touched him. But then, contrary to everything the animal was feeling, he could now sense that this boy's hand was moving toward him so gently. So very, very gently. Then the touch, the very first contact that he, the great horse, felt on his shiny coat from this small boy was so smooth, so slow and gentle, that the great animal melted. He melted, and every inch of his entire thousand-pound body began to concentrate down tight on the smooth, easy feeling of this boy's gentle touch. Jose, who'd made tame many wild horses before, continued stroking the great fire-red stallion on the neck—not the head, not near the eyes, which would be obtrusive between two individuals who didn't know one another yet, but on the neck—up by the mane, where the stallion could watch the boy's movements with his great large eyes and feel, feel, feel, with all the power of his being.

And so the first contact was done, complete, and now Jose spoke to the horse again, gently, softly, but with confidence and substance, too. And it was all like magic to the great animal, and he relaxed even more. Quickly, smoothly, Jose now kept cooo-cooo cooo-ing to the stallion like the turtledove of love . . . as he moved his hand down the animal's great neck, past his mighty chest, along his back—being careful not to come near any of the tickling areas—and then to the horse's rump and down his hind leg, where Jose suddenly grabbed little Juan and leaped away.

The great horse, who'd forgotten all about the little pulling nuisance on his hind leg, now suddenly remembered everything, and as he saw them both leap away, he exploded! Jumping five feet straight up into the air, gigantic muscles knotted with all that bottled-up fear that he'd been feeling.

No, the great horse hadn't really wanted to hurt the little infant—whom he'd known didn't mean him any harm—but the child's behavior had been driving him absolutely crazy with confusion, and so now the huge, powerful animal was rearing and kicking, exploding with power, until Jose now came back to him without Juanito in his arms anymore and touched the great horse again. Immediately, the big horse calmed down, trembling still. The boy's touch was like magic. It was so gentle and calm. The great horse turned his head, sniffing the boy, and Jose continued stroking the animal slowly, gently, smoothly.

"You are wonderful," the stallion heard the boy telling him. "You are absolutely wonderful. Now, now, now; it's all over and you're safe here with us. We love you very much, big boy. And we wish you no harm. You are a great, wonderful horse, and all is safe here."

The magnificent animal relaxed, calming down, down, and the people began to breathe normally again. It was over; Jose had saved the day, and now everyone began to openly admire the fine horse that Don Juan had brought home. People asked Don Juan how much he'd paid for such a great animal, and how fast could he run, and if he'd already thrown any colts.

But Don Juan couldn't answer even one question that they were asking of him. All he could do was stare at this skinny little dark Indian son of his who'd handled the stallion so brilliantly. And Don Juan's heart ached. For never in his life had he seen such fine horsemanship . . . and from a boy so young and small and dark. Why, the term in Spanish to train horses wasn't "breaking" a horse, as it was said in English in the United States. No, in Spanish the term for training horses was *"amansar,"* which meant to "make tame," to "make love," to "make a friend" of the animal. And that's exactly what his son Jose had just done—and with such ease.

Don Juan turned and looked at his *familia*—at his dark, short Indian wife who was now holding their child Juanito, and he looked at his other dark, short offspring, too. Then he glanced around at his tall, white, fair-haired children, who looked more like himself, and suddenly, not knowing why exactly, Juan Jesus exploded into an insane rage of screaming shouts.

"Get away from that stallion!" he bellowed at Jose. "You had no right to do that! I could've shot him between the eyes and he never would have moved. I'm a man! A man, you hear me? And I know what I do! I'm not some skinny little backward Indian-savage who knows how to talk horse to horses, but I can shoot! You hear me? I can force the entire animal kingdom to its knees in the name of GOD-GIVEN CHRISTIANITY! Get the hell away from that animal, so I can shoot him! You've ruined him! May you burn in DAMNATION FOR ALL ETERNITY!"

And bellowing all this, Don Juan once again raised his .45 to shoot the horse, but this time Doña Margarita intervened with little Juan still in her arms.

"No!" she screamed. "Please, dear husband! Do not shoot that horse! We all know you can do it! But don't!"

Don Juan tried to push his short little Indian wife away so he could fire, so he could kill the stallion, but she kept right in his face, talking the whole while. "No, Don Juan! No! You don't mean all those awful things you've said! You're just upset be-cause your little son Juan, who was named after you, was almost killed. You love that horse, and you love Jose, and you don't mean any of these things that you've said. You don't. You love us all too much!"

But Don Juan just kept raging and screaming. "Get the hell away from me, you stupid, backward Indian fool! I know what I'm doing; I come from kings! Do you hear me, KINGS! I don't see how I ever allowed myself to get mixed up with the likes of you and this whole tribe of imbeciles! Get away or, so help me God Almighty, I'll shoot you, too, woman!"

"No! I will not get away! Those are just words! Only words! You look at me in the eyes, Juan, and open your heart! You're a good man, Juan, a very good man, and you love that horse and you love your son Jose and tomorrow you'll feel terrible about this whole thing!"

And for an instant, Don Juan turned away from the horse that he was trying to kill and looked his wife in the eyes. And he began to melt, to calm down, as his good wife reached up and stroked him, gently, gently. "There," she said, "there, Don Juan, everything is going to be all right. Now take that horse away from here immediately, Jose," she added to her son without ever once taking her eyes off of her husband's eyes.

Instantly, Jose was on the horse's back, ready to race off like a shot, but Don Juan went crazy-*loco* again.

"No!" he screamed. "Get off my horse, you no-good Indian-savage bastard!" And he now took aim, trying to shoot his own son.

But Doña Margarita slapped Don Juan with every bit of power in her tiny body, and his exploding gun didn't hit its mark. "He is no bastard!" she yelled as Jose now raced away on the great stallion. "Part Indian, yes, and maybe no good, but not a bastard! For we are married, Don Juan; married in your Holy Catholic Church before God Himself, and you will have respect for your own faith, if not for me!"

She was only a tiny, skinny, five-foot-tall woman, and he was a huge, powerful, six-foot-one man, towering over her like a mighty oak, but still her words reached him and he began to calm down once again. She raised little Juan up to his face and added, "Here, Juan, take the little child that you named after yourself and give him love. That's all you really wanted when you came into the house shouting for us to come out and see the fine horse you'd bought. Love, only love."

But instead of hearing her words and taking the child, Don Juan took a step back as if he'd been hit by a club and he raised up both of his huge fists into the air. "Get away from me, woman!" he screamed. "I never wanted to name that little big-headed Indian *cabezón* after me! But you insisted that he was our last child, and so you forced me to do it!" He fired the .45 up into the air again and again until it was empty, then he bellowed, "I'll still kill that horse if I want! I'm a man; do you hear me, a man! And Jose is never to set foot in my home again as long as I live, so help me God Almighty!"

Doña Margarita bit her lip, saying no more, and, trembling, went into the house, carrying Juanito in her arms. Outside, the children were divided; some agreed with their father, others did not. Alejo, who was the oldest, became the angriest of all, saying that yes, indeed, the horse did need to be shot and that his father would've handled the whole thing perfectly well if Jose hadn't sneaked in with his little sneaky Indian ways. Alejo was large, well-muscled, and blue-eyed like his father.

Inside the house, Doña Margarita lit a candle to the Virgin Mary and then began to pray quietly as she rocked little Juan in her arms. Her daughters, Luisa and Emilia, came inside and put a shawl over their mother's shoulders, giving her warmth. Luisa and Emilia were both fair-haired like their father, too, but neither had his crazy-*loco* temperament. They began to pray, and pray they did as little Juan went off to sleep, feeling the fear and yet comfort of the three women talking with God.

Riding off across the little mountain valley on the great stallion, Jose didn't hear his father's words that he was never to set foot in his home again. But, no matter; for those were the very same words that were passing through Jose's mind as he rode away in a hoof-pounding fury of speed. He would never allow himself to come near his father again. For if he did, and his father ever insulted his beloved Indian mother again as he'd just done in front of everyone, then he would have to kill his father as sure as the Father Sun came up each day. And, he really didn't want to kill his own father in cold blood. For how could he? He was his son, and he loved his father more than life itself. Why, his father was a god and he, the son, was merely a lost, broken human being.

And so, broken-hearted to the bottom of his soul, Jose raced the stallion, Four White Stockings, to the far *barrancas,* a group of steep breaks that knotted up with oaks and boulders before dropping down into the great central valley of Mexico. And there, Jose leaped across *arroyos* that no horse had ever leaped before. He unsaddled the horse and rode him bareback. The animal was magnificent. Why, he could fly. Jose came to know the horse and love him. The horse came to trust this fearless boy and love him, too. That night they slept together under the stars in a small meadow surrounded by oak trees. Jose counted the passing clouds, and the stallion grazed alongside him. And when Jose began to weep, feeling so lost and all alone, the great animal came near him and nudged him with his nose. Jose stroked the horse's head and spoke to the animal like a human being speaks to his best friend. The great horse felt the softness of Jose's words, and so he, too, opened up his own heart and spoke back to Jose in horse sounds of equal tenderness. They were both strong, young males far from home and very unsure of what to do next. They smelled of each other and the great animal lay down and he and Jose slept so closely together that even the great jaguar who spotted them in the meadow didn't know what to think of them.

From that day on, Jose slept in the barn with the animals, and he never set foot in his home again unless he was sure that his father was gone. And no matter how much Doña Margarita tried to soften her husband's heart, nothing worked. For Don Juan Jesus had come from kings. And people who came from kings could never apologize for what they'd done, or the whole course of human history would run amuck.

And so the wounds of father and son bled on, never healing. But, on the other hand, Doña Margarita was able to see her son Jose Maria Villaseñor become a man so great with horses that his reputation spread across the entire region, and other young men—who'd lost their father-gods—began to come to him to learn the art of "making horses tame" in the full moonlight by giving them love with a slow, gentle hand. Soon the room in the barn where Jose lived became a place where young men gathered—not to drink and go wild but to learn how to cope with life's terrible twists and turns.

Walking home that day from church to ask her son Jose to go over to the widow's house, Doña Margarita's heart was very heavy. And she thought back to the day that she and her sister Marcelina had first seen the two tall, handsome Villaseñor brothers come riding into their village. The Father Sun had just been going down, slipping off the distant horizon, when they'd ridden into their little mountain settlement, looking like two young gods *tan bien sentados,* so well-seated on their fine, dancing, gray-white horses. They'd been dressed in their full *charro* outfits of suede and silver *conchos,* and their jeweled bodies and great *sombreros* had made them look like the knights of old, coming into town on their fine steeds to save the young damsels in distress. Marcelina, being older, had gripped her heart and quickly said, "The sensitive-looking one is mine!" screaming from her deepest female yearnings.

"All right," had said Margarita graciously, for she'd already put her mark on the larger, more muscular one who had all the well-honed arrogance of a fighting cock. "I'll take the larger one," she'd added oh-so-quietly.

"Of course, you're smaller, so you'd want the bigger one!" had said Marcelina, giggling with anticipation.

But the two well-dressed brothers had paid no attention to the two young, dark-eyed beauties as they'd ridden past them and up to the front of the *ramada.* They dismounted and followed the young Indian boy who'd guided them into the settlement to see the father of these two young women, Don Pio Castro—the local overseer—about the possibilities of maybe buying some land and cattle so they could start a ranch of their own.

And as the two young men came under the far end of the Castros' large, spacious *ramada,* they'd had to take off their great *sombreros* so they could fit under the rafters. And at this moment of removing their *sombreros* was when Marcelina and

Margarita had seen their startling fine-red-hair, and their breath was taken away from them. For these young men had hair that looked like it was afire, just like the glow of the going sun, and the color of these young men's eyes was such a bright blue that it looked like their eyes had come straight from the Father Sky himself. Neither young girl had ever seen such tall, magnificent, handsome young men in all their lives.

Marcelina had given a smile to the more slender one with the soft, quiet movements and he, Teodoro, smiled back at her, nodding his beautiful, well-made royal head.

But Margarita hadn't dared smile or give anything to the other brother, for she could already well-tell that this one had a burning fire deep within himself that was so great that it paled even the going sun. Why, this man had all the powers to part the seas and light up the night. And so, even though Margarita had only laid her eyes on this man just a few minutes ago, she already intuitively knew that her life with him—if that's what she chose to do—would be a very difficult one. She'd be forever needing to go very slow and easy in handling this godly man, if they were to survive and not kill each other. For to show him her full power, right from the start, would be to open herself up to do battle of such terror that even the spirit of the great female serpent, who'd guided Margarita in her life, would crawl away and hide.

So young Margarita now lowered her eyes, pretending to be a quiet, obedient, young, innocent *mestiza,* but all the while she was already instinctively concentrating with all her being into the holy warrior-steps of being a woman as she walked out of the *ramada* left-right, left-right, gathering up all of her female powers. Because, yes, she'd decided that this was, indeed, the man whom she was going to marry and have her children with and their number would be great; and all the world would come to know what happened when children came from the loins of a woman of the earth and the sperm of a god from the heavens.

And for the first ten years of their marriage, she and Juan

Jesus had truly loved each other with such passion that they'd sung away the days *con gusto* and danced the nights away in love, making a glorious new child almost every year.

But then had come that cold winter, and the crops had died and the starving wolves had come down in packs, attacking their livestock, and Juan Jesus had turned ugly, as if thinking that God Himself had turned on him. He'd started to hate the weather—enraged that he couldn't control it—and hate the wolves and blame God for everything. And no matter how much Doña Margarita had tried to calm him, telling him that this, too, would pass and all would turn out for the best in the end, *con el favor de Dios,* he hadn't been able to hear her. And he'd gotten uglier and uglier, until his hate filled his entire soul, and he'd then begun to hunt down the poor hungry wolves with a vengeance, killing them even in their dens before their very own mothers; not once realizing that these wolves had been here since the beginning of time and they were, in fact, his brothers and sisters and he could've learned so much about the cold weather from them, if only he'd opened up his eyes to see. And then, as it was, the cattle had died by the thousands the second cold winter anyway; cattle that the wolves would have thinned out, helping the weather to develop a new type of cattle that would be fit to survive for thousands of years and not just for a decade or two.

But in his great fear of lack of money and losing their fine life-style, Juan Jesus had not been able to open his eyes and see beyond his little immediate concerns, and he'd fought where he could have let go, hated where he could've loved; and there, in these rich soils of self-doubt and self-hate, was where he'd chosen to plant the seeds for the forest of the later years of their marriage. A forest that would become so huge and dense that later they'd have absolutely no comprehension where it had ever come from.

And so thinking these thoughts, Doña Margarita now went down the cobblestone street from the church to her home at the other end of the settlement—a distance of no more than a rock's throw—to tell her son Jose about the young widow Mariposa needing help. And as she went down the short little street, Doña Margarita fully realized that, yes, indeed, her father Don Pio had warned her against marrying this man Juan Jesus. Her father had come in from the state capital of Guadalajara three days before her wedding and he'd told her that Juan Jesus Villaseñor was the talk of all of Guadalajara. Not only had he been shamelessly in love with his very own cousin-sister, but he'd killed the prominent lawyer-*político* that she was to marry, and he'd done it in a duel only hours before their wedding. The authorities had come after him, and he'd killed six more. It was only because of his rich father's influence that he'd been allowed to escape. And his cousin-sister—who everyone said looked identical to him in height and beauty—was then sent to live out her days in a convent; and he, Juan Jesus—the most promising of all nine male children of the powerful Villaseñor family—was banished from all the civilized world for eternity!

And his brother Teodoro, the poet of the family, had agreed to go with Juan into the land of darkness. For he, too, loved his brother's wild soul every bit as much as their cousin-sister had loved Juan's untamed *alma de corazón.*

"So, *mi hijita,* this man is an outrage to the soul," Don Pio had told her. "And all people who love him and follow him will come to disaster. For, believe me, he doesn't walk in the grace of God's beauty, but, instead, in the path of the mad-imbalance *del Diablo.*

"Please, my daughter, I beg you to understand that my words don't come from ignorance or jealousy," he'd said to her, "but from a father who knows men; and I tell you this man is destined to come to hate you every bit as much as he loves you now."

"But, Papa," she'd said, feeling her heart breaking, "how can you be so sure? He loves me so much right now, and I love him so much, too."

"Because, *mi hijita*, as your mother Silveria and I have been telling you all your life, these bright-eyed Europeans are not of our Mother Earth. No, they are Sky People who destroyed their own *planeta* tens of thousands of years ago and then were cast to live among us against their will, just as this man Juan Jesus was cast among us against his will, too. And so he has no respect for us or for our sacred *tierra madre*, and so he will love your fair-skinned children, but hate the dark ones who come from your loins. I'm sorry, *mi hijita*, but, please believe me; this man is exactly—exactly, I tell you—the type of man that I've been doing battle with since I was nine years old, fighting first against those twelve big, greedy German families who stole our lands of southern Mexico, and then against the invasion of the French."

"But he's Spanish, Papa!" Margarita had said, trying so hard to hold on to her love.

"Oh, yes, Spanish and so romantic," Don Pio had said. "Why, this makes him even worse than the French and the Germans, because at least those never pretended to love us. I beg you, Margarita, *amor de mi corazón*, do not marry this *hombre!* For he will cause a war between our very own blood that will last for generations!"

"Papa," had said Margarita calmly, with tears running down her face, "I've heard every word you've told me and I know that you are the wisest, kindest man that the earth has ever produced, but understand, the great mother serpent herself arose last night in all her diamond-glistening glory from out of the heart-center of the earth, and she spoke to me, telling me everything that you've just told me. And, well, I still say that in my heart of hearts, I love this man, and so I will marry him, Papa. For, you tell me, how are we ever going to bring peace to *nuestra sagrada tierra* if we don't take in these lost Sky People with love?"

Margarita would never forget how the tears had come to her father's old eyes when he'd heard these words, and he'd looked at her silently, crying and crying. "Well, I guess I've raised you well," he'd finally said, "for no truer words could ever be spoken. And so today I will shave off my beard, and never again will I touch another sword or gun. For if I have either near me while I see you go from difficulty to difficulty, I swear that I won't be able to control myself, and I'll kill this man and rip out his heart, as I've done many times to the likes of him in the heat of battle. I will shave my face this very day, *mi hijita,* and cut my hair, and never again will you ever hear me speak of this matter, so help me God!"

And her father had, indeed, kept his word, never bringing up the matter again. But, oh, it had been so difficult for Don Pio, especially when Juan Jesus had banished their little son Jose from their home, the very house that her father had built with his own two hands and then had given to her and her husband when their family had grown so large.

And so, now, walking into the *ramada* of the house that had once been her father's home, Doña Margarita found her littlest son, Juan, and her eldest daughter, Luisa, in the kitchen laughing and laughing. Luisa's husband-to-be, Jose-Luis, was telling them a story and, as was proper, little Juan was sitting at the kitchen table between his sister Luisa and Jose-Luis, playing chaperon.

"Hello," said Doña Margarita, taking off her shawl. "Where is Jose?"

"Where he always is, down at the corrals," said Jose-Luis, still laughing at the funny story he'd just told. Jose-Luis was a big bear of a man. In fact, he was one of the few men in the area who was even larger than Don Juan himself. "He's working with that new colt of Four White Stockings. What a beauty!"

"Oh, the dark sorrel one," said Doña Margarita, going to the stove to fix herself a cup of *yerba buena* tea. She always liked to drink a little tea and eat something sweet after she'd been to church. "Well, go get him, Juan, and tell him that the widow Mariposa needs some wood cut and so I promised her that he'd go over and help her as soon as he could."

"The widow needs someone to cut her wood for her?" said Jose-Luis, grinning. "Why, I bet there are a dozen able men in this valley alone who'd give their right arm at the chance to do anything for her!"

"That's exactly what she doesn't want," said Doña Margarita, taking down the jar of honey to sweeten her tea. "Another crazy-eyed suitor bothering her when all the poor woman really wants is to be left in peace."

"It's strange," said Jose-Luis, laughing, "but I guess we men, Juanito, will never understand women. The way in which Camacho treated her, I'd think that she'd be happy with all the attention that she's been getting lately." He laughed a big belly laugh, mouth-wide-open, truly enjoying himself. "Once I found Camacho picking flowers in a field and I thought he was getting them for his wife, but then he went over and fed them to his burros. Oh, how that man loved his three burros. But I guess I can see why—they were fine, strong, hardworking animals."

"Oh, so that's what you think of me when you bring me flowers, eh?" said Luisa. "That I'm nothing but a big, strong, hardworking *burra?*"

"But you're not so big," said Jose-Luis, howling with laughter and slapping his thigh. "Not compared to me, anyway!"

Luisa howled, too.

"All right, Juan," said Doña Margarita, ignoring the two crazy-acting lovers, "go on now and give my message to your brother."

"Yes, Mama," said Juan, getting up to go.

"Hold on," said Jose-Luis, "I got to get going, too, so I'll go with you, my little *hombre.* My horse is tied up down at the corrals."

Little Juan and Jose-Luis had no more than gone out the door when Luisa stopped her laughter and turned to her mother, looking very serious. "But, Mama, are you really sure that you want Jose going over to Mariposa's house? A lot of men are going to get very jealous, and problems could start."

Doña Margarita took a deep breath. "Yes, I know, and I considered that," she said. "I really did, but only for about half a second. Then I said to myself, 'To see my son smile just one more time, one more time, I'd take the chance of sending him to the Devil himself to make that possible!'

"Oh, *mi hijita,*" continued the old woman, sitting down, "the tragedy of that day seven years ago still hangs here inside my heart and soul as if it had only happened yesterday. So many, many hearts were broken that day of the stallion. And not any less than your own father's heart, too. For he'd come home so proud of having purchased that fine horse—so proud, I tell you —only to have it all turn to *caca* inside his lost, prideful mind. Oh, the day God gave us this mind so we could do all this prideful thinking was the beginning of the end for us as a species, I'm sorry to say."

"Well, then, why did God give us this mind to do all these prideful things, if He knew it would bring us to such disaster, Mama?"

Doña Margarita took a sip from her tea and bit her sweet bread. "God only knows," she said, chewing her sweet bread with her one good tooth. "But I'm sure God has His plan. And, who can say," she added with a shrug, "I keep praying, so maybe the future will still turn out for the good for all of us, *con el favor de Dios.*"

And saying this, the old woman made the sign of the cross over herself. The younger woman watched her in awe. For the life of her, Luisa couldn't comprehend how her mother could just keep going so calmly day after day, year after year. Why, that day of the stallion had destroyed their home, ripping their hearts and souls apart, and yet her mother had continued loving their father and going on with life, *la vida,* with such power and purpose and confidence.

"Mama, tell me, how is it that you can just keep going with such strength and wisdom and unshakable faith in front of such disaster?"

A twinkle of mischief came to Doña Margarita's eyes. "Because," she said, laughing, "what other choice do we women really have, eh? Life and more life is all we have to give, unless, of course, we decide to eat up all of our children like the angry mother pig and take everything back inside of ourselves."

Both women laughed, really enjoying themselves. Oh, laughter truly did cleanse the soul. After all, laughter and tears were the two saving graces of every woman's sanity since the beginning of time when God created the heavens and the earth and made all things in sets of twos, including man and woman and the Twin Sister Planets, too.

Walking to the corrals, Juan tried to keep step with Jose-Luis, but he couldn't. When Jose-Luis realized what Juan was trying to do, he purposely opened up his long stride even more, and then began to hop and skip. They were both laughing uproariously by the time they passed under the great oaks and came to the corrals. Jose was inside the main corral, working the colt. The young animal was a spitting image of the original Four White Stockings, who was now so old that Jose didn't work him very much anymore.

"Jose," called Jose-Luis, "your little brother here has a message for you from your mother."

Jose rode over to them. His dark face looked as sad and as serious as always. He and Jose-Luis had been friends for years. In fact, Jose was the first real friend that Jose-Luis had made when he and his mother—who wasn't married—had moved into their valley some years back. A lot of loose talk had immediately started up about Jose-Luis's mother. For no unmarried woman should have a child and then move into a mountainous community and just go about her business with such arrogance and ability. A lot of people had thought it had served Jose-Luis's mother right when, years later, a passing mule-train driver beat her and raped her and put her with a second child.

"Go on," said Jose-Luis, turning to little Juan with a big smile, "tell your brother the message."

"Well," said Juan, "Mama came home from church and she said that she promised the widow Mariposa that you'd go over and cut some wood for her as soon as you can."

Without expression, Jose turned and looked at Jose-Luis. Ever since Jose had been forced to leave his home at the tender age of twelve, he'd been very careful to never show any of his feelings. Jose-Luis, on the other hand, had suffered so much at never having had a home or friends, that he smiled and laughed and showed his feelings every chance he had.

"Well, that's the message," said Jose-Luis, grinning ear-to-ear. "So you better get your butt over there as soon as you can."

Jose said nothing. He just sat there on the horse, thinking over the situation very carefully. Over the last seven years, Jose had become as cautious as a night owl. "All right," he finally said, and began to turn his horse to ride away, but then stopped. "Juanito," he said, turning back to his little brother, "I'll want you to go with me."

"Oh, yes, good thinking!" said Jose-Luis, now laughing openly. "You'll need all the chaperoning you can get!"

Jose's face flushed as red as the skin of a bright-hot chile pepper, but he said nothing. Juan looked from one man to the other.

"But he's only going to chop wood," said Juan.

"Oh, yeah, sure, of course!" said Jose-Luis. "Only chop wood!" And he walked off, whistling happily. He went to his own horse, tightened up the cinch that he'd loosened to go courting, and said, "I'll see you tomorrow, *amigos!*" He mounted up and took off toward home, laughing as he went across the valley to the little place where he and his brother and mother lived.

"What's so funny?" asked Juan.

"Nothing," said Jose very evenly, looking after his large, bear-like friend going across the open, green valley. "That's just how some people behave when they're in love." He put the colt next to the fence. "Come on, climb on back and we'll put Little Stockings away, then go and see about this wood."

Saddling up one of his well-seasoned horses, Jose mounted and put his little brother up behind him. They rode out of the corrals, past the house, and through the little settlement. His horse's hooves clattered with quick-footed sound on the cobblestones until the end of the town. Passing by the front of their little church, Jose and Juan both made the sign of the cross over themselves and then continued up the main red-dirt road past the fields of corn and alfalfa to the widow's house, just at the edge of town. Jose didn't say a single word to his little brother the whole way. No, his mind was exploding. He wondered why his mother had done such a thing without consulting him first. He no more wanted to go over to the young widow's house than he wished to fly. Oh, his heart was pounding so fast that he was beginning to sweat and the reins were getting damp in his hand.

For years, Jose had been admiring Mariposa from afar, long before she'd become the great beauty that she now was. For knowing horses, Jose had well known that it was possible to buy a shaggy, scroungey mare from right under another horseman's nose and then take that same horse and turn her into a gem within six months. And all it took to do this great feat was for a man to feed the mare properly and groom her with a steady, gentle hand that the mare could come to trust and love. And for years, he'd been doing this very thing—buying mistreated mares right from under other men's noses and then turning them into jewels, so he could then breed them to Four White Stockings. So, it had come as no surprise to him when Mariposa had suddenly blossomed. Her eyes, her movements, her well-hidden confirmation, had always been there, just waiting to bloom.

The only thing that puzzled Jose was the fact that Mariposa's entire transformation had literally happened overnight. This Jose had been marveling about ever since Camacho's death, as he lay alone at night in the barn with the animals. For a mare, no matter how good, it still took at least three or four months to turn her about. And so how could this woman have done all this to herself in one single night? Oh, this young widow truly was a marvel, an angel from heaven, and a treasure for the man who learned how to stroke her. And to learn which stroke would work with Mariposa wasn't a thing a man could know quickly. For, over the years, Jose had come to understand that each mare had her own way, and so it was never for a lover of horses to just come up to an animal and start touching the beast. No, each had to be studied and watched for a long time before the first stroke. Quickness rarely brought about trust. And love, of course, was never gained without patience.

"All right," said Jose to Juan, as they came up to the widow's house, "you can get off now, but don't go far." Helping his brother slide off the horse, Jose glanced around. He could see that Camacho had built a good house for his wife and a good barn and corrals, too. Why, the house and little barn even had red tile. "And keep in mind, Juan, I want you to stay close to me at all times," added Jose.

"All right," said Juan, looking at his brother. Juan could feel that Jose was nervous, and it confused him. For his brother Jose was one of the bravest and most respected young men in all the region. He could leap *barrancas* that no one else dared, so why would he now be afraid to come up to this woman's house?

Dismounting, Jose led his horse over to the little one-cow and three-pig barn to tie the animal up, and at that moment Mariposa came out of her house. She was wearing a long black dress. Juan thought that she looked old and ugly. "Hello," she said to the two of them. "I didn't mean that you had to come over so quickly, Jose. I hope I didn't cause you any inconvenience."

Seeing the widow, Jose took off his hat. Oh, just the sight of her was intoxicating, she was so beautiful. "Oh, no," he said, "I was just, well—ah!" He scratched his head vigorously, trying to figure out what to say, but couldn't. So he finally blurted out, "Where's the wood?"

"It's right here," said Juan to his brother. "Don't you see it?"

"Oh, yes," said Jose, turning all red when he realized that the pile of uncut wood was directly in front of him. "I just didn't, well—ah!" He scratched his head again, even more vigorously than the first time, quit talking, and went to the woodpile and got the ax to go to work.

"But don't we need to talk about the price first?" asked the widow.

"What price?" asked Jose.

"To pay you. How much should I pay you?"

"Pay me for cutting wood?" he asked.

"Well, yes. Didn't your mother explain to you that I need quite a few things done around the house? So I need to talk to you first to see how much I'll need to pay you before you get started," she said.

Jose swallowed, taking a deep breath, then looked straight into Mariposa's eyes for the first time. And she was so beautiful and light of skin and so, so—oh, he could hardly breathe when he looked at her. "You don't need to pay me," he said in all honesty of heart. And he wanted to say more; he wanted to say, "I love you, Mariposa, I've loved you for years, and I have a string of the finest horses in all the region, and I've been saving my money and now I want to groom you with gifts and bathe you with adoration and—and—oh, it was such a joy for me to hear that Camacho had died," he wanted to tell her, "for you have always been a queen, a glorious angel, in my eyes, and he was killing you, damn his greedy soul!" But Jose just held, saying nothing. How could he? For to tell a woman what you really felt inside would be saying that you could talk the tongue of angels; and Jose could no more talk the tongue of angels than he'd been able to tell his father all these years how much he loved him. And so Jose now said nothing, and he just held, looking at this woman with trembling nakedness of heart.

And Mariposa saw his eyes, his burning dark eyes, and the small boy-like features of his face, and she didn't know what to think or feel. Yet she knew the story of his life, as did everyone else in the valley, and so her heart went out to him. For she, too, knew what it was to suffer at the very hand that was supposed to love you. Tears almost came to her eyes, but she managed to hold them back.

"Oh, no," she said, holding herself strong. "I wish to pay you. I'm sorry your mother didn't make that plain to you, but I really don't want any man—I mean anyone—helping me."

Looking into her eyes, Jose now understood what she meant and so he nodded. "All right, then, but I can only come twice a week for half of each day. So, well, I'll charge you for one whole day's work per week which, let's see, the going price right now is at about ten cents a day."

"Ten cents!" she said, astonished. "Well, all right, but I'll only be able to afford that for a short time."

He looked at her, and she looked at him, and their eyes held. He took a deep breath. "Then it's a deal?" he asked.

"Yes," she said. "I guess it is."

"Good, then let's shake on it," he said, putting out his hand.

But she didn't take his hand. No, she looked at it first. And she saw that it was so much smaller than her husband's had been. Why, it was almost childlike in size. She took it and looked into his eyes, and the touch of his hand was so warm and gentle that it felt magical. It wasn't thick and calloused like most men's hands. No, it was so soft and soothing, and yet firm and strong.

"A deal," she said, smiling in spite of herself.

"A deal," he said, feeling that he'd touched paradise. Why, just the feel of her hand was shooting him through the clouds and up into the heavens. He smiled, and it was his first smile in years, and it was a beautiful smile. "All right, then, I'll go to work now."

"All right," she said, seeing how handsome his pale, dark face looked when he smiled. She began to hum as she went back inside. Something had happened to her; something magical had come to pass inside of her, but what it was, she didn't know, nor did she care to know. All she knew was that she felt kind of safe and happy and all warm.

Juan looked from one to the other. He, too, knew that something was going on. Then Juan watched his brother Jose roll up his sleeves and go to work, whistling. Juan had never heard his brother whistle before.

"I didn't know that you knew how to whistle," said Juan, gathering up the wood that his brother was splitting.

"You didn't?"

"No," said Juan.

"I'll be," said Jose. And he continued whistling as he put each piece of wood up on the big stump and then split it with one mighty blow.

Juan said nothing more as he rushed in and out, getting the wood that went flying off his brother's ax. Then the widow came out again, and she had an *olla* with her. She'd done her hair and put on another dress. This one was blue, just like her eyes.

"I've prepared some fresh wild strawberry water for you," she said.

"Oh, my favorite!" yelled Juan. "Did you add honey? Jose and I have been working real hard! Look at all the wood I've piled!"

Seeing how forward Juan was being, Jose and the widow started laughing, and in that instant Juan knew for sure that something very strange was really going on. Why, these two people were beginning to behave as ridiculously as his sister Luisa and her husband-to-be. Juan joined their laughter, feeling very good. It felt kind of wonderful to be around people who were so happy.

Getting home late that afternoon, Juan found his mother in the kitchen. She immediately asked him how things had gone at the widow's house.

"Oh, I worked so hard, Mama," said Juan, snatching up a hot tortilla from the little wood-burning stove. "But Jose didn't work as hard as me. He kept stopping to talk with the old widow every time she came out with strawberry water or sweet bread."

His mother laughed. " 'Old widow'? Well, just how old do you think she is?"

"Oh, I don't know," said Juan in all honesty. "But I know that she's way older than old Four White Stockings, so she must be near dead."

Doña Margarita howled with laughter. "Well, I'll be sure to never ask you how old you think I am. I'm probably close to three times her age, and so I must be way past dead." She took a deep breath. "So she gave the two of you strawberry water and sweet bread, eh?" said Doña Margarita. "Then you must not be very hungry, so no more tortillas or you won't eat dinner."

"Oh, no, I'm starved! I'll eat dinner!" said Juan, devouring the corn tortilla. "I worked so hard, I tell you!"

"Then you finished up all the work she wanted done?" asked the old woman.

"No," said Juan, finishing the first tortilla and reaching for a second one.

"Stop that! You'll spoil your dinner, I said."

"I won't, Mama, please, I could eat a horse and then start on a mule!"

He stole the second tortilla off the stove, put a pinch of salt on it, rolled it up, and began to eat.

"Then she came up with more work?" asked his mother.

"Yes, Jose and I are going to have to return tomorrow," he said, chewing vigorously.

"I see," said Doña Margarita, smiling, "I see." She continued working. "But, you know, maybe you shouldn't go over there with them tomorrow. You have chores to do here and Jose, I'm sure, can handle the work she has for him by himself."

"Oh, no, he can't!" said Juan. "He told me so. He said that he needs me to stay close to him and help him every time he goes over there. In fact, he's willing to give me part of the money that she's paying him. I got to go with him, Mama. Jose can't do all that work without me!"

"Well, all right," said his mother, "if that's how your brother stated it, then he must know."

Doña Margarita began to hum to herself as she worked, and then whistle a happy little tune.

"Jose was whistling a lot today, too," said Juan.

"Really?"

"Yes, and he can whistle real good. I didn't know that he knew how to whistle, Mama. I'd never heard him do it before."

His mother's eyes filled with a sudden burst of tears.

"What is it, Mama? Did I say something wrong?"

"Oh, no, *mi hijito,* you said something very right."

"And you cry? I guess Jose-Luis is right; we men will never understand you women, Mama."

The old woman took a big breath. "Come over here. I need a hug, *mi hijito.* A big, tight *abrazo.* "

Quickly, Juan went to his mother, giving her an *abrazo.* She stroked his head of curly hair and began to breathe more easily.

"After dinner, you sit with me," she said, "and I'll tell you a story about the she-fox and the male-coyote that will help you understand women. For, believe me, when men say that they can never understand women, they mislead themselves miserably. Women are the easiest people to understand in all the world."

"They are?"

"Yes, of course."

"And men, Mama, are they easy to understand, too? Because sometimes I get so confused. Like Domingo, he never has any fear, and I get scared all the time."

"We'll talk about that, too, *mi hijito,*" she said, kissing him. "Because fear is only natural, and we all have it."

"We do? Then why are men always saying that they never have any fear? And Papa—he wasn't even scared when he was unarmed and that man tried to shoot him with a gun last year. He just picked up a rock and knocked his teeth out."

"Yes, it's true that your father did that, *mi hijito,* but that doesn't mean that he didn't have fear. In fact, maybe it was fear that drove him to act so quickly, and now we'll never know if that man really meant to shoot your father or not. And, sadly, he now has another enemy, poor man. Oh, *mi hijito,* we have much to talk about. You are my special gift given to me by heaven for my old age, and I swear to you that I will not allow the mistakes that happened to my other male children to happen to you, so help me God."

"What mistakes, Mama?"

"I'll tell you in time, *mi hijito.* I have so many, many things to tell you."

"Good, because I love your stories, Mama! They're always so much fun!"

"I'm glad to hear that, *mi hijito,* because that's what life was really meant to be—a great big fun story given to us by God to be lived, and enjoyed with *gusto y amor!*"

"Really? But I thought life was all hard work and dangerous, with God and us always needing to fight the Devil. That's why we all need plenty of guns and knives," he said with relish, "and fast horses and lots of rosaries, too!"

The old woman laughed uproariously. "That's only a rumor, *mi hijito.* Life doesn't have to be like that. Just a few years back, before the last great flood, the whole world was still full of fun and happiness and, believe me, it will be again, once we've rooted the last of these lost cousin-brothers of ours to *nuestra tierra madre.*"

"Oh, good! So, now, tell me what happened to the she-fox and the male-coyote, Mama?"

"Later. I'll tell you after dinner, *mi hijito.* Remind me."

"Oh, all right," he said, looking disappointed. But then he snatched another tortilla and took off running before his mother could stop him.

"*Sinvergüenza!*" she yelled after him, laughing.

Twelve people sat down to eat dinner that night: Don Juan, Doña Margarita, Teodoro, Agustin, Jesus, Mateo, Luisa, Lucha, Maria, Emilia, Domingo, and Juan. Jose always had his food taken out to him. But, this night, he wasn't eating alone. Their cousin-brother, Everardo, who'd just come in from the United States, was staying with Jose in the little place that he'd fixed for himself to live next to the saddle room. Jose's brothers, Alejo and Vicente, were also eating with Jose this evening so that they, too, could visit with their cousin-brother Everardo. All four boys were very close. When their parents—the two Villaseñor brothers and the two Castro sisters—had married, all four of them had sworn to raise their children together like brothers and sisters, and they'd done so.

Don Juan surveyed the table, counting heads, saw that there were twelve persons present, the twelve that was necessary to have a proper Christian meal, and he bowed his head to pray. Everyone followed. Little Juan fiddled in his seat, staring at the table covered with all these wonderfully good-smelling dishes of rice and beans, meat and cactus, sweet potatoes and fresh corn. Oh, it was a feast from heaven, and how Juan sometimes hated his father's prayers. They went on and on for so long that the dinner got cold. And then after praying so much they, the children, weren't allowed to speak at the dinner table.

"Dear Lord God who reigns in the heavens, we, Your humble

and unworthy servants, ask You to please bless this food that we are about to . . ."

The prayer went on and on, just as Juan feared, and he began to get restless watching all the food getting cold. Doña Margarita saw that Juan was fiddling about, and she winked at him, quickly signaling for Juan to keep still before his father got angry. Juan winked at his mother and pretended to be praying along with his father. But he wasn't really into it. In his estimation, God wasn't dumb and so why didn't his father just cut it short, figuring God would catch on.

Finally, they were ready to start eating, but by now Juan had gotten sleepy and he began to doze off.

"Wake him up," said Don Juan to his wife as he served himself the *carne asada*.

"Let him sleep a little," she said. "He ate a few tortillas before dinner."

"Why do you let him do that? Pass the beans, Teodoro!"

Everyone was now passing plates and serving themselves anxiously. Every evening a great feast of five or six dishes was prepared, but then almost every evening the food got too cold to enjoy.

"You're spoiling that one," Don Juan continued.

"I hope so," said Doña Margarita.

"What did you say?" demanded Don Juan in a powerful tone of voice.

The table went silent and for a split-second it looked like Doña Margarita wasn't going to repeat herself, but then she spoke. "I said I hope so."

"You said you hope so? But how can you say such a thing in all good conscience?" he yelled. "You know very well that in the Bible it says—"

"Please," said Doña Margarita, closing her eyes in concentration, "don't be quoting the Bible to me. Please, not one single word!" she added with authority.

Don Juan saw her face, her determination, and he chewed his

jaw, cheek muscles jerking in rapid ripples. And he wasn't going to say another word, he really wasn't, but he just couldn't help himself. "Well, at least I don't read it on the toilet!" he said under his breath, shoving a big tortilla-scoop of *carne asada* into his mouth.

Doña Margarita began to laugh. "But you should try it sometime, dear husband," she said joyfully. "Why, reading the Bible on the toilet every morning as I take my first good *caca* of the day cleanses me out in more ways than you'll ever know. Truly, I recommend it," she added, laughing. "It could maybe do you wonders."

"Disgusting!" he said. "I swear that all the purity of our Holy Catholic Church got twisted here in this God-forsaken, backward country!"

"Disgusting?" said Doña Margarita, laughing all the more. "Why, reading the Bible on the toilet isn't any more disgusting than reading it at childbirth or funerals or any other of the great miracles of life, Don Juan." She was as happy as a bird singing in a treetop. "Why, to fart, a good *pedo*-fart and crap as you sing the songs of King David is beautiful, indeed."

Don Juan just chewed his food and said no more. Ever since he could remember, once his wife started behaving like this, he'd never been a match for her. Don Juan ate the rest of the meal in silence, and his bigger, older sons followed his manly example. The only male who spoke was little Juan when he awoke and began to eat, keeping up a constant chatter of words and silly jokes along with his mother and sisters.

When the dinner was over, the men quickly left the table and the women stayed behind and started to clean up. At this point, little Juan also quickly left to join the men, figuring that he'd gotten the best of the women's part of the meal and now he'd take advantage of being a male so he wouldn't have to clean up, too. And, also, very important, it was rumored that tonight Jose was going to maybe trade one of his finest horses to Everardo for the beautiful .38 Special that he'd just brought back from a place called Huntington Beach on the coastline of California.

But then, just as Juan was going out the door, he remembered the story about the she-fox that his mother had promised to tell him after dinner. He ran back inside.

"Oh, Mama!" he said excitedly. "I really want to hear your story about the fox and the coyote but, you see, Jose and Everardo are going to maybe do a bargaining tonight, and I don't want to miss that!"

A bargaining, a trading of valuable goods between men or women, was a huge event. Sometimes it went on for days, but other times it lasted only minutes. You could never tell, and so a person had to be there at the very beginning to get the feel of the whole business or it meant nothing.

"The story can wait, *mi hijito,*" said Doña Margarita, smiling. She felt full of mischief. She truly liked how she'd stood up to her husband tonight. Tonight she hadn't bowed down to Don Juan's ways, as she usually did. No, tonight her son Jose had whistled, and everyone knew that whistling was the trumpet of the human soul, and so now she just knew that good days were up ahead. "You go and enjoy yourself, *mi hijito,* but remember that we need to talk later, because for a man to not understand women is the single biggest mistake he can make in all his life."

"All right! Thank you. Bye, Mama!" said Juan, and he took off racing to catch up with the other men so he could watch the bargaining. But then as he ran out the door and past the *ramada,* Juan saw something so strange out of the corner of his left eye that all his life he'd wonder if he really saw it or not. Over behind the *ramada,* he saw his father—like in a far-away dream—and his father looked so sad and lonely as he glanced up at the full moon, that it gripped little Juan's heart. He almost stopped and ran over to give his father a big *abrazo,* but then he figured that he'd made a mistake because his big, strong father couldn't possibly be sad or lonely. Also, he knew better than to take the chance of his father maybe getting angry with him and hitting him on the head, so he just kept running toward the corrals to catch up with the other men who were now all going into the barn to watch the bargaining.

But what little Juan had seen out of the corner of his left eye was, indeed, correct. Leaving the dinner table, Don Juan had lit up a big cigar like he usually did every evening. And he'd been prepared to walk up the cobblestone street of their little settlement as he had seen his own father do almost every night when they'd lived in the state capital of Guadalajara and he had been a boy. But this night, Don Juan was just too much in pain to walk up the cobblestone street, and so he'd gone into the shadows of their home and he'd thrown down his cigar and looked up at the heavens, wondering why God was continuing to punish him.

Oh, at times it felt to Don Juan as if God was just out to get him. For he'd never meant to fall madly in love with his own cousin-sister, whom he'd known ever since they'd been babies, and start all that trouble. But, oh, when he'd seen that no-good womanizer go after his beautiful young cousin-sister, who was only seventeen years old like himself, he'd gone crazy-*loco* insane with love. And he'd had to do something. He couldn't just let that older man abuse her. Then he'd been on the run and it had taken a fortune for his father to pay off the other family and stop the whole situation from developing into a disastrous feud. He'd been sentenced to the land of darkness, and to his complete surprise, his brother Teodoro had volunteered to go with him. For years they'd wandered, until that magical day when they'd come upon the highlands of Jalisco—a place of drinking and music and the finest little sure-footed horses of all of Mexico.

Then that day as the sun was going down and they'd followed a young Indian into a little mountainous settlement of commerce and promise, they'd met Don Pio—a fine, honorable family man—and Juan Jesus had felt like he'd finally found his home.

He and his brother Teodoro had then met Don Pio's two beautiful, dark-eyed daughters and they'd begun to court them. A peace of mind had come to him that he'd never dreamed possible before. The days had become clear and purposeful, and the nights became a time of magic and laughter.

And so they'd married; he and Teodoro had a double wedding with the two Castro sisters, just as his own parents had had a double brother-and-sister wedding, too. And the first few years of their marriage had been a blessing from God, and Juan Jesus had thrown himself into working the land as he'd never worked before, hoping to build up a ranch so great and wonderful that he'd dwarf the dreams of his father, who'd refused to speak to him ever since the day of his banishment. But then had come that terrible winter, and in two seasons all of his dreams had been destroyed. And, oh, he'd tried so hard after that, so very hard, working day and night, but, well, God had turned against him once again, and that was that. Why, even his hopes of building up a herd of fine horses had come to nothing, too.

Don Juan now looked up at the heavens, staring at the moon, and for the life of him, he just couldn't figure out what had gone wrong *con su vida*. He'd loved his father so much—he really had —and he'd tried so hard to be the best possible son, but it just seemed to be his fate that everything he touched went to hell. But on the other hand, his brother was doing pretty well. Teodoro just seemed to thrive on getting along with these God-forsaken Indians. His brother was broke, had no money or power, and yet it just seemed like he didn't have the good sense to realize that he'd been beaten and left by God. Oh, sometimes Don Juan could have sworn if he didn't know better, that his brother had turned into a woman. Hell, half of the time all he did was just pray.

Don Juan now saw his littlest son Juan come rushing out of the house, and he saw him turn his big Indian head in his direction, and for a moment, it looked like he was going to come to him and embrace him, but then he just turned back around as if he hadn't seen him and he continued to the barn where all the other men were going. And this barn, this damned barn—the place to where he had banished his son Jose to live in shame—was now a place of joy.

Don Juan glanced up at the moon, hurting inside so much that he just didn't know what to think or do. All his life he'd always done everything that had been asked of him. And he'd prayed to God almost every day, too, and so why in the hell was it that life treated him as if he'd been condemned by the stars above from the very start? He put his boot to his cigar, crushing it into the earth.

Inside the barn were gathered over a dozen young men. Some were rolling cigarettes, others were just keeping still, waiting for the action to start. Jose, who was famous for being such a slow eater, was just finishing up his dinner, chewing every morsel as if it was the last bite of his life. Little Juan came bursting in, all full of energy.

"Has the bargaining started?" he yelled.

Everyone froze. Juan had just said the worst thing a human could possibly say at the beginning of a bargaining. For to ask this question so bluntly, so directly, destroyed the very core of what a bargaining was all about.

You see, a bargaining was when two individuals had something that the other wanted, and yet neither ever admitted what it was that the other had that they wanted. Bargaining was an art form that took great cunning and patience. Bargaining had begun aeons ago, way back in the beginning of time, when humankind had still been hunter-gatherers and had lived in small tribal units. And, when one tribe had come across another, they'd make camp together and visit, trading stories, knowledge, and showing off to each other the different things that they'd found along the way or had made with their very own hands.

And when two individuals, man or woman, finally saw something the other had that they wanted, they began to dance around each other, sharing food and stories, laughing a lot, but always being very careful to never mention the piece that the other had that they wanted. The reason for this great caution was because, way back then, each and every article that a human being owned was, indeed, a very personal treasure, a sacred piece of heart-felt art or a very basic tool which they loved and needed for their survival. And so to trade away one of these pieces was a huge emotional event called a bargaining—a giving of heart and soul—too deep and sacred to be spoken about directly.

No one knew what to say. Juanito, in all his innocence, had just, maybe, destroyed the whole evening. But then Jose, who knew how to talk horse, spoke.

"Yes, Juanito, it has started. It started long ago just over there above that little hill, when the Mother Moon spoke to the Father Sun, saying, 'Do not fear, O Big One, there's room for both of us here in the heavens,' and hence began the biggest bargaining of all time between the Night Sky and the Day Sky, darkness and light, good and evil, and men and women."

Everyone laughed, loving it. Jose had handled it so well. "Come and sit with me," Jose continued goodheartedly, "but no more words from you tonight, Juanito. Our special guest here, cousin-brother Everardo, was just telling us about Huntun-tun-tun Beach and how all the best mule drivers down there in California are *mejicanos* from up here in our very region."

"It's true," continued Everardo, a big, handsome man who looked almost identical to Alejo. And the reason that these two cousins looked so much alike was because they carried the same blood from the two Villaseñor brothers and the two Castro sisters. And so Everardo and all his brothers and sisters were, in fact, not just cousins, but blood-brothers with little Juan and all his siblings. "Some *gabachos* are good with horses, no doubt about that; but, as a whole, they're so rough and abusive that their animals end up working against them and not with them, like they do here. Jose, I tell you, you come back down there with me and we could get rich with all you know about horsemanship.

"Here, watch, I'll show you why," said Everardo, pulling his knife. He began to draw a map on the earthen floor. "You see, this is Mexico up here, and down below us toward the bottom of the world is the United States. And the *gringos*, the *gabachos*, are trying to build a road from the Mexican border all the way through California down to San Francisco. It will take them years, and we could break—I mean, tame—enough teams of mules and workhorses for them to get rich, Jose."

All the young men were very excited and deeply impressed with Everardo's knowledge of the world. Most of them had never even been as far as Guadalajara, three days away by horseback.

"I'll think on it," said Jose calmly. But he already knew that he was never going to leave these beloved mountains of his. He could never leave his mother alone with his father, who'd become less and less tolerant over the years and more and more religious than ever.

And now, there was also the widow Mariposa that he had to consider. Ever since her husband's death, Jose had been keeping an eye on her home at night. A couple of times when some lecherous drunks had come up to her house making obscene noises, trying to attract her attention, Jose had come out of the shadows, acting like he was just passing by, and he'd taken the drunks in hand, telling them that they could come over to the barn with him and sleep it off. Only once had it turned into a fight. But being sober, Jose had easily roped the drunken man before he'd been able to pull his gun and he'd knocked the man to the ground and dragged him off. But now, since men would be seeing him working at her place a couple of times a week, he could no longer just play the innocent boy passing by with his rope in hand.

Her suitors were becoming more aggressive each day. Particularly that new colonel who'd come up with his troops last month. That man was so big and handsome and full of charm, but yet Jose had smelled the evil coming off the colonel's body at a fifty-meter distance as surely as a deer can smell the lion's piss. All these men would just see Mariposa, find out that she was a widow, and demand her. They just didn't think that a woman—given to man from one of his very own ribs—had the right to have such beauty without a man performing his God-given duty over her prostrate body.

Jose fully realized that he'd have to start carrying a gun if he continued working for the widow. For a man without a gun up in these mountains was like a deer among a pride of hungry lions, especially when it came to this new colonel and his herd of ruthless *Rurales,* the local Federal law.

"So tell me," said Jose very gently, "what else did you learn down in those United States?"

"I learned that their gold coins weigh less than ours and yet they are worth more," continued Everardo. "I learned that the people down there aren't friendly and don't touch and hug each other like we do up here. Also, I learned that when a *gringo* is smiling at you, he can also be hating you with all his heart, but you'll never know it because for them the heart and head aren't necessarily connected, and so they can smile at you and yet be angry *de corazón.* And, also, very important, I learned that our slick old fox the *Presidente* here, Don Porfirio, is giving himself the most expensive 80th birthday present ever given to a human being in all the history of the earth—20,000,000 *pesos* in gold! And yet, here in Mexico, we don't know anything about this *desmadre!*"

"No!" said Vicente, who liked books and read a lot. "Impossible! Why, that's more than it took to build the Vatican, and we're in difficult times here! There's got to be a mistake!"

"It's no mistake," said Everardo, glancing at his cousin-brother Vicente. "Haven't you people noticed how the *Rurales* are combing the countryside harder than ever, forcing their will over all the people?"

"Well, yes, we've seen how this new colonel and his *Rurales* have been more ruthless than ever. In fact, just last month they shot a boy from our valley here, just for taking an ear of corn to feed himself down in the lowlands."

"Doesn't that terrible act tell you something?" said Everardo.

"You mean like a great plan or something? Oh, no, these are just isolated incidents, I'm sure," said Vicente.

"Isolated incidents, my ass!" yelled Everardo. Like Alejo, Everardo liked to argue with a loud, powerful voice. But he meant no harm. He just thought that was the Villaseñor way. "Look, be honest, Vicente, how many times have you been more open with your friends than with your own family, eh?"

"Well, yes, sometimes it is easier to speak the truth with your friends away from home than with your own family."

"You see!" snapped Everardo. "And that's the way it is between the leaders of nations! This ass Don Porfirio just loves to brag to his friends from other countries about his wealth and what a big celebration he's giving himself. Hell, it's in all the newspapers in the United States. Even President Teodoro Roosevelt is going to attend. But here, in Mexico, no one knows *caca* about nothing, so that way our fine *Presidente* can keep playing the sly fox, saying how his heart is with us, his children —the people of Mexico—but he lies! That's why I want to get a horse, so I can go to the capital myself and see this *desmadre* of 20,000,000 *pesos* in gold with my very own eyes!"

"Oh, so then you want a horse," said Jose softly, calmly, cutting into the conversation with a small sharp knife and finally bringing the bargaining back on course.

The young men in the room all marveled. Jose had done a wonderful job of just sitting back, Indian-style, and waiting patiently until the other bit bait.

"Well," said Everardo, realizing that he'd been caught flat-footed by a very patient hand, "yes, it's true that I've thought that, well, maybe, yes, I'd like a horse."

"Well, I happen to have a few pretty good ones," said Jose, smiling. "But, frankly, I don't know if you have anything I'd like to trade for."

Everardo grinned. He loved the way in which Jose had given him an "in" to the conversation. "Well, how about my .38 Special; you know, the one that you haven't been able to take your eyes off of."

"Oh, that little gun?" said Jose, smiling. "Well, it's all right, I think, for shooting rabbits. But for a serious matter, nothing compares to my father's Colt .45."

"Let's see," said Everardo. "Who here has a Colt like Don Juan's?"

No one had one.

"I'll go get Papa's!" shouted Juan excitedly, and he took off running before anyone could say anything. "Papa! Papa!" he yelled as he ran out the barn door. "We need your Colt .45!"

No one moved. No one said a single word. Juanito, in all his excitement and innocence, had just broken another rule. Don Juan had not come inside the barn while Jose was present in nearly seven years. They were all nervous. They didn't know what was going to happen. Would Don Juan just send his .45 along and refuse to come? Or would Don Juan show up and then Jose would have to call off the entire bargaining for the evening? Oh, little Juan just didn't know how to keep still. He spent so much time around the women that he had no real sense of the ethics between men.

"Well, well," said Everardo, trying to change the subject and yet, maybe, save the evening by keeping matters moving ahead, "I've heard that our grandfather, the great Don Pio, is thinking of maybe going himself to the capital for this celebration, too."

"Yes, that's true," said Jose. "Last week he sent up word

from Fat Rock, asking me if Four White Stockings could make the trip."

"And what did you say?" asked Everardo.

"Well, I said sure, why not, as long as he goes easy on him and doesn't push him hard like a young horse. You know," continued Jose, his eyes lighting up, "I bet Four White Stockings is still the fastest, strongest horse in all these parts for one good run. It's only when you need a horse for run after run for days on end that he's too old to come through anymore."

"Just like our *abuelito* Don Pio with his new bride, eh?" said Alejo, slapping his thigh and laughing *con carcajadas*.

If anyone else had said this, weapons would've been drawn instantly and there'd be blood on the ground in seconds. For no one, but no one, spoke disrespectfully of the great Don Pio—their grandfather who'd first settled this whole region—and got away with it. But Alejo was Alejo, the oldest male of the Villaseñor family, and even though he had a temper almost as bad as that of Don Juan himself he also had their mother's humor and was always coming up with things that no one else dared say.

Everyone burst out laughing. For it was true, the whole town had been completely taken by surprise when Don Pio, who was in his eighties, married the young twenty-year-old Indian maid who kept house for him within a year of his good wife Silveria's death. And then, within the first month, the girl was pregnant. Oh, it would've been a thing of ridicule if it wasn't for the fact that it was easy for everyone to see how much she loved him. She adored him, and openly told everyone that no man had ever touched her heart and soul like he and, even if her years with him were few, they'd still be the finest years of her entire life.

Just then, as they were all laughing, the barn door suddenly opened and there stood the mighty Don Juan Villaseñor with his Colt .45 in his hand. Juanito was at his side.

"I told him," said Juanito, still out of breath, "that we needed his .45 so we could try it out against the .38. So Papa has come, too, to show us which shoots straighter," added little Juan proudly.

Everyone stopped laughing. Even Alejo, who was Don Juan's favorite and could have kept laughing and wouldn't have gotten in trouble.

"All right," said Don Juan, glancing around the room at all the young men, "there's no better time than the present, so let me see this .38 and I'll show you in a minute which shoots straighter."

A couple of the younger men almost laughed because, yes, they knew that Don Juan had once been a very good shot back in his day, but that had been more than a hundred moons ago. And, now, everyone knew that the finest shot in all of the region was Jose, and so he should be the one to test the two weapons— not an old relic from the past who hadn't even been invited to the bargaining in the first place. But no one dared voice his opinion, and quickly the .38 was given to Don Juan. It was a double-action Smith and Wesson with a six-inch barrel—a totally different weapon from Don Juan's trusty old single-action five-inch-barrel Colt .45. He checked the .38's balance, its feel, and shook his head.

"No, this one will never outshoot my Colt. Its balance is off. It doesn't sit back by itself in your palm. But let's see; maybe I'm wrong. Who knows?"

They all went outside and walked down the road in the bright moonlight. They wanted to get far enough away from the barn so that their shooting wouldn't scare the livestock. Six white rocks were placed on the side of the road against an embankment, so in case the bullets went wild, they'd stick in dirt and not hit a horse or cow in the field beyond.

"All right, who wants to shoot first?" asked Don Juan.

No one spoke up.

"Come on, Jose," said Vicente. "It was you who said that the .38 could never match our father's Colt .45 in a serious matter."

"You said that, Jose?" asked Don Juan, feeling so good that his son had said this of him and his weapon.

Jose nodded. "Yes, I said that, Papa."

"Well, then, let's see if you're right. You do the first shooting," said Don Juan, offering his gun to his son with a big, handsome smile.

Jose felt so honored that he didn't know what to do or say. He glanced around and became embarrassed. Never, for the life of him, had he expected his father to show up with his gun when Juanito went to get him. And not in a million years had he expected his father to actually offer him his gun like he'd done when Jose had been a boy. Tears almost came to Jose's eyes and he was just getting ready to say, "All right, I'd be happy to shoot your gun, Papa," but he never got the chance to speak.

Because seeing his son's momentary hesitation, Don Juan began to anger, thinking that Jose resented the fact that he had even come to the barn at all. So he now said, "All right, then, don't shoot, you backward Indian! I'll do it, or you, Alejo, you do it!"

"I'll do it, Papa!" said Alejo instantly, stepping up and taking the .45 from his father as fast as he could.

Jose drew back, feeling all embarrassed. But he really didn't feel like he'd been mistreated or shoved aside by his father or brother. No, it was more like he, Jose, could now see very clearly for the first time in his life how truly well his brother and father communicated. They were both so quick and decisive, and had that same kind of fast-action type of behavior. Whereas he, on the other hand, was less quick to decide things. He was slower and liked to chew his cud like a cow in the springtime before he made any move. In fact, maybe his father was even right in thinking of him as a "backward Indian" because, the truth was, he was socially backward in many ways.

Just then the .45 exploded, and the first rock shattered into pieces. Then the second rock shattered, too. Alejo was a good shot. Everardo now handed the .38 Smith and Wesson to Alejo.

Standing up tall again, Alejo took careful aim at the third rock and fired, hitting high. He took an even more careful aim and shot again and hit even higher on the next stone. Everardo laughed, taking the .38 back.

"You see," he said, "that's one of the big differences between that old .45 and this new .38. The .38 shoots faster; that's why it's hitting high and is so accurate at longer ranges. But, yes, the .45 is excellent, too, throwing a much bigger, heavier bullet for a short range like this."

"But Alejo missed both shots with that .38," said Juanito.

"Yes, but he hit exactly right above each stone each time. A dozen more practice rounds and Alejo will be shooting just as accurately at short distances with this .38 as he did with the .45, and also, he'd be able to shoot at longer distances with the .38 than with the .45."

"Let's see," said Don Juan, not liking that his trusty .45 was being criticized. "Words are just words, but doing is truth! So let's get back, way back, and see."

They all went back up the road. Now the white rocks looked tiny in the bright moonlight. Some of the livestock were calling. The shots had stirred them up.

"Here," said Everardo to Jose, "you're the best shot, so you shoot from this distance."

Jose's heart leaped. Oh, how he wished that his cousin-brother hadn't said this. "Oh, me? I'm really not that good," said Jose. "I'll shoot in the daylight. The night gives me trouble sometimes," he lied.

"Well, how about you, Don Juan?" said Everardo.

"Me?" said Don Juan, still staring at his dark Indian son who'd just been called the best shot. "I only shoot my .45 but, hell, why not." He took the .38 and started to take aim.

"Just squeeze the trigger real easy, Don Juan," offered Everardo. "It's got a hair trigger and so you have to—"

The gun suddenly exploded, before Don Juan had even taken aim. He missed the target by ten feet.

"What kind of piece of crap is this?!" he yelled. "Give me back my .45. This distance is for fools! Real men face each other up close, not back here like little *putos, cabrones!*"

He took aim on the tree stump nearby, and he fired quick and true, exploding the stump as fast as lightning. Everyone was very impressed, giving Don Juan compliments. The older man loved it. Jose came up to him.

"That was good shooting, Papa. Very good shooting," he said in all heartfelt sincerity.

Don Juan turned and looked at his son, at this boy of his who'd become a man. "Well, at least I tried," he said with power. "Come on, best shot, you try!" he added viciously.

Jose swallowed. He didn't know what to do. His heart was pounding wildly. He started to take the gun, but then couldn't. He really didn't want to shoot in front of his father and these other people any more than he ever trained his horses in front of others. Oh, he was so good, so fantastic with guns and horses that it confused him. It was like he didn't know where it came from, but it came to him like magic. And the last time he'd performed magic in front of people, he'd been driven from his home forever.

"No," he said at last, "I can't."

"What do you mean you can't?!" said Don Juan. "Come on, stop being a backward, stupid Indian like your mother and show us what you can—"

Hearing his mother being called a stupid, backward Indian, Jose grabbed the .45. He asked for some bullets. He loaded it and then loaded the .38. He told everyone to get back. Then he breathed, breathed again, and put the .38 in his belt. He picked up two little pieces of the stump that his father had exploded and he tossed them behind himself high into the air over his left shoulder. Then he whirled, dropping into a crouch, shooting in rapid-fire like a machine gun, bursting the two pieces into smithereens in midair. Then he drew the .38 and, whirling about, exploded the white stones in the distance into pieces, too.

Everyone was silent. No one in all his life had seen such shooting. Jose handed both empty weapons to his father and turned, walking off. And he had no idea where he was going, but he knew he had to leave. Then, once he was out of sight from everyone, Jose fell to his knees, screaming to the heavens, crying and crying, asking God to please help him! Then he got up and took off running. And before he knew it, he found himself standing before the widow's home, and she opened the door as if expecting him and . . . and . . . and then, in the bright moonlight, they flew into each other's arms, barely re-membering to close the door behind them.

Inside the house, leaning against the hardwood door, they began to kiss gently, softly, tenderly. Tears ran down Jose's face. She saw his tears and was moved to the core of her being. She began to kiss each tear, licking them off his face. He laughed, and they began to giggle like little children. They became em-barrassed and stepped back away from each other. It had all happened so suddenly. All she'd done was open the door.

"Well, ah," she said, being very self-conscious, "are you hun-gry or something?"

"No," he said.

"Are you thirsty?" she asked.

"Yes, a little," he said.

"Oh, good," she said, moving toward the kitchen. "Can I fix you some wild strawberry water?"

"No, please," he said, breathing deeply, and the tears began to flow again.

"What is it?" she asked.

"I . . . I . . . I don't know, but you see . . . I've . . . I've dreamed of kissing you for so long, that just to be in the same room with you and having kissed you is so, so wonderful, so—how can I say—so incredible that now for you to offer me some wild strawberry water is too much."

"Well, then, how about just plain water?"

"Yes," he said, laughing. "That would be just right."

She got him a cup of water from the large *olla* in the corner, and he drank it all down.

"You really were thirsty," she said. "What happened tonight? I could feel it. I could feel something bad happening to you, and then I knew that you were coming to me before you got to the door."

He shook his head. "Please, I really don't want to talk about it. Please, don't ever ask me." But he then broke down, sobbing. "My father, I love him so much and yet he hates me. I can't understand it. I'm his son, and yet he treats me as if I were his enemy."

"Oh, dear God," said Mariposa, coming to Jose and taking him in her arms again. "It's not your fault. Believe me, I know, it's not your fault. I loved my husband before I married him, I really did, and yet from the very start he treated me like I was his enemy, too. I just don't know what gets into men, but that's how so many of them are. My father was the same way with my mother, always saying that he, the man, had to keep her in her place. Now I understand why so many women go to church every day and why so many other good, passionate women become nuns. It's all a woman's way of just trying to find peace and a real love that she can depend on—not a love that suddenly turns on her and becomes hateful and mean."

"It's the same thing with horses," said Jose. "I buy mares that have been neglected or abused and I train them into these wonderful creatures within six months by just grooming them, feeding them, talking to them, and giving them a slow, gentle hand. All of life wants to be treated with a love that they can trust; not just women."

"A slow, gentle hand," she repeated with a smile. "Why, that's what I felt today when you touched me. You know, when we shook hands on our deal. The gentleness of your handshake —oh, it was so wonderful, that it was magical."

He smiled. "Your touch . . . sent me flying to the heavens!"

"My touch? Really?"

"Oh, yes, your touch. You see, I've known for years that you were an angel—way before Camacho died and you suddenly became so happy and beautiful." He breathed. "You are gorgeous, Mar-i-posa."

"Me? Gorgeous?"

"Oh, yes, you are gorgeous! The most gorgeous butterfly the world has ever seen!"

"Really? I mean, you really think I'm beautiful?"

"Why, of course. Don't you know that? All these men are constantly after you, just wanting to touch you."

"Oh, but they don't really see me, Jose. They only see these large . . . you know what I mean. They didn't get enough breast when they were babies," she added, laughing.

He laughed, too, and he looked her in the eyes. "You are an angel, Mariposa," he said. "You are a queen. You are the most beautiful woman in the whole world!" He started crying again. "I've been so madly in love with you for so many years, my sweet butterfly. Oh, I hated it when Camacho mistreated you and then would brag to the other men that that's how to treat a woman and keep her in her place." He took a deep breath. "All these years, whenever I saw you walk by, I'd see this *mariposa,* this butterfly—just as your name says—of such wondrous beauty, that my heart would ache.

"And then, when Camacho died and all these men began to come by at night, making coyote howls to your home and bragging how they'd be sure to be the one to get you, I'd get so enraged with pain here in my soul that I'd—"

"Then you're the one, aren't you?" she said, cutting him off. "The one who's been staying by my house at night and driving the men away!"

He nodded. "Yes."

"Oh, my God from heaven!" she shouted. "At first, I thought you were just another one of those men. But then, night after night, I'd hear this angel drive the men away, and I came to believe that this was, indeed, my guardian angel sent to me by God to protect me. I gave you the name 'Archangel Gabriel,' and—oh, Jose, you really are my very own special angel, aren't you?"

"Yes," he said, "I am."

She looked at him, really looked at him, and saw that, yes, indeed, this boy who'd been living with the animals since the age of twelve was an angel, and she took him in her arms. But this time she wasn't so gentle, as she began to kiss him in a frenzy, cupping his boy-like face in both of her hands and drawing him to her hungry lips. She began to devour him, quickly kissing her way down his neck and to his shoulders. Then she began to undress him, kissing every inch of his small, tight, muscular chest. She led him to her bed and laid him down.

And there in the moonlight coming in the open window, Mariposa began to make love to this angel-boy of hers with all the passion that she'd kept dormant in her thirteen-year-long marriage. She was twenty-nine years old, and she'd never once experienced love-making while she performed sex with her husband. But now she was on fire with love, completely aflame with burning passion, and she lost herself, disappearing into that wonderful world of the beyond. Kissing, kissing, feeling, feeling, trembling as still as a hummingbird in midair, and then she began slipping, sliding down through the tunnel of love itself and . . . and . . . and she came screaming out the other side. Screaming, clawing, as she approached Saint Peter's gates. Oh, she was going crazy-*loca*, and she wanted to stop and not go any farther, for fear that she might die.

She held, suspended in time, and thought of returning back down that long tunnel to the other side, where all was safe and normal. But then, oh, God, Jose began to help her, too, touching her with such incredible, slow, gentle hands, coo-coo coo-

coo-cooing in her ear like the turtledove of love as he stroked her, soothed her, loved her. And his calm, easy manner gave her the assurance that she needed to let herself go farther and farther to a place within herself where she'd never been before. And suddenly she burst, going *loca*-insane as she danced up the wild steps of heaven and shot through Saint Peter's gates. And, way down below her, the earth EXPLODED in an avalanche of body-jerking, thrashing, leaping movements, and her love-soul was released, and gone, spent, no more, and oh, so happy.

Laughing, smiling, lying back in great joy, she now gripped him close with her powerful thighs, milking him to herself again and again as she kept dancing up and down the wild steps, truly enjoying herself as she never had in all her life. Oh, it was so fine to let go and be wild! It was just so fine to finally let go. And now she was all cuddly as a little kitten, going off to sleep, dreaming, dreaming as peacefully as a newborn child. And he was with her. Oh, my God, yes, he was with her; she could feel it, and they were gone together again, having left the earth far, far behind, shooting across the heavens.

And when one awoke, the other did, too, and they'd start again, playing like children of God until the sunrise of a whole new day took them by surprise.

Jose wanted to get dressed and leave as quickly as possible so her good name wouldn't be ruined. Laughing, she put a naked thigh over him, holding him fast, and said, "No, my love, I want the whole universe to know that for the first time in all my life, I know love!!!"

Smiling she felt tears come to her eyes. Lots and lots of tears, as she gazed at her Archangel Gabriel. Then she reached out and touched him, stroked him, moved the long black hair out of his eyes, and then rolled over on top of him. And, together, they began at the beginning . . . once again, and, oh, it was wonderful. Two starving souls had finally found their earthly substance: love.

2

And so the heavens smiled once more and he, the nine-teenth child, the baby of la familia, *watched as all around him the gods and serpents did battle.*

Once again Juan picked up a stick, tossing it high into the air over his left shoulder. Then he whirled about and, with his right hand, threw a rock at the stick . . . and this time he hit it. His eyes went big with joy and he screamed, "I did it! I did it! I'm almost as good as Jose!"

"And you are almost as good," said a big, deep voice. "But the trick is to do it every time, if you ever expect to be as good as your brother."

Juan turned and saw that it was Jose-Luis, his sister Luisa's husband-to-be, who'd spoken. Beside him stood Jose, looking so small and child-like compared to Jose-Luis.

"But how can anyone do it every time?" asked little Juan. "I've been out here for hours and that's the first time I've hit the stick."

"Easy," said Jose-Luis, laughing, "your brother will show you. Hell, I've never been able to do it myself, and Jose has shown me a dozen times, each time telling me that it's the easiest thing in all the world. Go on, Jose, show him."

Jose glanced at Jose-Luis and shook his head, then started over to help his little brother. Juan was beside himself with joy. Ever since Jose had demonstrated his incredible marksmanship, every little kid in the whole valley was trying to learn how to do it, too. Some kids were already getting pretty good with sticks and stones and someday they hoped to be able to do it with a real gun. They were saying that if they could all get as good as Jose, then a dozen of them alone could take on the whole band of abusive *Rurales* who came through their mountains every month, and run them out of the whole country.

Another young neighbor boy from town had been killed just three days ago by the no-good *Rurales* because he'd stopped by a rich *hacienda* down in the lowlands to cut a little alfalfa to feed his horse. Oh, that colonel and his band of no-good Federal troops were the worst criminals anyone had seen since the band of ruthless outlaws that Don Pio had run out of these mountains thirty years ago.

"Come here," said Jose to his little brother, "and stand right beside me, facing away from those cattle over there. That's right, now they're behind you, and you can't see the cattle anymore, right?"

"Right."

"Well, now, listen, this is a trick I learned from training horses at night. I don't know why, but at night when a horse doesn't see as well, then he pays more attention and learns faster, and sometimes even learns things that he could never possibly have learned in the daytime. I don't know why, but it just seems like—hey, you know that old blind woman in town and how she just walks to church, over the stones and curves of the trail, without ever falling? Well, I asked that old *india* one day how she does it, and she said that God gives blind people a special vision that comes straight from the heart. In fact, she told me that that's why people with good eyes have such a hard time knowing God, because they're distracted by seeing so much all around them.

"Do you get it, eh? What she was saying is that the less we see, the more we really see, especially when we open our hearts and just let our bodies go free. You've seen how she comes dancing down that trail, stepping lightly between the stones. She's a marvel to watch. And you, too, are a marvel, Juanito; you don't have to take aim with your eyes to spot an eagle in the sky. No, you just shoot your vision up to the sky and your eyes do it all for you, and there is the eagle, plain as day!

"All right, are you ready to try it?" Jose asked his little brother. "Now, you haven't seen those cattle behind you for quite a while, eh, Juanito? You don't even remember where they were here inside your thinking-mind, right?" Juan nodded. "Good, but, believe me, here inside of your heart-eyes you know exactly where they are. Watch, I'll show you.

"Take this stick and point it straight out like a spear, and when I say go, you turn around as fast as you can in a natural low crouch and shoot those cows closest to you with your eyes and spear. Ready?"

Juan nodded. Oh, he was so excited. "Ready!"

"Good. Now, remember, as fast as you can without thinking or aiming, just shoot that stick straight out at them like it's a magic bolt of lightning, and trust yourself like that old blind woman trusted herself, dancing her way down that rocky path to church. Ready, now go! Do it!"

Juan whirled about, sticking his hand straight out like a spear, shooting as fast as he could with his magic lightning bolt. "Bang! Bang! Bang! Bang!" he yelled at the closest cows, eyes all focused with joyful excitement. "Oh, boy! I got them! I got them all! I really, really did!"

"Of course, you did," laughed Jose. "You see, when a man stands up straight and takes aim, he stops all the natural flow of his body. That's why with aiming you can only get so good, no matter how much you practice. But when you whirl, not seeing, not knowing, your mind doesn't have time to get in the way of your body, and so your heart vision and your eye vision will become one. Oh, I don't know how to say it, but it's like, well, magic! Now, you want to try it with my gun?"

"Your gun?!" said Juan, not able to believe what his ears had just heard. "A real gun?" He was all choked up. He couldn't think or talk. All he could do was nod his head again and again.

Jose unloaded the .38, the one that he'd traded Everardo for one of his best horses, and he handed it to Juanito. "All right, now without bullets the first time, you throw that stick behind your back and then do it! Just do it!"

Juan took the gun, feeling so powerful and wonderful. He picked up a stick, threw it over his shoulders high into the air, and then whirled, pretending to fire the empty .38 and, yes, indeed, it was like magic, for he knew that he'd gotten the stick dead center without a shadow of a doubt.

"I got it!" he yelled. "I got it!"

"I'm sure you did," said Jose. "I'm sure you did."

Giving the .38 back to Jose, Juan hugged his brother with all his might. "Oh, I love you, Jose. I love you so much. How I wish you were our father."

Jose took a big breath. "Yes, Juan, sometimes I wish I was our father, too," he said. "Or that I was able to . . . to . . ." He stopped his words. And the tears began running down his cheeks.

Juan began to cry, too. Their father had never liked him since that day of the stallion, either. Jose and Juan were two of the darkest brothers of all the Villaseñor *familia*.

As he watched them crying, tears came to Jose-Luis's eyes, too. Jose-Luis had known Jose ever since they were little kids. And Jose-Luis had always thought that he'd had it hard not knowing who his father was, until he'd seen what happened to Jose. Now Jose-Luis was glad that he'd never had a father to abuse him. Lifting up his huge bear-like arms, Jose-Luis came forward, embracing both brothers.

A few weeks later, Juan and Jose were at the widow's house, mending fences, when the colonel and his thirty-six *Rurales* came up the valley on their fine, well-fed horses. Jose's .38 was lying on a rock beside him, and so he casually took off his shirt, stretched, then covered the gun with his shirt. Instantly, Juan understood. This colonel was a dangerous man, and Jose had prepared himself. The colonel's name was Alfonso Montemayor de los Santos. He rode a big, beautiful, well-groomed grey stallion, and his uniform was always impeccable.

"Just keep working," said Jose quietly. They were both dressed in poor workman's clothes. "We don't want any problems."

Juan nodded.

The colonel rode up to the widow's house with his force of men. They were all very well armed.

Inside, Mariposa—who'd also seen the *Rurales* coming—was trying to figure out what to do. For she didn't want to see the colonel, especially now that she and Jose were lovers. Jose was her angel sent to her from heaven. She would have married him instantly if he were not so young. But what could she do? She was going on thirty, and he was just nineteen years old.

The colonel glanced around at the place, then his eyes came to rest on Jose, who was doing his best to look very inconsequential. But he wasn't quite able to pull it off. The colonel had been in many gun battles, and there was something very interesting about this skinny little Indian boy and the child.

"Tell me," said the colonel to Jose, "do you know who I am?"

Juan laughed, almost saying, "Well, with thirty armed men and such an expensive uniform, we know you aren't the poor priest or the local drunk, you ass!" But Jose kicked him. "Ouch!" said Juan.

"*Sí, señor,* I know who you are," said Jose.

"Well, then, why won't you look at me?"

Jose took a big breath, looked at him, then spoke. "I'm sorry if that offended you. I meant no harm. I'm just trying to finish my work here, that's all."

"Oh, I see. And from the looks of it, you and that child have been doing a lot of good work here for the lady. Does she pay you?"

Jose glanced at the house. He could see where this was leading. If he said no, then the colonel would guess that they were lovers and probably pick a fight with him and have his men execute him on the spot. He swallowed.

Inside, Mariposa was going crazy because she could hear what was being said and she knew where the colonel was trying to take this. Yet, if she stepped outside, how could she ever hide from the world all the love that she felt for Jose? For the love, the absolute insane love, that she felt for Jose could not be hidden any more than the burning sunrise could be hidden by a couple of clouds.

"Yes, she pays me," said Jose, realizing how smart Mariposa had been to have insisted on this.

"How much?"

Jose took another deep breath. Oh, how he wished to say, "None of your business, you fat-ass arrogant shit," but he didn't, and instead he glanced around at all his armed men who'd already carefully maneuvered themselves around him, surrounding him in a circle. Jose held. "Ten cents per week," he said, and he was going to explain that this was because he only worked two half days, but the laughter that erupted from all thirty-six men and the colonel himself was so great that it broke all tension.

The colonel was suddenly very happy, deciding that he'd clearly overestimated this stupid Indian boy's importance and he was strictly a simple, ignorant *indio sin razón* and that he, the colonel, was just too jumpy and had completely overreacted.

Seeing his brother being laughed at made Juan so angry that

he stood up as tall as he could and started to say, "No one laughs at my brother! He's the finest horseman and best shot ever seen! Why, he could kill half of you before you even moved!" But before he'd gotten one word out, Jose kicked him again.

"Ooow!" screamed Juan.

The colonel stopped laughing. "Why do you keep kicking your son?"

"Because, well, I, eh—"

Just then, Mariposa stepped out, saying, "Oh, Colonel! How are you?" Her face, her body, her whole being, radiated such beauty, such love, that Jose and Juan were completely forgotten and every male eye was on her breathing, rising breasts.

The colonel took off his hat. "My," he said, "you look even more stunning than last month when I stopped by. I'll definitely start coming by more often just to lay my eyes on you." He dismounted, calling over his men with their pack mules. He was a tall, well-built, handsome man. "I took the liberty of bringing you some silks that I purchased for you in Guadalajara."

Mariposa wanted to glance at Jose and see if he was all right, but she didn't dare look. She took a deep breath, knowing damn well that this colonel hadn't purchased anything for her. He just confiscated whatever he wanted anytime he wanted in the name of Don Porfirio's great modern society, and now he'd confiscate her, too, if he had his way. She smiled.

"Oh, thank you, that's very kind of you, but I don't wear silk, thank you."

Instantly, the colonel's eyes turned mean. But then, thinking better of the situation, the man smiled a great big, beautiful smile full of charm. "There's a wedding coming up in a few weeks at my good friend Juan Villaseñor's house, just down the road, and I'd be honored to have you come as my guest and wear this beautiful dress." He handed her the dress. "I'll send a carriage for you along with an escort," he added with authority, then he took her hand, kissing it.

Mariposa said nothing. What could she say? He hadn't invited her. No, his had been an order.

"Well, goodbye for now," said the colonel, then he turned to Jose and Juan. "And you two!" he yelled at them with power. "You better keep working hard for those wages you're getting! Ten cents a week is too much for the likes of you!"

His men all laughed once more, and Juan was going to say that they were Juan Villaseñor's children and that he was a fat burro's ass, but Jose put his hand on his shoulder. "Don't," he said, squeezing him. Juan said nothing.

"And you, Mariposa," said the colonel, having mounted his horse, "I'll see you at the wedding."

And he turned and rode off with his men, never once waiting for her answer or asking if she was available that day or if she even wished to go with him. A couple of his men trampled the fence that Jose and Juan had just mended. They figured that Jose was such a stupid fool for working for such incredibly low wages that ridiculing him was the only proper way to treat his stupid Indian kind. Then they were gone, going up the beautiful, long mountain valley.

"But why didn't you let me tell him that we're our father's children?" asked Juan of his brother.

Jose breathed. "Because he never would've believed you. And, worse, if he had believed you, then he would've just gotten all confused. And a confused man is a very dangerous animal, especially if he's in a place of authority."

Jose picked up his shirt, putting it on. Seeing the gun exposed once more, Juan's eyes went big.

"How many could you have killed, Jose?"

"How many bullets do I have?"

"Five," said Juan, "because you never put one in the chamber where the hammer rests, in case you drop the gun."

"Exactly. So that's all I could've gotten, five. But remember what our grandfather always tells us: that a smart man is never wild or stupid, but has all the patience of the lion, and the lion and the jaguar aren't in the business of getting hurt or taking chances. No, they wait and plan very carefully until . . . one mighty rush and that deer is theirs for sure. Surviving is their goal. Not showing off their bravery or strength."

"Our grandfather, was he really a colonel at one time, too?" asked Juan.

"Yes," said Jose, "and he was one of the best men that Don Benito Juarez ever had."

"But he was never like this colonel, right?"

"Of course not. Our grandfather comes from the poor, and his heart has always been for the underdogs of life. This colonel is with the rich—and not the good, hardworking rich, either— but with the cowardly rich who hide behind the laws of the land."

Mariposa came up to the two of them, taking Jose's hand. The colonel and his men were now far in the distance, passing by Jose-Luis's mother's house, who grew the finest peaches in all the region. Juan watched his brother's fingers soothing Mariposa's hand. Their hands looked so beautiful together—one dark, the other light.

Then it was the week before Christmas, and everyone was going crazy around the Villaseñor *casa*. Luisa's wedding was going to take place right after Jesus Christ's birthday, and much had to be done.

After dinner, Domingo got up and went out the back door, signaling for his younger brother Juan to follow him. But Juan didn't want to go outside with Domingo. No, he wanted to stay indoors with *la familia*. But Domingo made a face at Juan that said, "You better get out here quick or you're going to get it real bad later, when nobody's around to protect you." Domingo, who was five years older than Juan, towered over him.

Glancing around at everyone, Juan swallowed and decided that there was no way to escape Domingo's wrath, so he got up and went out the back door, too. Once they were out of sight from all of the adults, Domingo quickly grabbed Juan and gave him a sharp knock on the head with his middle knuckle.

"Come on, you big *cabezón!*" said Domingo. "You know that they're waiting for us by the creek behind the pigpen!"

Getting to the creek, they met Lucha. "Where have you two been?" she said. She was two years older than Domingo, had blue eyes and reddish-brown hair, just like him. "I slipped out the front door when no one was watching, and I've been waiting for you."

"Is Emilia coming?" asked Domingo.

"No, you know how she is. She's a coward."

"Yes, just like chicken here," said Domingo. "I had to knock him on the head to straighten him out."

Suddenly a pig squealed an ear-piercing screech right behind them, taking them all by surprise. The dogs at the house yelped and the neighbor's dogs began to bark and a coyote family answered in the distance. The full moon slipped behind a soft, white-laced cloud, giving the whole night an eerie feeling.

"What is it?" whispered Lucha.

"Probably nothing," said Domingo, glancing about nervously, "or it could mean that those coyotes are a lot closer than they sound and something is up."

"Oh, I don't like this," said Juan. "Couldn't we wait and do it some other time?"

"No!" said Domingo. "You know that this is the last night of the full moon, so you must do it tonight!"

Juan gulped. "But why?" he asked. What they wanted him to do was go to Jose-Luis's house and summon the Devil because they all knew that Jose-Luis's mother was a witch and that once Jose-Luis married their sister Luisa, then they'd have a witch in their family and all their souls would be in danger of eternal damnation. "Wouldn't it make more sense," continued Juan, "to wait until *La Bruja*'s power's weakened so that I'll have a better chance of doing it for sure?"

"Eh, he has a point there," said Lucha. "We don't want to fail. Our entire family's future depends on this, so maybe it would be best to wait."

"Lucha!" said Domingo, becoming as indignant as an enraged priest. "Have you forgotten everything we've been taught at church? The Devil is strong, remember? At one time he was God's most glorious angel, and so if we expect to show him that we are not afraid of him, then we can't do it when a *bruja* is at her weakest. No, we must do it when *La Bruja*'s power is at her greatest! Then, and only then—like the good priest says—does the faith of a good Christian break the evil spell that has been put upon *nuestra familia.*"

Juan's whole body shivered with fear, he just couldn't help it—he was so frightened. He glanced up at the bright, full moon and then across the little creek to the far side of the valley. It was a beautiful night, and in the distance, just this side of the oak-covered hills, he could see the tiny light of Jose-Luis's house and his mother's orchard of peach trees over to one side. He took a big breath. His little heart was pounding.

"Look," said Lucha, drawing close to Juan, "if I could do it for you, little brother, you know I would. But I can't. I'm older than you and not pure of heart anymore, and so it would mean nothing for me to go and confront *La Bruja.*"

Juan brushed Lucha's hand away. Of all his sisters, Lucha was the one who Juan trusted the least. She had big, beautiful eyes and was always flirting and acting all lovey-dovey to get her way. He knew that she would no more do for him what had to be done than a fat pig would give up his food for another pig. "So why aren't you pure of heart anymore?" asked Juan.

"Oh," she said, acting like some *gran dama*. "What kind of a man are you to ask a lady a question like that?"

"A boy," said Juan. "A very scared boy who doesn't want to go to the witch's house for all the money in the world. And you're older, Lucha, stronger, faster, and so I want to know why you can't do it."

"Well, if you must know," said Lucha, playing with a long strand of her hair, "last summer I—but you must swear to never tell a soul!"

"We wouldn't!" said Domingo excitedly. "I swear it! So come on, tell us," he added quickly.

"Well, ah," she said, smiling and looking at them from the corner of her eyes, "you know our cousin Agustin. Well, when he stayed with us, he and I, well—" she turned all red, "—we kissed."

"You kissed Agustin?!" said Domingo. "But he's our cousin-brother! How could you do such a thing?"

"Well, we just kissed. It's not like we're going to get married or have a baby."

"You better not!" said Domingo. "It would have a long pointed tail because it would be a baby conceived of the Devil!"

"I know, that's why we only kissed, but by the hours," she added, laughing.

"You mean that you enjoyed it?" asked Juan.

"Yes, very much," said Lucha.

"Eeeuuuuu!" said Juan, making a face of pure repulsion.

Lucha went to hit Juan, but Juan only laughed, dodging away. "I'm going to brain you!" she said.

"Enough! Stop that! Both of you!" snapped Domingo. "What we have here tonight is very serious. It's about saving the immortal soul of our entire Villaseñor family."

Juan and Lucha immediately settled down because they both knew that Domingo was right.

"All right now, do you remember what you're supposed to do?" Domingo asked Juan.

Juan nodded. "Yes, I remember."

"Well, then, repeat it. I don't want any *pendejadas.*"

Juan lowered his head. "I'm supposed to go up to her house and—" He could barely talk, he was so scared.

"I can't hear you! Talk louder! And look at me in the eyes,

like a man!" demanded Domingo. "You know very well that a
good Christian never shows any fear to the Devil!"

Juan lifted up his little face to his brother. His eyes were
brimming with tears. He was truly terrified. But, still, he
straightened up the best he could, trying to look like a man.
"I'm supposed to go up to her house," he repeated, "then say
aloud that I don't fear her powers or the Devil's, either, then—
then—"

"Then what?!"

Juan's eyes became huge, like in a trance. "Then I'm supposed to make the sign of the cross and yell, 'We walk in God's
love and we fear no evil!' "

"Exactly," said Domingo, "exactly!"

"But—but—but what if her five big dogs wake up?" asked
Juan. "Maybe I should just whisper it and not say it aloud." He
had to squeeze his legs together so he wouldn't pee. "That huge
black dog, the one called *El Diablo* . . . oh, my God, if they
wake up, they'll kill me and eat me! You saw what they did to
that stranger last year. They took him down, with his horse, too,
and half-ate him before she could call them off."

"We've been over that!" said Domingo impatiently. "That's
why you circle her house, coming in through the peach orchard.
Her dogs sleep on the other side of her house. They won't even
hear you, if you do it right."

"Oh, Domingo," said Juan, his little heart going crazy, "why
can't you do it for me? I'm scared and not as fast or as strong as
you."

"Look, *indio cabezón,* we've been over this a dozen times! I'm
older than you and not pure at heart anymore! You know that!
I'm mean to you and kick dogs and torture ants and swear all
the time!"

"Look," said Juan, "I'm not so pure, either. I've kicked goats
and tortured bugs, too, and last year when the priest came and
found the poor box empty at the church, it was me who took the
money."

"You took that money?!" yelled Lucha. "How awful! And you never spoke up when the priest kept accusing us all of stealing! That was terrible!"

Domingo looked at his little brother with new, manly respect. "You really did that?" he asked.

"Oh, yes," said Juan, "and I've done other bad things, too!"

"Like what?" asked Lucha.

"Well, I've sneaked up and watched how you girls have to squat down to pee, and we don't."

"You've watched us?!" yelled Lucha. "Oh, you're dirty!"

"No, I stand up to pee," he said proudly.

"I'm going to hit you and tell Mama!" yelled Lucha, grabbing Juan and trying to hit him on the head, but he kept ducking. Domingo separated them.

Just then some other kids came running up. It was Mateo, Domingo's best friend, and his two smaller brothers, Alfonso and Pelon, and their sister Carmelita. Immediately, Mateo wanted to know what was going on. He and Domingo were the two best fighters with rocks in all the region. In fact, they were so feared that even some adult men wouldn't go against them in a rock fight *a las todas*.

"My little brother is ready to do it," Domingo announced proudly.

Mateo took a good long look at Juan. "He doesn't look ready to me. He looks scared, and everyone knows if you show fear to the Devil, then the ground will open up and swallow you whole! Down, down, down, into the very depths of hell itself!" Mateo laughed, truly enjoying himself.

Domingo whirled on Juan. "Are you scared?" he yelled, hitting him. "Ah, tell me right now! Are you scared? Ah, what's wrong with you? Don't you love your mother? Don't you love your father?"

Mateo appreciated Domingo's righteous anger, so he hit each of his brothers a couple of times, too. "You see, *burros,* what happens to you if you're not brave? You got to be brave at all times so that the Devil doesn't come in and steal your souls."

Both Alfonso and little Pelon lowered their heads and took their older brother's blows, just like Juan accepted Domingo's. After all, this was the way it was up here in the mountains of Jalisco. As the good priest had told them, a boy had to endure much in order to become a proper Christian.

Just then Emilia came running up. She was almost sixteen years old and older than all of them. "Stop hitting him!" she told Domingo. Although Emilia had hair and eyes just like Domingo and Lucha's, she wasn't strongly built like them. No, she was slender and as delicately made as a beautiful wildflower blowing in the breeze on a hillside.

"I thought I'd catch you out here bullying Juan again," she said, taking Juan by the shoulders and gently turning him around to face her. "You don't have to do this, you know," she said in a soft voice. "When the priest marries them, he is going to bless their wedding and so all this foolishness of witches and evil spells will be taken care of."

"But that's not true!" said Domingo. "Why, the priest won't dare to ever mention that Jose-Luis's mother is *una bruja!* You know very well that ever since the witch sent that basket of peaches and the fine fat chicken to the old priest in town and he choked to death on the chicken bone, no one—but no one—dares to even bring up her name, for fear of her putting a spell of death on them, too!"

"Well, yes, that's true," said Lucha. "You have to admit that, Emilia. This new young priest is never going to mention her name." She made the sign of the cross over herself. "May the soul of the old priest rest in heaven, dear God," she added.

Emilia looked from Domingo to Juan, and her eyes filled with tears. She took her little brother in her arms. "Oh, Juan, Juan, my little baby brother Juan, I just don't know what to do. Maybe we should just go ask Mama or Luisa. They always know what to do."

"No!" shouted Domingo. "That would be the worst thing we could do! Luisa can't possibly speak out against her future mother-in-law. And our mother—what can she do, except tell us to pray? Or worse still, have us go talk with the priest, and we all know that he's deathly afraid of *La Bruja*. Remember, he's the one who heard the old priest's last words, 'Josefina, Josefina,' just before he—"

"Oh, my Lord God!" said Lucha. "You just said her name, Domingo!"

Instantly, Domingo dropped to his knees, quickly making the sign of the cross over himself. "Oh, please, dear God," he said, "I didn't mean to mention her name! Oh, please, dear God, Who lives in the heavens, protect me!"

Everyone else fell to their knees, too, crossing themselves and praying as fast as they could, except for Juan, who'd remained on his feet.

"Eh, wait," said Juan, deep in thought. "Just how could the old priest's last words have been—" Everyone stared at him. He stopped himself. "I mean, when someone is choking on a chicken bone, they can't talk, can they? Every time I've almost choked, I couldn't talk. So how could the old priest have said *La Bruja*'s name if he was choking to death, eh?"

"Are you questioning the good priest's word?" snapped Domingo, still on his knees.

"Well, no," said Juan, "of course not. I'm just thinking that maybe—"

"Stop thinking!" exploded Domingo, getting to his feet. "You know very well that 'thinking' is one of the cardinal sins that caused our fall from the Garden of Eden in the first place! Doesn't the priest constantly tell us never to question the word of God? That ours is to believe, not to question!"

"Yes, I know that," said Juan, "but I was only trying to say that—"

"Stop it, Juan!" demanded Domingo. "Not one more word of this! It's time for you to stand up like a proper Christian and do what you have to do to save our family! Don't you love your mother? Eh, answer me!"

"Well, yes, I do, of course," said Juan.

"And don't you love our father?"

Juan wanted to think about this one. At times he wasn't quite sure if he did. His father was always so mean to him, hitting him on the head and calling him *"indio cabezón,"* that he wasn't quite sure if he loved his father or not.

"Well, answer me!" ordered Domingo. "You love your father, don't you?"

Glancing up at his brother, Juan saw that at times like this, Domingo looked so much like their father that it was scary. His whole face was red with rage and his blue eyes were all glassed over, looking almost white.

"Yes," said Juan, not wanting to get hit any more. "I love our father."

"Good," said Domingo, "then go do it right now!"

"But how are we to know if he really goes all the way to *La Bruja*'s house and does it?" asked Mateo. "He could just go halfway across the valley, and we'd never know. The way the moon is going in and out of those clouds, it's going to be hard to see him after he crosses that first rock fence."

"That's true," said Lucha, looking across the valley into the darkness. "After that first fence, we won't be able to see what he does if the moon goes behind the clouds."

"Oh, just leave him alone!" said Emilia, tears coming to her eyes once more. "It's enough that he's even attempting to do it! If you bigger ones are so doubtful, then why don't you just go along with him or, better still, do it yourself!"

"Well, no, we can't do that," said Lucha defensively. "We'd, ah, well, be sure to wake up her dogs because there'd be too many of us and then we'd all be killed."

Domingo shoved Lucha. "That was really a dumb thing to say," he said. "We're trying to give him reassurance, not scare him." He turned to Juan. "Look, Juan, it's not her dogs that we're afraid of. Right, Mateo?"

"Yeah, sure, right," said Mateo.

"The reason that we don't go along with you, little brother, and protect you is that then you wouldn't have the chance to prove how brave you are. And, after all, that's the only thing that defeats the Devil . . . when a man is willing to meet *El Diablo* all by himself with nothing between him and eternal damnation but the faith he has in Almighty God."

"That's true!" said Mateo, making the sign of the cross over himself and kissing the back of his thumb, which was folded over his index finger in the form of the cross. "The only weapon a true Christian needs against all evil is the faith he carries here, inside of his chest! Oh, I envy you, Juan. When you succeed doing this tonight, not only will you be saving all your family, but you'll be saving the whole world, too. For, remember what the good priest says: One man's battle in overcoming the Devil's way is all mankind's salvation!" Mateo smiled, feeling proud of how well he'd repeated the words of God that they'd learned in church.

Juan saw Mateo's straight white teeth smiling across his wide, handsome Indian face, and he felt a sudden strength come shooting up into his chest. Mateo was absolutely right. He just hadn't looked at it like that. This was, indeed, a chance for him, Juan, to prove—not just to his family but to all the world—how much he loved them, just as Christ Himself had done on the cross.

"I will not fail," said Juan. "I swear to you, I will not fail! And the earth will not open up and swallow me, for I love my mother, I truly do, and I will save us all!" He turned and started for the creek, eyes crying but his heart strong.

Quickly, Pelon rushed after Juan. The two boys were friends. Over the years, their older brothers had forced them to fight each other many times, but their hearts had never really been in it. "Here," said Pelon, giving Juan his special rock. "I found this little rock inside the church one day. I think it came from Jesus' feet when they were repairing the walls."

"Gracias," said Juan, taking the well-worn, smooth little stone.

Pelon gave Juan a quick *abrazo* and then watched him go down the slope to the creek and hop from rock to rock so he wouldn't get wet.

"But how will we know if he goes all the way?" asked Mateo again.

"That's right," said Lucha. "How will we know?"

Domingo thought a moment, then shouted after Juan, who was quickly disappearing into the night. "Bring back a peach!"

Juan just kept walking.

"Maybe he didn't hear you," said Lucha, so she screamed out, "Bring back a peach, so we'll know you went all the way!"

"Quiet!" said Emilia. "What do you want to do? Wake up the dogs, so they'll be sure to kill him?"

"But he didn't answer," said Lucha.

"He heard us," said Domingo, smiling. "No more shouting. Emilia is right. We don't want to wake up the dogs. My little brother needs a fair chance." He took a big breath. "Look at him go. He really is a brave little kid, isn't he?"

"Yes," said Pelon quietly, tears running down his wide Indian cheeks. "Very, very brave."

" '**B**ring back a peach!' they yell after me," said Juan in disgust to himself as he kept walking. "What do they think I am, one of the wise men to bring them Christmas presents? My God, the last person who tried to steal some peaches off her trees, she hit on the head so hard with a club that it's said that the poor old man lost his memory and now thinks he belongs to her and she works him like a slave from sun to sun."

Juan wiped the tears that came to his eyes and continued talking to himself as he walked across the valley, rubbing the little stone that Pelon had given him. "Oh, Lord God, why does it always have to happen to me? Ah? Why me? If I'm not getting hit for losing a goat to the coyote, then I'm getting hit because the pigs ate the chayote plant. Oh, I pray for the day that it isn't me that needs to get hit on the head, dear God.

"By the way," Juan continued, getting a twinkle in his eyes as he came to the first fence made of stone, "next week is Your Beloved Son's birthday, right?" He put his right hand on the rock fence and looked up at the heavens. The moon was smiling down on him between two great white clouds. "Well, then, Dear God, I'd like to dedicate what I'm about to do tonight as a Christmas gift to Your Most Beloved Son for His birthday. How about that?"

And having said this, Juan laughed and climbed over the first rock fence on his way to the witch's house. He felt pretty good now. He liked the way he'd slipped this one in on God. After all, since he'd offered to dedicate what he was about to do tonight to God's only Son, God couldn't very well let him fail, could He? So now it was in the bag, because God had to make sure that he, Juan, succeeded so that His Most Beloved Son Jesus Christ wouldn't be disappointed on His birthday.

Feeling much better, Juan continued at a brisk pace across the valley. With God indebted to him, what could possibly go wrong? Nothing; absolutely nothing. The five big dogs would be sound asleep, and the biggest, juiciest peaches would be down on the lower branches so he could just pick them as easy as he pleased.

He stopped. He could now make out the individual peach trees by the side of *La Bruja*'s house. He took a big breath. It was said that the reason her trees were so big and green and had the biggest, sweetest peaches in all the region was that she fed the trees the blood and guts of her chickens.

And once, long ago when Domingo and Mateo were little, they said that they'd actually witnessed her feeding her trees. It had just been dusk when Mateo and Domingo had sneaked up to her place to steal some of her fine peaches. She'd come out of her house, singing, with a big, fat chicken under her arm. She was petting the chicken with such love, when she'd suddenly taken a little knife from under her dress and slit the chicken's throat so quickly that they could hardly believe that she'd done it. Then she'd begun to dance around her beloved trees, holding the big chicken upside down by its feet, singing with *gusto* as she fed the chicken's dripping blood to her trees. She'd raised the dead chicken to the sky, and they'd heard her summon the powers of the Devil to give her the greatest peaches ever seen. Domingo and Mateo had barely crawled away with their lives intact. Why, she'd been as quick as lightning with that chicken-killing knife.

Remembering this story, Juan took a few deep breaths. "Oh, Dear God," he said, "remember, we got a deal, so no matter how quick she is with that knife of hers, You got to keep brave and stay by my side ready to help me out."

He could now see that *La Bruja*'s house wasn't very far. He'd have to keep his wits about him and make sure that her dogs weren't out hunting in the fields around her house. Because if he came upon her dogs out in the open fields, then they'd get him for sure. It was said that she had the meanest dogs in all the region because she deliberately kept them half starved.

Getting to the second stone wall, Juan stopped to catch his breath. Her house was ahead of him now, and her peach orchard started on the other side of that last rock wall. He glanced up at the full moon and then back across the valley to where he'd left Domingo and the others. But he couldn't see them anymore. In fact, he could barely make out the dark outline of the pigpens and the horse corrals behind them. But he could see his parents' house easily. The bright light from the kitchen could be seen through the window. He wondered if he couldn't just turn around now and go back home. After all, to have come this far in the dark, he'd already shown the Devil that he was pretty darn brave.

"Look, God," he said aloud, "people ride their horses clear around this side of the valley so they don't have to come near her orchard. I've already come closer to her place in the night than most mortals dare. So what do You think, eh, God? Do I really have to go any farther? The Devil can already see that I'm pretty brave."

Suddenly the moon went behind some dark clouds, and the night darkened and turned cold. Instantly, Juan's eyes got big.

"All right, all right, God!" he said quickly. "I'll go all the way, just don't take my moonlight away. I need all the light I can get!"

The moon came out from behind the clouds, and the night was bright with light once more.

He took a big breath and made the sign of the cross over himself, kissing the back of his thumb, which was folded over his index finger in the form of a cross, just like he'd seen Mateo do. He blew out and continued across the open field toward the witch's home—this woman, this person who grew the finest peaches in all the region.

Suddenly Juan thought he heard something, and he stopped dead. Slowly, carefully, he glanced around, hoping to God that it wasn't her dogs that had sneaked up on him, but he saw nothing. And the moon was now out from between the clouds, and it was so huge and bright and big around that it illuminated the whole area around him almost as bright as day. He could see her house clearly, too. Why, he could actually begin to make out the individual stones of the rock fence around her home.

Then, as he was studying her place carefully, he spotted her huge dog. Juan's heart stopped dead. Good God, it was her famous dog named *El Diablo,* and there he was up on her porch, stretching and yawning with his huge mouth aimed toward the moon. Juan was sure that his entire leg could fit inside that enormous mouth.

Juan swallowed, not moving a muscle. The huge dog continued yawning and stretching. If the monster dog *El Diablo* was up and about, then Juan figured that her other four dogs were up and about, too. Without moving his head, Juan quickly rolled his eyes to the left and right, carefully searching for the other dogs around the house. For Juan well knew that the most dangerous dog for him this night wasn't *El Diablo,* her biggest dog, but *Cara Chata,* her smallest. In this area of Mexico, every ranch kept a pack of dogs, and among their pack they always had a nervous little dog that was a light sleeper so it would start barking at the slightest sound and wake up the larger dogs.

Juan searched her porch with his eyes, examining every potted plant, every basket and shrub, then carefully he looked all around her famous mango tree. It was said that mango trees couldn't live up in this mountainous region of Jalisco, Mexico, that mangoes were strictly tropical fruit trees, so they could only grow big and strong and bear fruit farther south in the regions of Guerrero and Oaxaca. And yet, there stood Josefina's mango tree alongside her house, as big and as strong as a fully-grown oak and full of fruit as huge around as bull's—

Juan stopped his thoughts. "Good God," he said to himself, "I just thought of her name inside my head! I wonder if she also knows when people think about her, too." Just then, as he had this thought, the door flew open with a bang and out came the witch herself. She was a tall, well-built woman with big, strong hands and large, callused, bare feet. It was said that she always worked barefoot and she was never without a shovel or hoe in her hand. She'd always done all her own work—building fences, planting trees, hauling dirt in baskets—until she'd hit that poor old man on the head a few years back and now she had him working with her from sun to sun.

"*¡Perrrros!*" she said to the dogs. "Here are a few scraps, but I'm not feeding you too much tonight."

Quickly, all the dogs got to their feet and she threw them the scraps. Juan crouched down into a little ball, holding as still as he could. He was out in midfield with nothing between him and the terrible witch. The rock fence that he'd just climbed over was quite a ways behind him.

"Oh, dear God," he prayed, "please don't let her see me."

"I want all of you dogs staying alert tonight," she said, petting her pack of hungry beasts. "It's a full moon, a good night for some no-good, lazy so-and-so to try and steal some fruit off my trees, so you keep alert or I'll cut your guts out and feed them to my trees, too!

"Here, *Diablito,*" she said to her huge black dog, calling him Little Devil, "you be extra ready tonight. I got this odd feeling that something very, very strange is going on tonight." Then she suddenly turned and looked straight out at Juan. "What is that funny little clump I see out in my field? Ah, answer me! Are you a rock that fell off my stone fence, or what?"

Juan squeezed his eyes closed, hoping he could just disappear. "Dear Lord God," he said to himself, "what are You doing? I thought we had a deal! Oh, please, dear God, help me! Help me! I'm just a little boy!"

"Oh, so you won't answer me!" yelled the witch at the clump that she thought might be a rock. "All right, then, take this!" And she picked up a stone from the pile of rocks she kept on her porch and threw it with all her strength at the clump, almost hitting Juan. "I can see you, you no-good thief! Don't you dare think I can't see in the dark! The full moon is my friend, and you come any closer to my winter peaches and I'll have my dogs on you in a second!"

Juan didn't dare move a muscle. He was rolled up in a little ball, rooted to the ground. His eyes wouldn't even open. They were transfixed, staring into the eternal darkness of his own forgotten soul. Then he heard her door close with another big bang, and he figured she'd gone back inside. He could hear her dogs gnawing at their bones and lapping up the scraps. He figured that this was maybe his last chance to escape with his life. But he didn't dare get up and run, so he began to crawl backward as fast as he could.

Just then the little dog named *Cara Chata* began barking.

"Oh, dear God," said Juan, "she's spotted me. I don't have a chance now. Good God, I was a fool to have let them talk me into doing this."

Then Juan heard the roar, the huge howling roar of *El Diablo*, and here came the pack of dogs flying off the porch straight toward him.

"Oh, dear God!" said Juan, almost peeing in his pants. "Now what am I to do? If I stay here, I'm sure to be ripped to pieces and eaten alive. But if I get up to run, they're sure to catch me, or . . . wait, what if I can make it to her peach trees over there and climb up a tree? Yes, that's it!" he said excitedly.

So Juan tried to get to his feet so he could run as fast as he could to her peach trees, but he couldn't get up. Something was holding him down to the ground like a gigantic hand. The pack of howling dogs was getting closer and closer, bellowing sounds of hell as they came, but Juan just couldn't get to his feet, no matter how much he pushed against the earth with both of his hands. This gigantic hand-like force was holding him down tight to the Mother Earth.

Finally he gave up. And in that instant when he gave up and relaxed, he saw that a female coyote was over there, not far from him, sniffing in his direction. He looked at the coyote and she looked at him, and their eyes held on each other for a long, heart-in-your-throat timeless moment. Then the coyote smiled —actually smiled—at him, glanced at the pack of howling dogs, gave a yelping howl, and leaped over the rock fence, passing over the moon as graceful as a dream.

Juan couldn't believe what his eyes had just seen: a smiling female coyote leaping over the full moon. And so he relaxed, feeling the warmth of the gigantic hand that was holding him down against the rich, good-smelling earth. Suddenly he felt much better; for he knew that he was safe now. All he had to do was stay still, and the dogs would follow the coyote.

The pack of dogs came racing up, hollering as they came.

Juan watched each one of them jump up on the fence, gather their feet under themselves, and leap past the full moon, too, but not nearly as gracefully as the she-coyote had done.

Then all the big dogs were gone, giving chase to the coyote. Now Juan thought that he was perfectly safe . . . until he realized that *Cara Chata* was staring at him, eyeball-to-eyeball. The little dog hadn't been able to make it over the fence, and her long tongue was hanging out as she now tried to catch her breath. Juan swallowed, not moving a muscle. "Oh, dear God," he said to himself, "I've been caught dead."

Back across the valley, Domingo and the others heard *La Bruja*'s door open with a bang and then they heard her shout into the night.

"Do you think she saw him?" asked Emilia. "Oh, Lord God, we should never have allowed him to go!"

"Quiet!" said Domingo. "Let us hear!"

They heard another shout, even louder than the first, and then the door slammed shut.

"What do you think, Mateo?" asked Domingo. "Did she spot him?"

"No, I don't think so," said Mateo, "or we'd hear her dogs."

They listened to the silence of the night, wondering what was happening to Juan. Then suddenly they heard the high-pitched barking of the witch's little dog, and then here came that huge, devastating roar of *El Diablo*, filling the whole valley with sound.

"Oh, good God!" yelled Emilia. "They're killing Juanito! Quick, let's go tell Mama!"

"No!" said Domingo. "Do you want us all to get in trouble?"

"Besides," added Mateo, "they don't have him yet. Those barks are of dogs giving chase; not of dogs ripping and killing."

"That's true," said Lucha. "Dogs sound very different when they've got their prey down on the ground. They're just chasing right now. Listen to them, our little brother must be really running," she said, smiling proudly. "He really went all the way. Wow, I wouldn't have ever really gone all the way. Would you, Domingo?"

"Quiet!" he said. "We need to hear! Those dogs are going crazy! Just listen to them. He must be in the orchard, climbing a tree or something.

"See, Mateo," continued Domingo, turning to his friend, "all these years I've been telling you that my little brother is brave. You're going to have to push Alfonso and Pelon a long way for them to match my little brother."

"We'll see, we'll see," said Mateo. "How do we know that the dogs aren't just chasing a coyote or something? For all we know, your brother could just be laying down by some rocks, hiding."

An adult voice suddenly startled them all. "What's going on?" asked Jose Villaseñor, coming up behind them. All six kids turned around and came face-to-face with Jose. And beside Jose stood Jose-Luis, as tall and wide as a giant.

"Eh?" continued Jose, glancing them over. "Why are those dogs barking? What mischief have you kids come to do behind the pigpen? Come on, answer me. Mama sent us down here, thinking you might be up to something."

His voice was calm. Jose always spoke very calmly. "Domingo," he said, "hear me good. Don't glance like that at Emilia again, or I'll take you down to size in front of everyone. Now talk. Quickly. What's going on?"

Mateo didn't dare do anything, either. The giant Jose-Luis had come in close to him and was ready to snatch him up by the throat if he so much as breathed. They were trapped. There was no getting around it. Emilia was the first one to speak.

"Jose," said Emilia, "they sent Juan to *La Bruj*—I mean to Jose-Luis's mother's house, and I told them not to, but Domingo kept insisting that—"

"Oh, no!" said Jose-Luis.

But Jose never said a word. He'd already turned and was running toward the horse corrals. In a matter of seconds, he caught a horse, jumped on it bareback, and was racing off at a full gallop, leaping across the little creek.

Jose-Luis got a horse, too, and took off after Jose. Domingo and the other kids watched as both men disappeared into the night, horses' hooves pounding the good earth with a fury of sound. The dogs continued howling in the distance, filling the night with terror.

The short little dog named *Cara Chata* caught her breath and started barking into Juan's face, calling the pack of howling dogs back.

"Oh, my God!" said Juan to himself as he leaped to his feet. "I'll run to *La Bruja*'s house and summon the Devil, then I'll race to her orchard, pick a bunch of peaches, and take off back across the valley before her dogs return!"

Thinking that it would be easy now, Juan laughed at the barking *Cara Chata* and dodged left, then right, then jumped over the short-legged little dog and took off racing toward the witch's house. But he hadn't gone more than ten feet before the stout little dog caught him by his leg, dragging him to the ground.

"You fool!" screamed Juan, kicking at her. "Don't you know that I'm about God's business?!" But the little dog didn't seem to care, and she kept hold of Juan, growling and biting and snapping.

Juan finally broke loose and took off running again. But *Cara Chata* was in fast pursuit, grabbing him and knocking him down every few feet.

"Now what are You doing, God? Having fun? Well, it's not funny to get past a pack of killer dogs only to have my feet chewed off by this little nothing dog!"

Then Juan heard laughter, a great ROAR of huge laughter, and he glanced up at the moon, thinking that God was now openly laughing at him. But then he realized that the laughter

was coming from behind him. He turned around, and there was
the witch herself, no more than twenty feet away, and she had a
shovel in her hand, holding it like a club up in the air to do him
in. His heart leaped into his throat. "What have we here? A
baby thief?" she yelled viciously.

Juan swallowed. "No!" he yelled, leaping to his feet. "I'm
here to . . . to summon the Devil and . . . and say that I
don't fear him, or you and your witchcraft, for our *familia* walks
in the path of Almighty God!"

The large woman stopped dead in her tracks, not having
expected this—especially not from such a small child. The little
female dog, *Cara Chata,* also stopped yapping at Juan and stood
there in the moonlight with her head cocked at an odd angle,
looking at him in a strange way, too.

Juan made the sign of the cross over himself, kissed the back
of his thumb that was folded over his index finger in the form of
a cross, and said, "The earth will not swallow me and no harm
shall ever come to my mother and my family, for I can truly say
to you that I carry God's love here inside my heart and soul,
and you are powerless before me."

Hearing these last words, *La Bruja* came out of her momentary surprise and said, "Powerless, am I? You little piece of
chicken *caca!* We'll see! We'll see!" And she charged at Juan,
swinging at him with her shovel.

But from so many years of getting hit on the head, Juan was
pretty agile, so he ducked her blows and took off running
toward her orchard, heart pounding so fast that he was sure that
his little heart was going to jump out of his mouth. He swallowed again and again, trying to keep his pounding heart down
in his chest as he ran. But here came *Cara Chata* again, grabbing his legs. Juan jumped and hopped, dodged and kicked, and
managed to keep going until he got to her peach trees.

Quickly, he glanced around for some fruit, but none was
hanging from the lower branches. All the peaches were up high
in the trees. It was strange; nobody in all the region had winter

peaches except for *La Bruja*. Juan was just deciding which tree to climb when he heard that huge, devastating roar of *El Diablo*. The pack of dogs was headed back his way.

Instantly, Juan climbed the tree nearest him as fast as a squirrel and picked one, two, three, four, five, six big peaches, swung down from the tree, gathered up his fruit and put it in his pouch, then took off racing as fast as he could. But the pack of dogs was on his tail, and the witch, too.

"Good God!" said Juan to himself as he ran, "I did it, God! I really did it! Even right to her face, so please don't let her killer dogs get me now!" He was racing across the open field as fast as he could go, hoping to get to the first rock fence, scramble over it and then—oh, he just didn't know what to do. The big woman was going crazy, yelling at her dogs to hurry up and get the boy. "He's a thief! A thief! Get him, *Diablo!* Get him and tear his no-good heart from his chest and eat it for your DINNER!!"

Juan got to the first fence and climbed up on top of it so he could look around. There came the pack of dogs no more than a hundred yards away, hollering to the heavens as they closed in on him. Right behind him came the witch, no more than fifty feet away.

Juan quickly glanced around and spotted a pile of big rocks not far out in the next field. "If I can get to those rocks, I'll have a fighting chance," he said. "But I'll need a club to fight the dogs off with. Oh, God, please help me!" he said, glancing up to the heavens.

Just then, as he asked for help, he saw the witch stop thirty feet away from him and raise the shovel above her head, whirling it around like a lariat. She sent it flying at him with all the power of her body, the whole while screaming, "May you burn in hell, you little no-good thief!"

Calmly, carefully, Juan watched the shovel coming right at him—long wooden handle following large spoon-like metal in a spinning circle of air-swishing noise. Smiling, Juan ducked, jumping off the rock fence, and the shovel passed right over him.

"Gracias!" yelled Juan to the old witch, and he ran over and picked up the shovel and took off for the pile of big boulders out in midfield.

"Don't give me *'gracias'!"* screamed *La Bruja,* getting to the fence. "May your thieving soul burn in hell for all eternity! I've worked hard for what I got!" She kept yelling after Juan, as she stood there by the fence she'd built with her own two hands. "And you have no right to enjoy the fruits of my labor! May you choke on the seed of my peaches! TO DEATH!!"

Hearing the words *choke to death* as he ran, Juan thought it had been pretty stupid of him to have stolen so many peaches because how could they really enjoy eating them, realizing that they came from the witch's trees and that an old priest had, indeed, choked to death while eating one of her fat chickens? He dropped the peaches. The big rocks were getting closer and closer as he ran, but her dogs were almost on top of him.

"Oh, dear God," said Juan, leaping over the grass and rough terrain as he went, "I did do wrong to steal her peaches, because she does work hard to grow them. I see that now; I really do. So could You please forgive me for my trespasses, like I forgive others for their trespasses? And from now on, I'm the biggest forgiver of trespasses You've ever seen! No kidding, dear God! The biggest!"

He could hear the dogs getting closer and closer. He turned and saw that the huge black dog was leading the pack. They were no more than thirty yards away from him, howling to the heavens with vengeance. "Oh, Mama! Mama! Help me!" yelled Juan. "I think God has forgotten me!"

He pumped his little legs as hard as he could, trying to get to the boulders before the pack overtook him. He figured that if he could just get to the rocks and scramble up, then he could maybe fight them off with the shovel. The rocks were getting bigger and bigger as his little legs went flying.

"You won't make it to those rocks!" the witch yelled at him. "And if you do, my dog *El Diablo* will pull you off of them and eat you alive!"

She began to laugh and sing. "Ha ha ha! You're going to get yours! Ha ha ha! All of you thieving men are going to get yours!"

"Boy, she's not very forgiving of others' trespasses," said Juan to himself as he ran.

And he was tempted to turn around and take a quick look at her to see if she was dancing as she laughed, but he couldn't. He knew that the dogs were almost on top of him. He could feel their breath, and they smelled awful. Then he reached the big rocks and was just scrambling up when he felt a sharp, tearing pain grab his left foot. He turned and saw that *El Diablo* had him by the foot, growling and biting and yanking and ripping. Juan kicked and jerked and SCREAMED at the top of his lungs and tried hitting the monstrous dog with the shovel. But then here came the other dogs, leaping on him from all sides, ready to devour him, too.

The last thing Juan saw before he passed out was the form of a huge horse-like creature with wings come flying out of the heavens, smashing into the pack of dogs. Then a mighty angel was swinging a club with a head of steel, lashing dogs left and right, cutting them to pieces, as they yelped in pain. Then a larger angel also appeared, and this angel grabbed *El Diablo* by the throat, strangling him.

All this time, *La Bruja* was weeping hysterically, yelling, "No, no, no! Please, no, no, no!" Finishing off *El Diablo*, the larger angel then turned and took *La Bruja* into his arms with such tenderness, calling her "Mama." Juan thought that was so, so funny. He'd never, for the life of him, thought that witches could also be loving mothers, especially not of angels. And that was the last thing Juan remembered, then he was gone, done, no more.

Waking up, Juan found that he was in bed under the covers in his parents' bedroom. His whole body was in pain. Why, it hurt his head to just move his eyes to look around the room. He tried to lick his lips but his mouth was so dry that he had trouble moving his tongue. He swallowed a few times. He was so thirsty that he didn't know what to do. Water. He needed lots of water, right now. He tried to get up to go get some water, but when he moved, his whole body screamed out in terrible pain.

"Oh, my God!" he said. "What happened to me?"

"Mama, he's woken up," Juan heard Emilia yell in the distance.

"About time!" Juan heard his mother answer from another room. "It's been three days!" Then he heard his mother's feet come rushing over the tile floor and his sister Emilia right behind her.

"So, you've finally come back from the dead," said his mother, smiling at him. "Oh, *mi hijito,* you gave us an awful scare. But what ever possessed you to do such a crazy thing? You know very well how Domingo and those wild boys are about everything. Did you really think that their interpretation of God's wishes would be any different than what they think of the rest of the world?" Gently, she took the back of his head with her right hand and lifted him up just a little so she could spoon-feed him the watery herbs that she'd specially prepared for him.

"Oh, *mi hijito,* I'm so surprised with you. You're my last-born son, and all these years I've been raising you to think for yourself. Doña Josefina is no witch. She's just a bitter, lonely woman. What you did was wrong, *mi hijito.* "

Juan heard his mother's words like in a faraway dream, and he wanted to tell her that he'd only been trying to save their *familia*'s immortal souls, but then he was sound asleep once more, dreaming, dreaming, seeing that flying horse and angel come swooping down out of the heavens and once more scatter the pack of mad dogs. Then, here came that female coyote again, and she smiled at him. Suddenly Juan felt all warm and good, with the female coyote at his side. Then his head was being raised up again and he was spoon-fed some more warm watery liquid and, when he opened his eyes, he saw that his mother was, indeed, the female coyote, and she was smiling down on him as she fed him. Now he realized why that female coyote had been so willing to lead the pack of dogs away from him. Why, the female coyote had been his own beloved mother.

"Drink up," his mother was now saying as she fed him with the smooth-feeling wooden spoon, "and keep in mind as you grow stronger that all these years I've been raising you to be a gentle man—not another lost male, *mi hijito,* who destroys all he lays his hands on because he feels so left out of the joy of giving birth.

"Oh, I love you so very much, *mi hijito,* so very much, but you must promise me to never do such a thing again without consulting me first. You've become a little man, *mi hijito,* and a man always needs a woman's opinion in order to round out his decisions. Like the broken cliff rocks that fall into the stream need the river waters to smooth out their rough edges and make them round and smooth and whole, so do a man's decisions need a woman's influence to be complete.

"Domingo and those others were wrong, *mi hijito,* very wrong. Doña Josefina is no *bruja,* any more than I am. She's just a lonely, lost woman who has tilled her garden alone all these years because she was wronged by a man in her youth—as so many women have been wronged by men since the beginning of time. And so she has strange ways and doesn't trust anyone, especially not since that old mule driver abused her, too. But she's basically a good woman, *mi hijito,* just a little crazy and scared like so many of us when we lose our faith in God. Believe me, she's no witch; those are just the rumors that people like to pass around, especially men who can't stand to see a woman doing well on her own.

"Now, drink up. We got to get you strong again. Christmas is only a few days away and then a week later we have the wedding. That poor woman, she works so hard for her peaches and she'd have none to sell if she didn't have you boys intimidated by her wild ways."

Then Juan heard heavy footsteps, and into the room came Jose and Jose-Luis.

"Juan," said Jose, "Jose-Luis is here to see you. He's been coming to see you every day since the accident."

"That was no accident," said Jose-Luis with *gusto*. "That was a message sent to Luisa and me straight from God! Now we can go into our marriage with open hearts! Juanito, you saved the day for us by bringing everything out into the open that everyone has been talking about for years all over the valley but has never had the guts to come and say to me or to my beloved mother's face!"

"Are you two the ones, the . . . the angels who got the dogs off me?" asked Juan, seeing Jose and Jose-Luis in a whole new way.

Jose grinned. "Yes, Jose-Luis and I are those angels."

Jose-Luis came close and took Juan's hand gently. "We destroyed all the dogs, *amo*. Now you can come by our home without fear anytime you please. I swear, *en el otro mundo no hay malo, pero en este mundo quién sabe con todo los miedos y celos que la gente esconde en sus corazones!*" In the other world there are no evils, Jose-Luis had said, but in this world who can know with all the fears and jealousies that people hide in their hearts.

"You are *mi amo*," continued Jose-Luis, "you are my soul, my hero, my savior. And my poor mother will come around to saying the same thing once she gets over the mourning of her dogs. Yes, we had to kill them all, except for *Cara Chata*. She wasn't trying to bite you when we ran up. No, like the proper little lady she is, she'd figured that she'd done her job of calling in the pack and so she was just sitting back and watching with that head of hers tilted at that funny little angle she always gets." Jose-Luis laughed. "You are *mi amo,* my hero, and I give you homage!" Then he kissed Juan on the forehead ever so gently.

"All right, no more now," said Doña Margarita. "That's enough for today. He needs to sleep so he can regain his strength. Oh, I knew those wild boys were up to no good when I sent you two to go check on them. I could feel it in my bones."

"And you were right, Mama," said Jose. "We just barely got there in time."

"Yes," said Jose-Luis, "and if Jose wasn't the greatest horseman in all the region, he wouldn't have been able to clear those rock fences with such ease riding bareback and get there before the dogs did even more damage."

Juan heard no more. He was off in a dream once again and the smiling coyote was by his side, keeping watch over him. He smiled back at the coyote, feeling so happy, and Jose-Luis's words *en el otro mundo no hay malo* continued singing in his brain. Then he realized that yes, indeed, even though his own beloved mother could turn herself into a she-coyote at will, this didn't make her a witch. No, it simply made her a powerful woman who was wild of heart. There were no witches. There was no evil on the other side. That was all just a rumor coming out of the fear and jealousy that people hide in their hearts and souls.

It was Christmas day, and the whole house smelled of cooking and baking. All the family was present—thirty-some cousins and cousin-brothers and their aunts and uncles and parents. Don Pio, Juan's grandfather on his mother's side, had also come up the mountain from the town of Piedra Gorda, Fat Rock, with his young bride. The great old man was fifty-five years older than the young Indian girl whom he'd married, but no one laughed at them when they saw them together. He looked stronger and better than he'd looked in years, and she was just glowing, she was so much in love with him.

Emilia and Jose came into the bedroom where Juan was staying. "Come on, lazybones!" said Emilia to Juan, smiling. "Mama has said to bring you into the living room, where we've set up a special chair for you!" She was so happy. It made Juan feel all warm and good inside to see Jose and Emilia's love.

Jose picked up Juan in his arms, being careful not to touch the leg that *El Diablo* had chewed up, and carried him across the house. All the kids came rushing to Juan. He was the talk of the whole valley. In fact, it was now said that Juan was a boy so brave that the blood ran backward from his heart.

Domingo watched all their cousins give Juan greeting and ask him if it was true that he'd faced the witch eye-to-eye in midfield and had singlehandedly fought her pack of dogs to a standstill. Seeing all the cousins speak to Juan with such adoration, Domingo's face filled with rage and jealousy.

Suddenly, out of nowhere, Domingo felt a powerful hand grip his shoulder. Turning about, he saw that it was his brother Jose. Christmas was the only day of the year that Jose was allowed under their roof while their father was present. "If you want people to look at you like that, little brother," Jose said to Domingo, "then next time you do your own dirty work and don't push people littler than you to do it for you."

"But he's the youngest!" snapped Domingo. "The purest of heart! And the priest has always told us that—"

"Don't give me that crap," said Jose, cutting him off. Mariposa stood a few feet away, watching. "We both know that you can always take the words of the priest or the Bible and twist them into any sneaky little act you want to commit. Remember that our mother always adds to the Bible or the priest's words 'Does it harm anyone? Does it cause pain and darkness? Or does it bring a little more peace to our hearts, and light to our souls?'

"Domingo," said Jose quietly but firmly, "look at me in the eyes. You're no fool. You're smart and could be a good leader, but you have got to stop sneaking off behind pigpens to do your glorious deeds." Eye-to-eye, both brothers held. "You know damn well that what you were doing was wrong, or you wouldn't have been hiding."

And saying this, Jose continued staring at his larger, younger, fair-headed brother. The tension became so great that Domingo was ready to explode. He just wasn't going to give an inch. But, just then, the front door opened, and in came Jose-Luis with his mother. The woman was all dressed up, and she had a basket covered with a cloth in her hand. In all these years, no one had ever seen *La Bruja* dressed up like a lady. The room went silent. Even Don Juan, who'd been talking loudly and drinking tequila with a couple of relatives, stopped his words. No one moved. Everyone stared in complete silence—adults and children alike. It was Doña Margarita, who was visiting with Don Pio and his beautiful young bride Herlinda, who finally got up and went across the room. She walked right up to the tall, handsome woman and her son, who both towered over her.

"Welcome to our humble home, Doña Josefina," said Doña Margarita. "This is, indeed, a glorious day for us to finally have you here with us under our roof. Merry Christmas!"

"Feliz Navidad," said the tall, powerful woman. Cautiously, she glanced around the room at the dozens and dozens of faces whom she'd seen at a distance over the years but never up this close. "The honor is mine, Doña Margarita. I feel . . . well, most happy that you've invited me and my son to spend this most holy day of Jesus Christ's birthday with you and your *familia.* "

Some people were heard to inhale sharply, being taken aback by the fact that the witch had dared pass God's Most Sacred Son's name through her lips.

But Doña Margarita wasn't surprised at all and said, "From

now on, you and your son will always be invited to pass the holy days of Christmas with us. For let it be known," she added, taking *La Bruja* by the hand and turning to everyone in the room, "that from now on, Doña Josefina and her son Jose-Luis are part of *nuestra familia* and they are both to be loved and respected as our family members here on earth and afterwards in heaven, too!"

A couple of the younger cousins giggled. "Here on earth, maybe, yes," one whispered, "but how is a witch supposed to ever get into heaven?" All the kids giggled.

Juan's mother turned toward Juan and the kids, saw them giggling, and came flying toward them, bringing the witch with her by the hand. "And, children, I want you each to meet Doña Josefina personally and shake hands with her."

The kids froze in terror. Domingo and a few others quickly tried to crouch down and sneak away, but there was Jose on one side of them, and here came Jose-Luis on the other side. Domingo froze and so did the others who'd been thinking of getting away.

"Come on, step forward one at a time and shake hands with Doña Josefina," said Doña Margarita once again. But no child would dare come forward. They all just held back in dread terror. They didn't care what Doña Margarita said; they knew that this woman was evil to the bottom of her heart.

Seeing how terrified the children were of her, Doña Josefina took a big breath and then said, "They don't have to shake my hand, Doña Margarita." Tears came to the large woman's eyes. "Children, after all, really do no more . . . than what their parents would really like to do themselves, but don't have the guts . . . to come forward and do it!"

A hush of whispers went all through the room.

Wiping her eyes, Doña Josefina turned to her son Jose-Luis. "Come, let's go. I'd told you it was a mistake for you to bring me here today. These fine people will never accept me in a million years!"

"But, Mama," said Jose-Luis helplessly, "we've got to try and—"

"Then stay if you like!" she snapped. "But I'm leaving!" And She turned with all the dignity she could muster and had started to go when a voice behind her said, "I'd like to shake your hand, *señora.*"

It was a child's voice. *La Bruja* stopped dead in her tracks. She and everyone else turned to see who had spoken. The group of children opened up, and there sat Juan in the big chair that had been prepared for him. He swallowed, then repeated himself. "I'd like to shake your hand, *señora.*"

"Eh, aren't you the one who—" The big woman stopped her words. Juan's hands and arms and legs were still all covered with swollen bruises and large reddish-black wounds.

"Yes," said Juan, "I'm the one and, well, I want to say that I'm sorry for—for—" Tears came to his eyes. The room was silent. Juan had to swallow several times before he could go on. "I mean, I know you work real hard to grow your peaches, *señora,* and I had no right to steal them, even if I think you are a witch."

People gasped. Others choked. The whole room was filled with a nervous hush of coughing and breathing. Some people began to fan themselves, trying to get air.

"Juan, you must apologize for what you said," said Doña Margarita.

"No, *señora,*" said Doña Josefina, "please don't have him apologize for simply saying what he really thinks. For the truth is that half of the good people in this room think the same thing, but don't have the nerve to say it to my face." She glanced around the room, looking from face to face. The room was absolutely still. Then she turned back to Juan. "Thank you, child, for acknowledging that I do work hard to grow my peaches. I accept your apology. And about you thinking I'm a witch, well, what can I say, except that—"

"You don't have to explain yourself, Mama!" bellowed Jose-

Luis, standing up tall. The cords of his powerful neck came up like ropes, he was so mad.

"But I want to explain," said his mother. "I don't want you to have to run away from this valley like your brother had to do!"

The talk had become so terrible about her second son, whom she'd had because of the mule driver, that the boy had finally had to run away, so he could start a life of his own. The large, well-muscled lady took a deep breath. Never in her life had she ever spoken publicly. She was terrified, but she saw no other way. "I'm no witch," she said to everyone—men, women, and children alike. "Do you hear me? I'm no *bruja!*" Tears came to her eyes. "Yes, maybe I've acted like one over the years, being overprotective of my trees. And using manure and animals' guts and blood to feed my trees has, I'm sure, caused much talk, too, but . . . but that doesn't make me a witch!" she said. "That just makes me a woman who doesn't have much trust in people —especially men—and shows that I know what I'm doing when it comes to growing plants and trees.

"My mango tree, my winter peaches, they aren't the accomplishments of witchcraft. No, they are the accomplishments of, well—" the tears streamed down her face "—of science, which the old priest in town taught me, along with so many other wonders of life." She stopped her words, weeping uncontrollably. Jose-Luis took his mother in his arms, holding her tenderly. Luisa also came up and hugged her mother-in-law-to-be.

A few people began to whisper, but no one spoke aloud. They were all stunned. They were shocked. They'd never expected in a hundred million years to see this big, powerful, wild-woman— whom they'd all considered to be a witch—to be crying like this, so tenderly, on her son's massive shoulder.

"All right," said Doña Margarita, stepping forward after a proper quiet moment, "as I was saying, I want each of the children to meet you, Doña Josefina, and Juan here has volunteered to be the first."

"Oh, yes, excuse me," said the large woman, "just let me dry my eyes, please."

And so everyone watched as this woman dried her eyes and then stepped forward to meet little Juan. "I'm so glad to meet you," she said, smiling. "In the last few days, my son Jose-Luis has told me so much about you."

She reached out, giving Juan her huge, hard hand. Juan looked at the big fingers and callused palm and then took it. It felt as heavy as a large stone.

"Merry Christmas," she said, eyes full of merriment, "and, look, I've brought you a basket of peaches." They were the largest, prettiest peaches anyone had ever seen. "And from now on," she continued to Juan, "whenever you want some, just come by the house and we'll pick them together. That way, you won't get green ones like you did the other night."

"Those were green?" asked Juan, astonished.

"Yes," she said, laughing. "Green-green!"

"Oh, no!" said Juan, laughing, too. Then, looking at the basketful of peaches and smelling the rich aroma, Juan took one and bit into it. "Oh, my God, this is heaven!" he said.

"Exactly!" said the tall woman. "And those were the exact same words the poor old priest always used to tell me, too," she said, tears coming to her eyes again. "Oh, he was a good man, a very good man, God rest his soul in heaven," she added, making the sign of the cross over herself. "I loved him; I truly loved him. He was my everything good and bad here on earth, all wrapped up in one blessed human being, so help me God!"

And in that instant, all the people in the room realized who Jose-Luis's father was. Why, this large, tall woman and the old priest had loved each other as a man and a woman.

Quickly, others started making the sign of the cross over themselves, too. For this was, indeed, a special moment, a holy moment. God had come down upon the earth and visited them, His people, in all His power and mystery and miraculous wonders of love.

Then a child spoke—the smallest child in the room who could speak. "If I shake your hand and let you hug me and kiss me," said the child, "will you give me a peach, too?"

People started laughing, melting, relaxing.

"Why, yes," said Doña Josefina, "certainly."

"Oh, good, Señora Witch!" shouted the little girl, throwing open her tiny arms for a big hug and kiss.

The whole room exploded with laughter. Even Domingo was finally caught up in the whole spirit of the moment.

So the child and Josefina hugged each other, and the people were filled with such relief that they just couldn't stop laughing and smiling. Don Juan went back to his drinking, and Doña Josefina went across the *ramada* to present Don Pio with a peach. After all, it had been Don Pio who'd come by the day that the mule driver abused her, and he'd had the man arrested, horse-whipped, and run out of the valley.

"I know this isn't much, Don Pio," said Josefina, "but I'd like to give you this fruit and ask for your forgiveness. I had no idea that he was your grandson. I'm so sorry."

"There's no need for that," said Don Pio. "After all, it's Christmas, a day of great celebration. And remember, how can we mere mortals not forgive one another our trespasses when God Himself sent down His only Son to die for our sins?

"Let us rejoice, Josefina; you are part of *nuestra familia* now, and among family, we must all do our best to live and let live, or, believe me, we could go crazy with our differences. You are a fine woman, and we're proud to have you and your son Jose-Luis as part of *nuestra familia.*"

Don Juan and a few others were watching as Josefina and Don Pio spoke together. Then it was time to eat, and everyone gathered around the long table of food that had been specially prepared all week long. And just as Don Juan began to say grace, Doña Margarita quickly stepped forward and asked her father, Don Pio, if he would do them the honor of leading them in prayer.

"Why, of course," said the grand old man. And yes, he'd seen that Don Juan had been ready to say the grace, but he didn't want to take any chances. Especially since this was the only day of the year that his grandson Jose was permitted to be in the house with them—the very house that Don Pio had built with his own two hands and then gifted to his daughter.

And so Don Pio led them all in prayer and the much-feared woman of their valley joined them. And the people now saw very clearly that, yes, indeed, she could make the sign of the cross over herself, just like any other good Christian, and the earth didn't part and swallow her whole. Why, she was just a poor lost soul like everyone else.

Then Jose and Mariposa sat down alongside little Juan to eat with him, and then Jose-Luis and Luisa joined them, too. Juan felt like a little king sitting in his throne-like chair with all these happy people around him. And when the time came for everyone to sing happy birthday to God's Beloved Son, Juan would swear that he actually saw Jesus stop looking so sad—hanging there on the cross over the doorway—and He straightened up and cast a big, beautiful smile at Juan, winking His left eye.

3

And suddenly one evening, the Great Father Sun gave birth to a Baby Shooting Sun who came flying across the heavens with his tail on fire, announcing to all the known world the beginning of God's new **paraíso de la tierra sagrada.**

And so they, *la familia,* were dancing, singing, having a wonderful time at Luisa and Jose-Luis's wedding when Colonel Alfonso Montemayor de los Santos and two of his *Rurales* rode up on their fine horses. The colonel was dressed in a gorgeous soft grey *charro* suit with silver buttons up and down his leggings, and he looked so handsome on his well-fed white-grey stallion. Don Juan Villaseñor met him at the entrance of their *ramada,* asking Vicente and Alejo to please take the colonel's horse and his two men down to the barn and care for the horses, then hurry back to join the celebration.

"Come right in, *mi Coronel!*" said Don Juan graciously. "I want you to meet my daughter and son-in-law. You just missed the wedding ceremony, but—like any wise man—you made it in time for the celebration and the great feast!"

Escorting the colonel through the crowd of people, Don Juan led him to where Jose-Luis and Luisa were seated together. Juan Villaseñor was a big man, six feet tall, and the colonel was almost as large, too. But when Jose-Luis stood up to greet them, he dwarfed both of them with his huge bear-like loose-limbed body and big *gran* smile.

"Coronel," said Juan Villaseñor, "I'd like to introduce you to my daughter Luisa and her husband Jose-Luis, whose mother grows the finest peaches in all the region."

"You mean the—"

"Exactly," said Don Juan, laughing. "That's Jose-Luis's mother, the woman with the—let's say—unusual reputation!"

"My, I never realized she had a son . . . and so large," said the colonel.

"He's a bull!" said Don Juan proudly. "The only man in the whole region who might be almost as strong as me!" he added, laughing happily.

And as they shook hands, the colonel felt his hand become engulfed in Jose-Luis's huge paw. "Why haven't I ever seen you before?" asked the colonel.

Jose-Luis laughed. "I work down in Leon, and also, a long time ago I learned that it's always best to avoid meeting up with authority!"

Hearing this, the colonel burst out laughing, too. "I can fully agree with you. Life is so much easier when one doesn't confront authority. In fact, that's been the secret of life since time began, but so many people—particularly nowadays—fail to understand this single truth. Why, at my home, we'd do anything to avoid my father's wrath."

"Exactly," said Don Juan. "We must all respect authority! Why, if you and your men didn't patrol these mountains on a regular basis, we'd have thieves running wild every-which-way. At least this way, we only got one good *chingón* thief that we can depend on regularly," he said, laughing. "Come!" he added, putting his arm about the colonel's shoulders, "let's get you some food and drink!"

The colonel didn't quite know how to take this last remark from his good friend, Juan Villaseñor. What the hell was he saying? That they, the *Rurales,* were thieves? But he figured that he was among good friends for a change, so he decided to just let it pass and went across the patio toward the long table, which was laid out with an incredible feast fit for a king. A whole steer had been slaughtered and barbecued, and a pig was being cooked into *carnitas.* And the tequila . . . why, it was the finest of all the region and was being served *a lo gallo* with Mexican lime slices and salt and great shouts *de gusto!*

Licking the top of his left fist, then putting a pinch of salt on the well-licked spot, the colonel lined up with the other drinking men and took a slice of sweet Mexican lime between his left thumb and index finger. He smiled to the others as he took the earthen shooter-cup of straight tequila that had been served to him. He nodded to Don Juan, and then both men together shot the tequila down their throats as they threw back their heads. Then they quickly licked the salt, bit the lime, and inhaled deeply, mixing the fire of the tequila with the salt and lime and a sudden gush of oxygen. They let out a yelping *grito de gusto,* feeling the instant rush of the liquor and fresh air hitting their brains with a *wamm-oh!*

The line of *charros* applauded the colonel, and so he and Juan did it five more times in rapid order. Then laughing, arm in arm, they turned to go to the banquet of beef and *carnitas,* beans and platters of tortillas, exquisite dishes of salsa and baskets of fresh fruit and vegetables. The colonel's stomach was empty. He hadn't been snacking all day as Don Juan had done, so his tequila-soaked brain was spinning.

And at that very moment, he saw Mariposa in all her wondrous beauty, dancing with Jose under an oak tree, along with Juanito and half a dozen other children. Around and around, the widow danced with Jose and the children, having so much fun as the musician played and the sunlight came down through the tree branches, giving them all a golden storybook-look of pure happiness.

The colonel stopped dead in his tracks, wiped his mouth, and marched directly over to them. Juanito and the children were the first to sense the powerful menace of the colonel coming toward them, and they stopped dancing. Then Jose and Mariposa stopped dancing, too.

"Where were you?" bellowed the colonel at the widow. "We came by with the carriage after hours of terrible labor to get here, but you were gone!"

The music stopped.

Doña Margarita, who'd been speaking with her elderly father, Don Pio, and his young Indian bride, Herlinda, stopped talking, too. Everyone in the patio was stunned by the colonel's sudden outburst.

"Well," said Mariposa cautiously, "I waited for you as you asked but, well, when it was getting late, I didn't know what to do, so I—I simply—"

She lost it, her face twisted, and her beauty was beginning to evaporate before everyone's eyes. Quickly, Jose took her hand.

"I asked her to come with me," he said, facing the colonel, "so she wouldn't be late for my sister's wedding. She didn't mean to offend you in any way or manner, *mi Coronel!*"

But the colonel never heard a word that was being said to him. All he could do was stare at Jose's small, dark hand, which had taken the widow's lovely white hand. And she'd accepted it so readily. Coming out of his trance, he screamed.

"How dare you take her hand, you Indian peasant fool!" He was outraged. Mariposa was so white of skin and beautiful. "I'll have you dragged and horsewhipped!"

The colonel's two men were just entering the patio, laughing and joking along with Alejo and Vicente. They'd stayed down at the barn to shoot down a few tequilas, too. And now, when they heard their colonel's shout, they instantly went for their guns.

But Jose-Luis—who'd seen them coming—was already behind them, and as easy as pie, he popped one on top of the head with his huge fist, dropping him to the ground like he'd been struck by a sledgehammer, and he slapped the other up across the left ear, grabbing his gun as he sank to his knees.

"Release her instantly!" the colonel continued shouting. He grabbed Mariposa by the arm, pulling her to himself. "You will dance with me! You will dance with me right now! And you!" he yelled at the musicians, "start playing again!"

They began to play once more, and the colonel pulled Mariposa around with him, lifting his feet high into the air as he'd seen the children and Jose doing. He wanted that joy; he really wanted that happiness that he'd seen them having with the children, but it wasn't working, it wasn't happening. And so he went into a rage again and slapped Mariposa, yelling, "What's wrong with you? I've treated you like a queen! I brought you silks and a golden carriage! What the hell more do you want?! You treacherous woman!"

Her ears were ringing from the slap, but she'd been slapped by strong hands before. And this time, hearing herself being called a "treacherous woman," something snapped inside Mariposa, and she was enraged—enraged even more than she was frightened or hurt. "What I want," she said, wishing that she'd spoken up in all those years of her marriage, "is to be treated with respect! And love!" Her heart was pounding and yet she stood up taller than she'd ever stood before. "No woman really wants to be treated like a queen, *mi Coronel!* A woman wants softness, kindness, and the confidence of a slow, gentle hand."

"His? This poor Indian imbecile's hand?" shouted the colonel. He was outraged. Why, not only had she talked back at him, but now she was shamefully admitting that she loved this stupid dark Indian boy. He pulled back his fist to slug her with all his might this time, but before he could deliver the blow, Jose grabbed his wrist, yanking him about.

The colonel was shocked. He was a bull of a man, just under

six feet tall, and this little, insignificant piece of Indian *caca* had grabbed his wrist with such force that he'd been turned on his heels. He couldn't believe it. It was all happening to him like in a faraway dream until, facing the boy, the colonel now saw his dark Indian eyes, and they were burning, burning. They were completely aflame with such raging anger that it put terror into the colonel's very soul.

The big man went for his gun. But, to his shock, it was kicked from his hand before he could even get it completely out of his holster. And then there were those huge dark eyes again, without any fear whatsoever, and they were bearing down on him. And in that instant, the colonel realized that he'd been right about this Indian when he'd first seen him at the widow's house last month, and he should've had him executed immediately, just as he and his men had been executing every Indian boy with eyes afire that they'd come across for over two years. For Mexico would never be at peace until they had stamped out all the bad Indians, as their good neighbor to the north of them, the U.S., had done. The colonel shouted for his men.

"Here they are," said Jose-Luis, calmly dragging them both up. "They fell. Poor *hombres*. But I'm sure that they'll be all right in a few minutes."

The colonel didn't know what to do. "Don Juan!" he demanded. "What is the meaning of this? Why don't you and your sons execute this Indian for me?"

Don Juan glanced around at all his *familia,* dark and light alike, and then walked over to Jose. "But this is my son," he said, putting his arm around Jose. "These are all my sons."

The colonel's eyes went huge with disbelief. He was speechless. He glanced around at everyone, and suddenly each man, each woman and child, looked Indian, or at least part Indian, and he felt naked.

He turned and leaped for his gun that lay on the ground beside him. But before he'd even moved, this skinny insignificant boy, who'd stood over there alongside his tall, handsome, red-headed father, was so fast, so incredibly agile, that he just flew over the ground, shot by him, and swept the gun away with his boot.

In a mad rage, the colonel lunged for his weapon again, wanting to come up firing, killing, massacring everyone. But once more the boy moved in a whirling-blur of motion and came up holding the weapon right between the colonel's eyes. *El coronel* felt utterly helpless. Why, he was a little fat rich boy again, and he didn't have a chance against all these wild kids of the street.

Jose removed the gun from between the colonel's eyes, unloaded it, and gave it to him, as one would treat a harmless child. *El coronel* took it and suddenly felt so tired, so completely exhausted and baffled, that he was no longer big and handsome; no, he was old and fat and ugly, and it looked like he might pass out.

Don Juan took him by the arm, leading him out. Vicente and Alejo brought up their horses, and all three men were put back on their mounts. Now the colonel was feeling a little safer and so he surveyed the people and then tried to shout at them, but it came out as a squeak.

"I'll be back," he squeaked, "and I'll get all of you stupid, imbecile Indians, so help me God!" The poor man took a big breath and now tried to bellow. "You backward, ignorant, savage Villaseñors have no right to live!"

Don Juan, who'd been holding the colonel's horse by the reins and feeling sorry for the man, now heard his family's great name insulted; and the rage that came to him was so incredible, that he wanted to break the man's face in two with his bare hands. But, also, he felt torn because the colonel had already been destroyed. So, instead, Don Juan swung at the colonel's well-fed stallion with all his massive power as he jerked down on the reins. And he caught the horse across the temple with the meaty bottom of his fist, and the twelve-hundred-pound animal dropped to the ground as if hit by a lightning bolt.

His horse knocked out from under him, the colonel yelled

with absolute terror, running down the road on foot, his fat, drunken ass wiggling as he went. Oh, it was hysterical, and the people howled with laughter.

Don Pio, the great man himself, now called everyone together. "Enjoy this celebration," he said. "Please enjoy this night with all your hearts and souls, for this is . . . the last celebration that we will have in years to come without burying many of our loved ones, so help me God!" He made the sign of the cross over himself, tears filling his eyes.

"That man, that coward, that bully," continued Don Pio, "will he now go back and tell his soldiers the truth? No, absolutely not! He will say that we abused him, that it took twenty of us to just handle him alone, then he'll say that with one hundred good men, they can come up here and exterminate us like the rats we are. Believe me, he'll lie and they'll believe his lie, and within the week he'll come to get us with a force of hundreds.

"I know; I saw this type of bully cowardice happen again and again in our wars against the rich German *haciendados* of the south and then again when we fought the French. These lands are going to run red with blood, so enjoy tonight. Truly, enjoy tonight! For *mañana* . . . our blood will paint the earth once more!"

Saying this, the great old man took his young Indian bride's hand and began to dance in bliss. And *la gente* watched and then joined them, dancing, singing, celebrating, as they had all been doing before the colonel's arrival.

Juan and the other kids went out back to see if they, too, could punch a calf in the head and knock it to the ground with one mighty blow. But once the cow saw what they were about, she let out a bellow and came charging at them. The kids ran out of the corral, screaming joyfully.

The Father Sun was going down. It had been another wonderful day upon God's wonderful earth. Jose and Mariposa were dancing together once more, and she was so beautiful again. Oh, love was in the air. It had been another magical day in *el paraíso de* Los Altos de Jalisco, and now it was going to be a magical night—a night of love, a night of sleeplessness, a night of people breathing in harmony with the cautious deer, the cleansing plants, the laughing stones, the joking insects, and, of course, the smiling guardian angels who looked out for all of them—the people, the deer, the plants, the stones, the insects, and the harmony of it all.

Two days later, Don Pio was ready to ride down the mountain with twenty-five men. He was going to go to the capital, Mexico City, to see his old friend Don Porfirio, the *Presidente* himself, and inform him of how abusive his *Rurales* had become in the last few years. He was going to see if he could get Don Porfirio to stop this mass slaughter before it began. Don Pio took Jose aside, asking Juanito to hold his horse, Four White Stockings, for him.

"Jose," said the great old man, "I'm leaving you behind, because if anything happens to me, then it is up to you to keep the sanity alive up in these mountains. I will not mention names, but some of us here have more pride than wisdom, more strength than cunning, and so it could become a battleground here very quickly if fighting isn't avoided at all costs. Do you understand?"

"I'm listening, *abuelito.*"

"Good, I know you are." He put his small, dark, wrinkled old hand on Jose's shoulder. "If they strike before I return, you run. You hear me? You run and avoid all fighting. And I know that what I'm asking you to do is against every young man's hot blood, but I don't want any killings, if it can at all be avoided, until I return. Also, by doing this, by running again and again, then they'll figure that we are cowards for sure. So, if we have to fight them someday, then we'll have them set up for such an ambush, that twenty good men with the right terrain can destroy two hundred."

Hearing this, Jose grinned. His grandfather was an absolute genius. He really had been one of Benito Juarez's right-hand men. He hugged his grandfather with all of the *amor de su corazón.* Oh, if it hadn't been for his grandfather's love, Jose didn't know what would've become of him since his father had turned on him. "All right, *abuelito,"* said Jose, "we will avoid all fighting until you return."

"Good. Thank you. You are a good man, Jose, the best. And don't ever let anyone convince you differently. And you, Juanito," said Don Pio, now turning to Juan, "of course were listening to every word, eh? That's why God gave you such a big head and those large ears. You are to learn from everything that you see and hear and become a great man like Don Benito himself. You little wonder," he added, hugging Juan, "coming to your mother in her old age. You are our gift from heaven, *pansonsito!* Little fat-belly, you!"

And Don Pio held little Juan in a warm *abrazo* for a long time. Then Juan held the stallion's reins and Jose helped their grandfather mount up. All the other horsemen were ready to go. Alejo, Vicente, and Everardo were going, too. All of them were dressed in their finest clothes and riding their best horses.

Juan went over to his mother's side. His father and Domingo were on the other side of Doña Margarita. They all waved goodbye to the horsemen. Don Juan and Alejo gave each other another quick hug. Alejo was certainly Don Juan's favorite. But Vicente was pretty close to Don Juan, too. Don Juan's eyes began to water as he saw his two fine-looking, fair-haired, blue-eyed sons go off with their dark little grandfather.

Don Pio's young Indian bride remained rooted to the ground, watching her true love go off, long after everyone else had stopped watching. Oh, how she loved that old man, her husband. She adored him with all her heart and soul.

The colonel didn't hit them that week, and he didn't hit them the following week, either. The rumors were that he'd been called away to settle some pressing matters to the north. Stories were going around that all over Mexico the people were beginning to openly oppose the ruthless *Rurales*.

Jose instructed Mariposa not to let the colonel's absence lessen her caution. "You must be very careful after I leave in the mornings to go to work in the fields," he told her. "You must keep alert, and on the first signs of the colonel's appearance, you have to disappear instantly.

"Because he wants to avenge himself on you, my love," he added. "So go to the church or hide at your neighbor's home immediately. All the people in the valley have been informed. We must all keep calm and work to avoid all conflict until my *papagrande* returns. Hopefully, Don Pio will be able to talk sense to Porfirio and turn things around before we end up in another revolution, *querida.*"

"Jose, you tell me this each day," said Mariposa, "so stop it and just kiss me. Don't you know? I don't care if I live or die, as long as you're with me. You are my life. Hold me, please, hold me, and tonight, let us make miracles again."

And she purred to him like a baby kitten, and then he went off to work in the fields for the day.

It was early evening, the sun had just gone down, and Juan and Domingo were coming up the *barranca* with a gunnysack full of oranges. They were herding home the goats along with their pet bull, Chivo, and their two giant uncles, Basilio and Agustin.

Basilio and Agustin were the children of Don Pio's older brother, Cristobal, and his union with a big, dark local Indian woman, who'd died shortly after the two boys' birth. Basilio and Agustin were grown men in their mid-thirties, but they behaved like children. They had no sense of money or private property and would give a perfect stranger the shirt off their back if the stranger liked it. They were huge men, the only men in all the mountains who were larger than Don Juan or even Jose-Luis. But they didn't have soft, bear-like bodies like Jose-Luis. No, these giants had muscles of iron piled up all over their bodies like they had been welded together with steel plates. In fact, they were so strong that they could lift a three-month-old calf by the tail with just their teeth, or raise a dead bull up off the ground with the brute strength of their mighty backs. They were men so powerful and so huge of sexual organs that it was said they could mate with no human female. They were the most shy and backward and happy of any two adult men in all the mountains, and when it would storm and the sky filled with thunder and lightning, they'd strip off their clothes and go racing naked through the forest of oaks, bellowing to the heavens, trying to outrun the bolts of lightning that streaked across the sky.

Oh, Juan and Domingo just loved being with these giants. They were so funny and outrageous that to spend the day with them was to spend the day in paradise.

It was the evening of the 17th of January, 1910, and Juan and Domingo were now coming up the *barranca* with Basilio and Agustin and their pet bull, Chivo, herding the goats home as they lugged a sack of oranges. Domingo and Juan had acquired the sack of oranges from an *arriero,* a muletrain driver, by trading a young goat. They'd lied to the two giants, telling them that they had their parents' permission to trade a goat for the oranges. But now they were trying to figure out what to do with all the oranges that they hadn't been able to eat. They didn't want to just dump them, because oranges were truly a huge luxury up in these mountains. Oh, Domingo and Juan didn't know what to do. If they showed up with the sack of oranges at home, their parents would be sure to find out that they'd traded a goat for them and they'd get in terrible trouble.

And so here they were, on their way home, when suddenly,

there across the evening sky, came a ball of fire right at them. They all stopped dead in their tracks—animals and humans alike—and stared in wonderment. The ball was huge, burning orange-red like the mighty coal of a hardwood fire, as it came shooting right at them at great speed, leaving behind itself a long trail of fire like a cock's great tail. Oh, it was a sight that they'd never seen before. And it was marvelous!

Immediately, Domingo dropped to his knees, making the sign of the cross over himself. "It's God coming to punish us!" he said. "Oh, please, dear God, Ruler of the universe, I'll never trade another goat without permission as long as I live! Just, please, don't kill me or let this be the end of the world! I'm still a virgin and I'd like to make love just once before I die!"

Domingo continued praying, but the giants only laughed.

"Oh, look!" said Basilio, watching the great ball of fire coming right at them. "God's ass is on fire and He's coming down upon the earth to play with us again!"

"Yes," said Agustin, stretching and loosening his mighty muscles, "and we're going to beat Him for sure this time!"

Quickly, the two giants began to strip off their clothes, pounding their mighty chests and getting ready to run a foot-race with the ball of fire, like they ran races with the lightning bolts every time it thundered.

And Juan was over to one side, along with their pet bull Chivo, and both of them stood rooted to the ground, staring at this wonder of wonders as Domingo continued praying in awful fear and the two giants stretched and stripped and laughed, getting ready to race the greatest race they'd ever raced against God Himself!

"My God!" said Juan in awe. "It looks like a baby sun with his tail on fire! Look how it lights up the whole sky!"

Basilio stopped stretching and took another good, long look at the shooting comet. "You're right, Juan," he said very philosophically, "that is a Baby Sun. You see, what happened is that last night God and His Great Friend, the Father Sun, had a *gran* feast together, and They ate too much and with a mighty fart They gave birth to this new Baby Shooting Sun." He laughed. "Come on, Juan," he said. "Join us! The time has come for all of us to race with God Himself and show Him that we're ready to return to heaven and play with Him again!"

And saying this, Basilio and Agustin took off racing through the oaks, naked as the day they were born, giving *gritos de gusto* as they ran, huge muscles pumping.

Picking up the sack of oranges, Juan took off racing after the giants, shouting at the heavens, too. Chivo, their huge black bull that Domingo and Juan had raised from a little calf, raced after Juan, bellowing as he went and grabbing up each orange that fell from the bag and devouring it. The goats ran behind the bull, cleaning up the sweet orange pieces that were left.

Getting to the cliffs just above their home, Juan came to a small clearing in the oaks and he stopped to catch his breath. He could hear Chivo and the goats bellowing and bleating behind him, and in the distance ahead of him, Juan could hear the giants racing through the forest, giving such shouts of *gusto* that their mighty voices echoed and echoed off the far *barrancas*.

Looking up into the sky, Juan now saw that the ball of fire was closer than ever, large and bright and totally magnificent as it shot across the stars and heavens. Oh, Juan's little heart was bursting, overflowing, and his eyes filled with tears of joy. Then here came his brother up the trail, still praying, still begging to God in awful fear.

"Domingo," said Juan, "don't you see? God isn't mad at us. Just look around; it's all so beautiful! Why, this Baby Sun has come to tell us that the time has come upon the earth for all of us to have fun again!"

"No, you fool!" shouted Domingo right back at him. "It's the end of the world! Don't you see that all the sky is catching on fire, and we're all going to hell!" And he continued praying in a frenzy, trying to make up in a hurry for all the wrongs that he'd ever done.

At their home, Doña Margarita and all the rest of the *familia* were outside of the *ramada* also watching this incredible spectacle. With bottle in hand, Don Juan took a long, hard pull and then passed the bottle to the other men as they watched in terrible fear. The women and children were holding close together and praying. Then they heard the mighty shouts of the two giants as they came racing over the hilltop and out of the forest, running through the pasture below the town—naked as the day they were born—and shouting with joy to the heavens!

Doña Margarita started laughing. "Oh, there they are, our very own two *gran inocentes,* and I bet you that they really do think that they'll catch this heavenly gift from God this time and wrestle it down to the ground before it reaches that distant mountain!"

"Woman," bellowed Don Juan, "stop talking nonsense! Those two damn fools are going to try God Almighty's patience once too often and bring us all to ruin!"

She laughed. "Oh, no, *querido,* they give joy to all the world and the heavens alike! Just listen to their happy shouts!" And saying this, Doña Margarita started shouting with joy. "Go, Basilio! Go, Agustin! Catch that shooting star and reopen Saint Peter's gates for all of us!"

The women loved it and took up Doña Margarita's chant. "Go, Basilio! Go, Agustin! And reopen *San Pedro*'s gates for all of us!"

"Yes!" yelled one woman. "Open up those mighty gates with those great keys you two carry between your legs!"

Hearing this, the women all burst out laughing, screeching with *carcajadas!* And that's when Juan came running over the hill, with Chivo and the herd of goats and Domingo right behind him, and he heard his mother's shouts of joy and all the women laughing.

Coming up the cobblestone street, dragging the sack of the

few remaining oranges, Juan saw that the women were laughing *con loquería,* but the men were drinking and looked pretty angry. Then one husband—who didn't like how his wife was carrying on—drew his gun, wanting to shoot the giants. But another knocked his hand away, and the husband ended up shooting at the sky. The women could see what was happening, and so they tried to stop their laughter and settle down, but they couldn't. Why, they were as excited as little girls, just giggling and laughing.

Don Juan now pulled out his own gun and bellowed, "No shooting stars frighten me!" And he emptied his .45 at the oncoming comet.

Hearing these shots, Chivo pawed the ground in rage, let out a bellowing cry, and attacked, scattering all the drunken men. In the confusion of Chivo's charge, the sack of oranges burst open, and sent all the fruit rolling. The women screeched when they saw the round, golden oranges rolling about on the cobblestones. Picking up the oranges and peeling them, they found them to be the sweetest they'd ever tasted. "Gifts from heaven," one of the women was heard to say.

Juan went up to his mother, handing her his last orange. "Here, Mama, this one is especially for you."

"Oh, thank you, *mi hijito,*" said the old lady, and she put her arm around her smallest child, drawing him close as they continued watching the comet shoot across the heavens. Oh, it was a glorious sight, and little Juan felt so blessed, so happy, so all at peace being at his mother's side and watching this great spectacle.

Domingo, on the other hand, joined the men and sneaked a couple of drinks from the tequila bottles that were being passed around. Oh, it was truly a miraculous night; each person had finally come to find what it was that their soul needed.

And the night sky was bright with wonderment; and the earth rejoiced with the sounds of laughter and the shouts of the two mighty giants as they continued to race after the shooting star, wanting to play with God Himself once again.

The next morning the colonel hit them—the day after Halley's Comet appeared in all its glory. But the people were ready for the colonel, and so they all just ran and hid in the forest of oaks before he reached the settlement.

Enraged at not finding anyone, the colonel and his men began tearing down fences and burning houses. But then, out of nowhere, there appeared a dozen young men on horseback. The young men were such bad shots that a couple of them unloaded their weapons at the colonel and his force of one hundred men, but never hit anyone. Quickly, the colonel and his men took off after the no-good boys, but they were such filthy cowards that they never stood up and fought. No, they just kept running and dodging through the oaks and then leaping across *arroyos*.

Finally, the colonel's large, well-fed horse was so exhausted that he began to stumble. The colonel and his men had big, strong lowland horses. They were no match for these quick little skinny mountain horses with the huge lungs. The colonel held up his hand. "Let them go," he said. "We'll return in a few days with extra mounts, and we'll hit these filthy cowards before daybreak! Mark my words; these Indian imbeciles are going to pay for the abuse they did to me!"

Two more times the colonel came, and two more times Jose and his group of young horsemen led them away so they wouldn't destroy their homes and fields. But Jose and his next-in-command, the short, freckle-faced boy named Felipe Juan Kelly, weren't so sure that they could do this much longer. Already two of their companions had suffered minor wounds. The colonel and his men were shooting to kill, and Jose and his men were only shooting to attract.

Late one afternoon, Don Pio returned from Mexico City. Everyone rushed out to greet him. It didn't look good. The old man was falling off his horse, and half of the people who'd gone with him were missing.

"They killed Alejo!" he said. "They killed Vicente! They killed Eduardo, Ramon, Cesar, and even my mighty old friend, Felipe, who fought so many battles at Porfirio's side! Oh, they massacred all of them! And the poor men were unarmed and carrying a white flag when they rode into the city!"

Don Pio broke down crying, and they took him off of Four White Stockings. The horse's stomach was all caved in. Don Pio had ridden him all the way home, almost three hundred miles, nonstop. "We've lost Mexico! Porfirio has turned rich, white, and French! His people wouldn't even allow us, *los meji-canos,* into our own capital!"

He kept babbling like a lost old man as they carried him into the house. He, this man who'd looked so strong when he'd left. His young bride came and took him into her arms, and he wept like a child—he, the *gran* Don Pio, the great, powerful man of war, man of peace, man of love and life, *la vida.*

Jose led Four White Stockings off, and he knew that the animal was finished. He'd never be any good again. He'd been ridden into the ground, and at his age, there was no coming back.

Don Juan broke that night, too. Receiving the news of the death of his two favorite sons, he went off into the woods to be alone. No one saw him for nearly two weeks; when they did, Don Juan was absolutely drunk out of his mind and looked old and ugly and completely defeated.

That night, Jose and his band of young horsemen also met in the oak forest, just north of town.

"All right," said Jose, "we were waiting for my grandfather's return, and he has returned."

There wasn't a young man in the group who hadn't lost a father or brother or uncle in that massacre in Mexico City. And they'd been unarmed and carrying a flag of truce, Don Pio had said.

"And so," said Jose, "the next time the colonel comes, we don't run. No, we lead him into our famous little hell-hole of no return."

"God help us, yes!" shouted the short, muscular Juan Kelly, *con gusto!* "I'm tired of being shot at and can't shoot back!"

"Do we get to keep the weapons of the men we kill?" asked Jorge, Mateo and Pelon's older brother. Jorge came from a large, poor family. He was the oldest son, and the only weapon he owned was an old, wornout machete.

Jose nodded. "Of course, that's how we'll be arming ourselves from now on: with their weapons and ammunition."

Jorge grinned, turning to his younger brother Manuel.

"Good!" yelled another boy. This one, Chango, had just turned sixteen. "And I'm personally going to kill the two bastards who killed my brother for eating that ear of corn, then arm myself with their weapons so we can finish off the *Rurales* across all of *Méjico!*"

"All right," said Jose, "now let's calm down and go over our plan once more. We got to stay calm and very well organized, or it will never work. Remember, they're not fools."

And so the next time the colonel came up the mountainside from Leon, Guanajuato, with his force of one hundred well-armed soldiers, he was met by Jose and two of his quickest horsemen, Jorge and Juan Kelly, right at the head of the valley. Jose and Juan Kelly had decided that the colonel might be a little reluctant to go on another wild-goose chase, so this time they deliberately rode out of the trees in plain sight of the colonel and his men.

"My dear Colonel," said Jose, taking off his *sombrero*, "did you ever tell your men the truth . . . that it was only one simple Indian boy who embarrassed you that day, or did you lie, saying it was twenty?"

"Why, you insolent, lying little bastard!" screamed the colonel. And he drew his gun, but before he could fire, Jose and his young companions whirled their horses about in a show of great horsemanship, bolting into the oaks.

Gouging his horse with his huge, sharp spurs, the colonel was after Jose and the two young men, shooting as he went. The colonel's men were right behind him, dodging through the trees, trying to head off the boys. But Jose and his young companions had played in these woods since childhood and knew every turn. The colonel and his men chased Jose and his two companions through the trees, leaping *arroyos,* and then across a flat. There, Jose turned into a wide, innocent-looking canyon, and the colonel and his men followed him. It still hadn't entered the colonel's mind that this young, dark Indian boy and his friends had any brains. He just figured that they were a bunch of wild fools of no consequence, and his men—who were used to having their way with people for years—accepted the colonel's judgment, too.

But then up ahead, the canyon suddenly dropped, getting deep and narrow. From here on, no horse could climb up its rocky sides. And just when the colonel was sure that they'd finally trapped the stupid boy, huge balls of burning brush were hurled down upon him and his men, igniting the knee-high grass with an explosion of sound. Their frightened horses went wild, bucking and twisting.

From up above them, hidden in the rocks, nine boys on foot began shooting at the soldiers from a distance of less than a hundred feet. And that's when Jose flipped his *serape* over his horse's head, blinding him as he'd done many times while training him at night, and he gave his mount the spurs, bolting him straight at the leaping fire and the colonel and his men, .38 Special in his hand, firing as he attacked.

Juan Kelly and Jorge were at Jose's side, their horses' heads covered, too, and they were also firing as they came. Jose gunned down five soldiers with the .38, then he drew his machete, and at close range, he cut down two more riders. And then he saw the colonel and the colonel saw him. And as the older man fired wildly at him, Jose gave *un grito de gusto* and came flying at the colonel, with his machete gleaming in the bright light of the dancing fire. Seeing the deliberate, steady coolness with which this crazy-*loco* boy was coming at him, the colonel turned his horse, fleeing in terror, trying to hide among his escaping men.

Juan Kelly's horse had been shot out from under him but, on foot, he was still shooting at the escaping soldiers. And the joy, the absolute joy, that came to Jose and his young men when they saw the terrible fear in the colonel's soldiers' eyes as they now raced off was wonderful. Pure ecstasy. Quickly, the boys came down from the rocks and rushed upon their prey, hacking the survivors with their machetes and stripping them of their weapons and ammunition. Thirty-five they'd killed, thirty-five, and they hadn't lost one single man.

"Oh, that was wonderful!" screamed Jorge. *"¡Los chingamos!* And you looked so great, Jose, leaping your horse through those flames, killing right and left! *¡Los chingamos a todo dar!"*

"Yes, and I killed one of the bastards who killed my brother!" shouted the sixteen-year-old boy. "Look! I cut off both of his ears, and I'm taking them home to my mother!" Blood ran down his arm as he held up the two ears for all the world to see. "Those bastards! Did you see the fear in their eyes?! Killing people for *nada, cabrones!"*

"All right," said Jose, trying to calm down. He alone had killed seven, eye-to-eye, and felt a little shaky. It had all happened so quickly. All his years of training had come in to play in just seconds, and now it was over and they had to get their wits about them again. "Now I want all of you going home for the night and saying your goodbyes. But don't be celebrating or bragging too much. Believe me, this is just the beginning. They will be back in larger numbers and full of treachery. We will never be able to do a massacre like this again. They now know who we really are, and we're . . . *chingonese, a todo dar!*"

"Yes!" screamed one young, baby-faced warrior. "We are *chingonese!*"

"Now let's go in groups of two or three," said Jose. "And be careful. Very careful; I don't want anyone getting ambushed on their way home."

"Don't worry," said Juan Kelly, "those bastards are going to run all the way home to their garrison with their assholes puckered up tight! Their eyes, did you see the fear in their eyes?! Oh, we really got those *cabrón* cowards!"

"Yes, but we have to calm back down, Kelly, and not let this go to our heads. Like I said, this is just the beginning."

Taking a few deep breaths, Juan Kelly calmed himself down. "Will you be going to see your grandfather?" he asked Jose.

"Yes," said Jose.

"Well, I'd like to go with you, since I'm second-in-command," said the dark, red-headed boy. "Jesus, I never really thought that it was going to work this well. We massacred those bastards, but good!"

"My grandfather told me," said Jose, "to never ever underestimate the ridiculousness of a prideful man. That colonel should never have followed us into this canyon," added Jose, as he and Juan Kelly rode off together. "He was a fool, but he won't be a fool again."

Riding down the mountain that night to the little town of Fat Rock, Jose was very quiet. He could now also see many of the other things that his grandfather had always explained to him over the years. One was that the human being was only centimeters away from becoming a wild beast again, and so a good leader had to be very careful of his own men, or they could very quickly become as lost and cruel as the very monsters that they were fighting. Those two ears that the boy had cut were just the beginning. The *Rurales* had been beating the people down for years, and there was a lot of hatred in these young men's hearts. And, also, once a man had the smell of the kill in his nostril, he was a very dangerous animal, his *papagrande* had explained to him. Oh, that whole canyon had filled with the sweet, pungent odor of blood. And the pure rush of excitement that he, Jose, had gotten as he'd raced head-on into those men, shooting as he came, had been so wonderful, that it was scary.

Approaching the town at Piedra Gorda, Jose and Juan Kelly reined in. This town wasn't very large or important, except for the fact that it stood at the entrance of the shortcut between the cities of Leon, Guanajuato, and Guadalajara, Jalisco. Each of these cities was the capital of its state, and the colonel and his men were responsible for keeping the roads safe between these two state capitals.

Riding into town, Jose and Juan were met by a couple of young men they knew. The two men informed the boys that the famous colonel himself had suffered a great defeat today, and that the whole town was celebrating.

Before Juan Kelly could say a word, Jose pushed his horse into Juan Kelly's mount. "Oh," said Jose, "we hadn't heard. Thank you."

Then he and Juan rode on down the street, with their horses' hooves echoing on the cobblestones. "But why didn't you let me tell them that it was us who did it?!" said Kelly.

"Because when the going gets tough," said Jose, "it's going to be one of our own friends who turns us in, and I don't want to tempt fate any more than we have to."

"Oh, no, you're wrong!" said Juan Kelly. "The people are with us! Everyone hates that colonel and his men as much as we do!"

"Yes, they do," said Jose. "But in the long run, my *papagrande* has always explained to me that it's seldom your enemies who do you in. It's your very own Judas every time." And saying this, Jose gave his horse the spurs. For there was no way on earth that Jose could explain to his young friend Juan Kelly the things that he knew. For the day he was cast aside to live with the animals at the age of twelve, Jose's whole view of the world had changed. No longer had he spent his time with other boys talking or playing. No, he'd begun to see the world all around him as if he were almost a stranger to the planet. And when his grandfather had spoken to him, he'd had the ability to really, really listen with all his heart and soul. And that's when he'd begun to see the world as something more than just interesting, and to watch all things with such concentration that the very act of watching became a passion in itself, and all of life took on dazzling new significance.

Take, for instance, the first time he'd noticed that old blind Indian woman coming down that rocky path to church. He'd sat there on a little knoll outside of town and he'd watched her with such fascination that he'd actually waited until mass was over, just so he could watch her again. And he'd sat there watching with such intensity as she now came dancing up the little rocky path from the church, that it was as if no one else existed in all the world except himself and this old blind woman. Why, she was a marvel of movement to watch, and yet she'd been doing it for so long that nobody in the community bothered to notice anymore. It was as if God Himself had presented them with this gift straight from heaven, but they'd lost their ability to see.

Finally, after watching her half a dozen more times and marveling at her ability, Jose had gone up to her and asked her how she was able to perform such a miracle. And when she'd told him that God gave blind people a special vision that came straight from the heart, there'd been nothing else that he could think of. But, of course, he was sure that it never would have entered his mind to start copying her and come down that same path in the dark of the night with his eyes closed, if he hadn't been a person so alone in the world. Neither would it have entered his mind to keep doing it again and again until the eyes of his heart opened, and he could also fly over stone in darkness like the old blind woman, if he hadn't been living all alone with the animals.

Oh, yes, he'd lost his home, his family, his father, whom he loved so much, but it was almost as if the heavens above had adopted him. For a secret angel had opened up inside of him and embraced his soul.

And so this night Jose rode in silence, knowing that there was no way on earth that he could ever explain himself to his young friend. But maybe his grandfather could do it. And so Jose introduced Juan Kelly to Don Pio that night, and they spoke all night long. And the great old warrior explained to them many things. He informed them that this defeat that they'd just handed the *Rurales* up in that canyon was happening all over Mexico.

"You see," said the great old man, "after they shot down your brothers at the capital, Jose, they hit our camp at daylight. And we were doing nothing but sleeping and preparing our breakfast. I swear, military men know no love or loyalty except to force itself. Here we were, the very men who'd helped Porfirio come to power, and now he'd turned his new forces on us, his own people. The few of us who managed to get away swore that we'd spread the word to every region of all of *Méjico*. So, believe me, God, yes, what you boys did up in those mountains today is happening all over Mexico, as we speak here, this moment."

He smiled. "These *Rurales* have been ruling this country for Porfirio with a fist of iron for nearly thirty years, but that's all going to change very quickly. *La gente* will take only so much, *mi hijitos*," he added, "and then they explode. But you two must be very careful. You're never going to be able to do a massacre like that again. That colonel is going to be very treacherous from now on. He's got to do all he can to save face."

"Yes, we know," said Jose. "We were speaking of that when we rode in, *Papagrande.*"

"Good," said the old man, looking carefully at his grandson and his young freckle-faced friend, "I'm glad you know that. And also remember, as I've told you many times, Jose, that in the long run it will not be your enemies who finally defeat you in life, but your friends and your very own greed."

"But does it have to be like that?" asked Juan Kelly. He just hated this idea. "My God, it almost makes it sound stupid to even fight your enemies, if it only ends up being your own friends or yourself who destroys you at the end."

The old man smiled kindly and reached out, stroking the young man's hand. "Exactly, Juan," he said. "Exactly. And this is why every young warrior must always fight the demons he carries here inside his own heart as much—if not more—than the demons he fights out here in battle. Just take a look at this *gran* Porfirio who, over the years, has grown to consider himself almost a god. It's his own friends and greed that are finally bringing him down, not his enemies. So believe me, Juan Kelly, look inside yourself very closely. Porfirio was a good man at one time, too. But then his pride won out and he stopped listening to his heart."

Young Kelly's head was reeling when they saddled up and went back up the mountain at daybreak. He was now beginning to understand why Jose knew so much and yet was still only a boy of nineteen.

"My God," he said to Jose, "I'd never heard someone speak with so much sense before. Why, to sit before your grandfather was like sitting before the throne of wisdom! Not once did he ever say don't do this or that like most adults. No, he just simply told us how to think clearly, what to expect, and that it was all up to us, whatever we decide to do. And I can now see that he's right, Jose, as we grow stronger and stronger, it's not going to be our enemies who we have to watch out for; it's us, here inside of ourselves."

Jose smiled. He could see how excited Juan Kelly was. He just couldn't stop talking. And Jose well knew how he felt. The first time that his grandfather had spoken to him, right after he'd been banned from his home, he'd felt wings. He'd been in the barn, crying his eyes out, thinking that it was the end of the world, that maybe even somehow it had been his fault that his father hated him so much. But then out of nowhere, his grandfather Don Pio had come into the barn one night, and he said to him, "Rise up from ashes of your broken heart, Jose, and thank Almighty God for this great challenge that has been bestowed upon you! For your father knows no more what he does than the men who executed Our Lord Savior at Calvary. Rise up, I say to you, and open your eyes and ears as you never have before and go forth with the power and the conviction that life is Holy, Holy, Holy, indeed, and each twisting, painful turn is only God's way of drawing you in closer to your own salvation!"

In the morning, Jose couldn't remember if it had all been a dream or if, in fact, his grandfather had really come to him. But no matter, for after that he'd begun visiting his grandfather often and seeing life completely differently. That's when he'd finally noticed the blind Indian woman and had begun to study her and learn to open his heart-vision. And after that was when he'd begun to train horses at night and become a shrewd horse trader. By the age of fifteen, he'd owned a string of some of the finest horses in the region, owned his own purse of money, and was as different from other boys his age as the stars in the heavens.

Oh, yes, he well knew how exciting it was to spend an evening listening to his *papagrande*. Juan Kelly would never be the same. He'd been given wings. Yes, indeed, the word was Holy.

Getting out of town, the two boys quickly took off. Their horses were rested and had been well grained. And, also, because they'd been trained so much at night, their horses had no trouble traveling quickly in the dark, early hours of the dawn.

It was late at night when Mariposa sneaked out the back door of her home. She was to meet Jose in the forest south of town. She hadn't seen him in nearly two weeks now, and she was dying to be in his arms again. She was with child, and she wanted to tell Jose that yes, yes, she would marry him.

But when she arrived in the middle of the woods, Jose wasn't there, and the night birds were making quick, nervous sounds. Instantly, the widow realized that she'd been followed and it was a trap. But before she could turn and run, she was surrounded by a dozen men, followed by the colonel.

"Gag her and drag her away. I'll personally tend to her later, but right now we're going to catch us this little fighting cock once and for all!"

They gagged her and dragged her away, and the colonel set up his men so that they could catch Jose when he came to meet Mariposa. Feeling confident that the trap was set, the colonel then went down to the creek where they held the widow.

"Well, my dear," he said to her, "so we meet again, eh?" He smiled. "My God, even with all that fear and hate in your eyes, you're still so beautiful. It's just not right," he added, reaching out and stroking her cheek gently, "to have so much beauty in one single woman.

"So you didn't like me treating you like a queen, eh?" he said. "Well, we can fix that. I'm an open-minded man. Let me see," he added, still stroking her gently. "You want a man to respect you, eh, and treat you with tenderness like this, eh?" He continued stroking her face gently, softly, tenderly, until she began to relax and not fight against the ropes that had her tied in place. Then, at that very instant when she was just beginning to relax, he suddenly gripped her cheek with his thumb and index finger, twisting it with all the power of his large muscular hand, and he yanked, driving his dirty thumbnail into her flesh until he drew blood, tearing her cheek open.

"There, you bitch! I treated you gently!" he yelled, signaling his men to get away. He began to undo his gun belt. "I'll show you how a real man does it! I'll show you what women were really put here on earth for, you miserable slut!"

He dropped his gun and holster and began to lower his pants. He loved the fear that he saw in her eyes. He loved the power he now had over this beautiful woman. She was his now, only his; and from now on she would always be his until the day she died, which couldn't be soon enough, in his estimation. Oh, how she'd embarrassed him, how she'd humiliated him in public and then caused him to run down the road afoot like a frightened child.

Kneeling down, he forced her legs apart. "I'm going to throw so much cock into you, you bitch, that you're going to cry in pain! I'm going to spread you so deep and wide that you'll think you're giving birth!"

Hearing his words, Mariposa knew that she was going to die. Forcing himself on her wasn't going to satisfy this crazy monster. No, he would beat her afterwards and then kill her. Suddenly, a great peace came over Mariposa. For, down deep inside her heart, she knew that someone loved her. Someone had, indeed, come down upon the earth, taken on the form of the Archangel Gabriel, and made genuine love with her.

She closed her eyes and she thought of Jose and then drew her angel-boy close to herself so softly, so gently, as this monster now lowered himself into her. Her heart and body disappeared as he drove into her again and again. Then, before her very eyes, she saw her soul rise up out of her body, and she wasn't here with this monster any longer. No, she was gone, way up there, about ten feet above the ground, as she now watched this brutal man tear her earthly body apart. But it didn't really matter anymore, because she was no longer with her body. No, she was gone, all safe and good, as she floated above the earth.

And, to further her joy, now came her child down from

heaven to her, and he took her hand in his tiny little dark hand. And the touch, the feeling she got from his tiny little hand was so wondrous, so angelic, that she knew that she was pure soul. And he was so beautiful, and she was so beautiful, and they were now together forever and ever, mother and son. And, yes, her son wasn't going to get to be born this time around, but this was all right, too, because he'd come to be born again some other time in the future, into a whole new world with all new circumstances.

Jose's unborn son took his beloved mother's hand and led her away, back up into heaven, as her earthly body was torn apart; a very empty, hollow victory for the man abusing her.

Jose was screaming. He was screaming, bellowing, thrashing against the men who held him down, but he couldn't get free to go and save her. He yelled and bit and screamed and threatened, but they just held him down with all the force they had. And he knew that she was being raped at this very moment; he could feel it in every fiber of his being, and he wanted to get free and leap on his horse and attack all of them single-handedly, if need be, and save her.

Oh, God how he loved her. She was his life, his heart, his soul! But Juan Kelly and three other of Jose's friends held him to the ground, not letting him go, saying, "Jose, Jose, it's a trap, and you know it, and you've been training us for years like Don Pio trained you to think of all the people of Mexico and not just of ourselves alone."

"I don't care about Mexico!" screamed Jose. "I love her! I love her! She's my life! Oh, my God, Mariposa! Mariposa! *MARRIII-POOOOSAAA!!!*"

But they wouldn't let him go, no matter how much he screamed and bit and thrashed. "Jose, Jose," they said, "we need you, you are our general, and we can't let you go and get yourself killed."

"Cowards!" he screamed. "You're all nothing but a bunch of useless cowards! I'll fight them alone!"

"We're not cowards, Jose. You know that. We'd follow you into hell itself, but we're only twelve, and there's over a hundred of them hiding in a trap."

And so they held Jose rooted to the earth, not letting him go to save his true love, as he thrashed and screamed and wailed. But then, suddenly, he stopped. His eyes got big and he passed out. She'd died. She'd died; he could feel it. And in this safe place of her death, Jose lost all earthly consciousness and he went out the other end of the tunnel to the great beyond. And in the great beyond, he now saw Mariposa in all her glorious beauty, and she was, indeed, an angel, floating over the earth's surface. She held a small child to her breast, and they both looked down upon Jose with such peace and love and serene happiness.

"I'll be waiting for you, my love," she said.

"Yes," he said, "I know. And I won't be long. Believe me, I won't be long. I love you so much."

"And I love you. Here, this is our son."

"Oh, my God! He's so beautiful!"

"Yes. He was conceived with love, and when he comes to be born next time, the world will hopefully be ready for him."

Jose's whole body jerked. "I'll make sure," he said. "God help me, I'll make sure." And his body went into quick-jerking spasms and then he went off to sleep. He slept for sixteen hours straight, and then when he came to, his eyes were large and bright and terrible in their absolute calm detachment.

He sat up, surveying his men. He took a deep breath and drank the water they served him. "I'm going home to visit my parents for the last time," he said. "And I'd like you to pick up her remains, put them in a coffin, and bring her to the settlement for a proper Christian burial."

He said nothing more and mounted his horse and rode home.

The whole *familia* was shocked to see Jose enter the house with their father being present.

"I'm home," he said to Doña Margarita, embracing her and his little brother Juan. "I'm home, Papa," he said, coming up to his father.

Don Juan was drunk; he'd been keeping himself pretty well drunk ever since Alejo and Vicente's deaths. Jose reached down to embrace his father, who was sitting down, but Don Juan jerked away, not accepting the embrace.

"I can't," said Don Juan. "All these years, all these years, and now Alejo and Vicente are both dead, and Jesus and Teodoro have gone north with Everardo to work in California. I'VE LOST ALL MY SONS!" he shouted, trembling and sobbing. "I've lost everything that I worked so hard for!"

Jose held, refusing to take the insult of his father's abusive words, and simply said, "I know, Papa, I know. You've worked so hard and it's all going. Come, give me an *abrazo.*" And he pulled his father to his feet and, chest to chest, they hugged in a big *abrazo,* and everyone—including Juan and Doña Margarita—began to cry. It was so beautiful, so fantastic, after eight years of separation; now here they were, father and son, together at last. "I love you, Papa," said Jose. "I love you very much."

The old man didn't respond to his son's words, but Jose just continued. "And I know you love me, too, Papa. I know it, even if you can't say it. I've always loved you, and you've always loved me, too. And the day you fought the great serpent, I was there and I saw you do it."

"You saw me?! Really? You saw me do it?"

"Yes."

"Well, why didn't you ever say so?"

"Because, well, I guess—I don't know. I . . . I . . . love you so much and have always admired you so much—wanting to be like you. The . . . the way you attacked that monster without a bit of fear, and the way you whirled the horse about because he was going crazy with fright, I, I get all tongue-tied just to think of it, and I . . . I can't, can't—"

"Then you saw me do it, you really saw me do it, and you admire me?"

Jose breathed. "Of course. With all my heart, Papa!" he said, tears coming to his eyes.

Don Juan stared at Jose, stared at his crying eyes and deep sincerity. "But I always thought you hated me and only admired your grandfather."

"Oh, no, Papa. You've always been my hero, my God, my— my father."

"OH, GOOD GOD!" screamed Juan Jesus Villaseñor. "Good God!" And he stood up tall, with all his great, massive power, and he was so mad, so enraged, that he didn't know what to do or who to attack, and so he attacked himself, biting his arms and shoulder. "I'm no good! NO GOOD!" he bellowed, as he bit at himself, tearing cloth and flesh.

Little Juan stared at his father in utter shock, not believing what his eyes saw—a huge powerful man devouring himself like a mad dog, his teeth and lips covered with blood as he ripped flesh and cloth from himself in wild madness.

Doña Margarita rushed forward and helped her husband to sit down. He was bleeding from his arms and shoulders, having exposed hunks of open flesh. But Don Juan didn't care. All he could do was look at Jose, really look at him—this small, delicately-made man who was his very own son, from his very own flesh and blood—and he broke down and started weeping like a lost little old man, almost child-like, angel-like in his vulnerability.

"I didn't know," he said. "I DIDN'T KNOW!" he screamed, and he opened up his huge, long arms to embrace his small, dark son with a big *abrazo*. "Oh, I love you, too, Jose. I love you too! I always loved you, but could never understand you. You . . . you . . . don't talk. All you do is . . . is feel. And I, I hate feeling. Good God, I hate feeling! It's not right!

It's bad! It makes you weak! That's what's wrong with this whole backward country!"

With tears of joy running down her face, Doña Margarita made the sign of the cross over herself and dropped to both knees. "Oh, thank You, God," she said, giving witness to this miracle of God's infinite love. "Oh, thank you, Lord God, Ruler of the universe, Creator of all miraculous wonders!"

Juan joined his mother, kneeling down, too, and so did Emilia, Lucha, Maria, and Luisa, and they all prayed together. Oh, they were all in absolute awe. Why, this was, indeed, another magic moment. God had come down upon the earth once again and was showing them yet another incredible side to human nature. Their beloved mother led them in prayer, and in the distance the church bells rang, giving sound and music.

The next morning, they had a huge funeral for Mariposa, and people came from as far away as two towns. Juan Kelly and the armed young men kept the entrance of the valley guarded. And little Juan saw that when the armed men spoke to Jose, they addressed him as *mi General,* and Jose listened to them with great patience, then told them what to do in such a soft, calm manner, as if he'd been directing men all his life.

For yes, indeed, Jose had found his voice at last, and this voice of his was the voice of the people, the voice of the angels, the language of an open, naked heart; the tongue of God Himself, which he'd been struggling to find all these years, ever since he'd seen his father's great heavenly spirit come down upon the earth in the form of *un charro de Los Altos de Jalisco* and fight the mighty serpent—a voice, once found, never forgotten, and never questioned, for Jose's soul was now one with God, and hence all his earthly deeds were now in alignment with the goodwill of the great beyond.

The funeral was over, and the Father Sun was going down, and the armed young men were anxious to go; but still, Jose stood by Mariposa's grave with his *sombrero* in hand, saying goodbye to his true love.

Juan and his playmates were all excited. They wanted to join Jose and his armed band and go with them and live in the hills. It was said that all over Mexico *la gente* were taking up arms, and Juan and his playmates wanted to join up before Jose and his band destroyed all the *Rurales*.

Then, just as Jose and his band of young men were mounting up and saying their goodbyes, Jose noticed the wild gleam of excitement in Juan and his little friends' eyes as they kept pleading that they wanted to go, too. Jose took a big breath and glanced around at each young boy—Domingo, Mateo, Pelon, Alfonso, Juan, and seven other small boys. He dismounted and called the young boys over to a private distance.

"Look," he said, trying to think of how his grandfather Don Pio would handle this situation, "I know that you boys think this is exciting and want to join our band, but understand; I need for all of you to open your eyes bigger, much bigger, and see—" he breathed, "—that all of you are already part of our band.

"Grandfather always explained to me that wars aren't won by the soldiers who are up in the hills fighting, but by the women and young ones and the old ones who stay at home. You see, we are the arms and legs of this struggle, but you are the heart, the stomach, our reason to keep going. And you young boys aren't just the keepers of our goats and pigs and corn so we can eat and keep strong, but you are the keepers of our homes, our mothers, our sisters and babies, so that our struggle for our way of life isn't all done in vain!"

Then he glanced around at each of them. And he saw their small brown faces and their large dark, hungry eyes. He could see that they were nothing more than children. His eyes began to water. "This is our home!" he said. "Please, understand, this is our home!" he shouted. "Our heartland! Our piece of earth for us to finally stand up for and say we will not move! And we will not die! We will live, no matter what! And mean these words to the root of our being! We will live! And we can only accomplish this by you young boys staying home and doing your daily work! Do you hear me? We need for you to stay home and give heart and soul to our land! Our homes! Our families! Our piece of Sacred Mother Earth!"

Juan's little chest was pounding—he was so filled with his brother's wondrous words. "Yes!" yelled Juan. "I hear you! And I'll give all of my heart and soul!"

"Yes!" yelled Domingo. "I hear you! And I'll give my heart and soul, too!"

"Yes!" shouted all the young boys. "We hear you! And we will give!"

And *la gente* began to gather, to come over and hear Jose Villaseñor's fine, true words, and his words moved their hearts to the core of their being, just as his grandfather's words had moved hearts two decades before.

"And, God forbid, if our struggle goes on too long, then each one of you will be called upon to take up your older brother's weapon; but until that day, I, we, the town, your families, need you to stay here, rooted at home!

"Domingo," he said, "and you, Mateo, for years now you two have been some of the most capable boys, fighting with rocks and sticks, in all these mountains. You've proven your-selves over and over again to be strong and loyal and capable. Well, now, we need you two more than ever. You, Domingo, I'm depending on you to get up early each day and do the milking and use all your power and cunning to keep the ranch running.

"You, Mateo, your brothers and I are depending on you to keep that corn growing that your family planted so we'll have food to eat this winter. And you, the smaller boys, who know every rock and tree in all this region, we need for you to help your older brothers do the work and keep your eyes peeled like the newborn chick and your ears alert like the gopher in the ground, and send word to us immediately of any movement of soldiers or strangers. For this is just the beginning. Believe me!" he shouted. "The great ugly serpent of Don Porfirio's monstrous power hasn't even shown its head yet!"

And as he spoke, Jose had no idea where this power, this wisdom came from. All he knew was that ever since he'd risen from the ashes of his true love's death, his heart had no more place to hide, and he now stood naked before the entire universe with a clarity of mind that was terrible in its power. Why, coming home and taking his father in his arms and straightening out the problem that had lain between them for so long had been easy.

Oh, to know love, to truly know love just once to the root of your being, was so powerful an experience that there was never any turning back again. Tears filled his eyes, and he spoke on, and the people continued gathering.

Doña Margarita made her way through the crowd, and seeing her son and hearing his words, she made the sign of the cross over herself. For she could see that, yes, indeed, a miracle had come to be, and it was gathering in force and getting ready to now shoot across the heavens in all its natural glory and new-found beauty. Love had been re-born. The child who'd been cast to the animals at the tender age of twelve had ascended on the wings of angels with all the wisdom and power of the ages. "Thank You, Lord God," she said. "Thank You that I lived long enough to see this great day!"

"To kill a hungry boy for just eating an ear of corn," continued Jose, "to kill another for just cutting a little alfalfa to feed his horse, to shoot down in cold blood a group of friends who come to visit you unarmed and under the banner of a white flag, these are the abuses of a sick, diseased government! And then to rape and kill a woman just because she—she—" Tears came to Jose's eyes, but he didn't wipe them away. "—she didn't love you, is the act of a people who are so drunk on their earthly wealth and power that they have lost their very souls!"

He stopped and wiped his eyes. He'd just turned twenty years old that week. He was still a boy and yet every eye was on him as if he were the wisest, strongest man the earth had ever produced. "I'm depending on each of you," he added calmly, glancing around. "For, believe me, you—every one of you—are already part of our band; for we are the band of our people, the band of our homes, the band of our hearts, the band of our . . . our mothers, our fathers, our grandparents, our children, and our children's children, so help me, God!"

And so, with tears streaming down his face, Jose now came forward and took Domingo in his arms. Chest to chest, they hugged in a big *abrazo*. Domingo was crying, too. Oh, how he loved his older, small dark brother.

Mateo's two older brothers, Jorge and Manuel, now came forward, too, and hugged their three younger brothers. Juan was crying, Doña Margarita was crying, everyone was crying; there wasn't a dry eye among them. For Jose had truly spoken with the voice of *la gente*, the meek of all the earth, touching each and every listener down to the core of their being, their heart, their long-forgotten soul, and given them wings of hope.

And then, when Jose came and took little Juan in his arms, hugging him, he whispered, "Take care of Mama, Juan, take care of Mama. For she is our very own angel, straight from God. Never forget that; that she's our *familia*'s very own special gift from heaven," he said, tears streaming down his face. "I love you, Juan, I love you so much, little brother!"

"And I love you, too, Jose," said Juan. "I love you with all my heart, big brother."

"Good," said Jose, kissing Juan. Then he walked through the crowd to their mother and took her in his arms. And Juan watched his brother and mother hug each other with so much love, so much feeling—such raw, naked emotion—that his little heart overflowed.

He glanced around at all the people and saw that they were hugging and kissing, too; mothers and sons, brothers and sisters, fathers and sons. And then Juan saw his own father, Don Juan, coming up through the crowd to see Jose off, too, and he couldn't believe it. But, yes, it was true. There came the huge, powerful Don Juan, who couldn't see Jose for all these years, and he now handed Jose his Colt .45, giving him *un abrazo* with tears running down his face.

Oh, miracle of miracles! Don Juan was hugging Jose with love, real love, and kissing him, too. Juan came up and stood alongside his mother, and she took his hand and together they rejoiced, watching Jose and Don Juan hugging each other with all their God-given souls!

Jose was now looking his father in the eyes and he was trying to talk, to say all he felt inside, but he couldn't. And this time it didn't make Don Juan nervous or doubtful that his son couldn't speak. No, for they'd touched, and once two people truly touched, then there was a basis of trust and love and plenty of room for differences.

"Well," said Jose finally, "I'll be going now, Papa. And thank you for the .45. I'll take good care of it."

"On the contrary, may it take good care of you, *mi hijito*," said Don Juan. *"Con Dios,* my son! *¡Con Dios!"*

"¡Con Dios, Papá!"

And they hugged together once more in another big, strong *abrazo*—one man pure European, tall and light of skin, with reddish-brown hair, and the other mestizo, part European and American Indian, short and dark with jet-black straight hair.

Jose then mounted his horse, Little White Stockings, and spun him about in a flare of horsemanship, and then once more he glanced around at all the young boys. "Remember," he said with conviction, "you are already part of our band! And we're depending on you," he added. "So stay home and give heart! Heart and lots of hard work!" Then he turned, going off with his group of armed young men.

The Father Sun was just going down, and they looked like

black silhouettes as they rode out, into the darkening land and bright yellow-orange sky.

Going home that night, Juan just knew that a whole new life was starting for him and his *familia*. His parents had their arms around each other and they looked so happy. Juan took a deep breath, realizing that he'd never seen his father and mother acting like this before.

And at the dinner table that night, they didn't have the twelve people for a proper Christian supper; but, still, Don Juan said grace—a short one, at that—and they ate their meal in peace. In fact, it was the first meal that Juan ever remembered having eaten so calmly and happily, that his stomach didn't hurt him afterwards.

4

And so the Father Sun gave birth to a Baby Shooting Sun so all the world could see that the Gates of Heaven had reopened, and now was the time for all of humankind to dance once more with a wild abundance of love.

Two more times the colonel and his men came up the mountain, expecting to draw Jose and his wild band of young men into an all-out battle, but they could never find them. And the reason the colonel wasn't able to find Jose and his band of young men was because Jose had taken his men into the woods right after Mariposa's funeral, telling them to avoid all fighting until he returned, that he had to go and see his grandfather and mourn his true love's death. And that this was not a sign of weakness, but the power of the bull chewing its cud. Juan Kelly assured Jose that he had nothing to worry about, that they would await his return.

Getting to his grandfather's house, Jose slept all night and day and then, when he awoke, his grandfather's young bride, Herlinda, fed him, and Don Pio explained to Jose that he had to understand that the colonel hadn't just killed Mariposa to avenge himself with her, but to make him so mad here inside of his heart and soul, that he'd do something wild.

"Remember, Jose, this is a military man, and military men know no love but the love of battle. He knows that he hurt you bad, *mi hijito*, and so he now expects you to come rushing out at him like a wild fool so that he can demolish you and your boys once and for all."

"But then what am I to do?" asked Jose, tears streaming down his face. "I loved her, *Papagrande*," he said. "She was my life! I can't just start running again." Oh, he was truly torn to the root of his being.

"Jose," said Don Pio, "look at me in the eyes; yes, look at me, and realize, *mi hijito*, as I've told Herlinda, here, that love is truly a gift from God, and nothing on earth can destroy a gift from God, especially not death."

Hearing these words, the tears poured forth from Jose's eyes even more. "I hope you're right, *Papagrande*. I truly hope you're right."

"Of course, I am. Just open your heart and see life in all its glory," he said, gently stroking his grandson's forehead. "Remember what you told me, when you first got here? You said that you just knew the moment of her death. You just knew it here in your heart without a shadow of a doubt, and then you slept like you'd never slept before, eh? And when you awoke you found yourself so calm and clearheaded that it dazzled your mind. You said that you felt like somehow you'd traveled up to the heavens and were now looking down upon the earth, seeing life as you'd never seen it before. That was why you were able to go home and settle matters with your father with such ease.

"You see, *mi hijito*," added the old man with a big beautiful smile, "what happened to you is that your soul did, in fact, travel up to the heavens while you slept, and you heard the angels sing." He took his grandson's hand, holding it. "I swear, it happens to all of us, *mi hijito*, if we just have the eyes to see and ears to hear. The heavens open up to us and invite us to learn the language of the stars. You see, the time has come for you to open your earthly eyes even larger than ever before and no longer ask me or any other mortal what I think or what you should do. No, *mi hijito,* the time has come . . . for us to ask you, for you have been chosen and the stars are with you."

"With me?" said Jose, taken aback.

"Oh, yes, of course," said Don Pio. "Do you really think that there wasn't a reason why you were run out of your home at such a young age?" Tears came to the old man's eyes. "I wanted to go to you. I wanted to kill your father. But no, I held on to my faith in God, and look what has come to pass. You performed a miracle; you yourself were able to settle matters with your father. Why, the heavens are rejoicing at this very moment!"

"And it was so easy, *Papagrande,*" said Jose. "It's like I suddenly couldn't see why I hadn't done it years before."

The old man couldn't stop grinning. "And this is how all of life, *la vida,* is when we finally let go of our earthly fears and accept the abundance of the Almighty's love; everything is easy."

"I'll be," said Jose with a huge, beautiful smile.

"And this is exactly why I can now say to you that my days here on earth are numbered, and I'll soon be gone. And now it's up to you to start trusting your own instincts, knowing that God is asking you to rise up from the ashes of yet another challenge that the stars above have bestowed upon you. For as I've told my young bride Herlinda here—bless her soul—many times, we're all only passing stars who have come by to give each other a little light for our few short days here on earth." He smiled, and it was easy to see that his smile was blessed.

"So I now ask you, Jose, what are you going to do? Eh, what illumination did you learn from Mariposa's love? This colonel has no wife or woman that he loves more than life itself, like you. For, believe me, military men are not like you and me, who see fighting as a tragic necessity. No, these men see fighting as the ultimate joy of their living and are happiest when they can find the opportunity to settle matters in this wornout method of administering pain and terror.

"Think, *mi hijito,* and know that he wants you to be so angry that you'll do something stupid, so he can then catch you out in midfield. Sleep on the matter, *mi hijito,* like you did to learn of horses, and let your dreams talk to you. And I know that you will come up with something so big and daring and unexpected that he will be caught completely with his pants down. For, remember," he said, closing his eyes in concentration, "in the long run, military men always lose, for their solution to life is fighting, and in fighting we never find the wisdom for loving or living life, *la vida.*"

He opened his eyes and took his grandson into his arms, and they held each other in a long *abrazo* and they both knew, without ever saying it, that they'd never see each other again.

Jose stayed one more night with his grandfather and then, just before dawn the next day, he saddled up and left. But he didn't go directly to his men. No, he rode down into the deepest woods that he could find so that he could wrestle with his demons demanding revenge. For he was still only a young boy, and his first reaction was to meet the colonel head-to-head in battle and tear him apart, limb by limb. But then in the early hours of the following day, Mariposa came to Jose and took him in her arms as she'd done the first time that they'd made love. And it was so wonderful, so fantastic, so beautiful, that when Jose awoke and didn't find Mariposa at his side, he started to cry out in anguish . . . until there, before his very eyes, he saw *paraíso.* And paradise was a living, breathing feast. And each tree, each blade of grass, was blazing with fire.

Then he saw Mariposa, and there she was by the creek that ran through the tall ferns between the oaks, and she was floating above the earth's surface, looking so beautiful with golden-white fire all about her, too. He smiled and she smiled, and the whole earth sang and hummed and vibrated with love's fires of illumination. And once more he knew that his soul was up above in heaven, looking down upon the earth with such terrible calm detachment that his earthly body was truly free to see life, *la vida,* as it really was: a living miracle.

Why, he could now understand without a shadow of a doubt that, yes, indeed, the day that he'd been banned from his home was—just as his grandfather had so well said—the greatest gift of his young life. For that day, he'd been forced to open his eyes and see *la vida* as never before. And, now, he could also see with absolute clarity that, with the death of his true love, he was being asked again by the great beyond to open up his eyes even larger.

He was being asked to stretch, to truly reach as high as he possibly could and learn the language of the angels, just as he'd been asked to learn how to talk horse in his youth. And he could now see that once people knew this language of the stars, then they were never alone again. For God's breath was then all around them, igniting each tree, each blade of grass with golden-white flame. And there was Mariposa, just right over there by the creek, floating above the earth's surface and, yes, indeed, she really, really had come and made love to him in the early morning hours of the dawn.

He laughed and she laughed, too, and he got up and went to the stream to bathe. He took off his clothes and carefully got down between the smooth river rocks into the cool, good-feeling water. Mariposa came to him and began to wash his arms and legs and hum to him like a turtledove. His grandfather had told him the absolute truth: love was, indeed, a gift from God, and nothing could destroy a gift from God, especially not death. And all it took for us humans to enter into this blessed conversation of the heavens was just to "get still" inside our heads and start listening with our hearts. But, oh, what a heavy hand it had taken for him to finally "get quiet" inside of his mind.

Mariposa disrobed and came into the stream with him, and together they moved merrily, merrily downstream. And he could now see that every little painful, loving thing that had ever happened to him was beautiful. For each had peeled away another layer of his eyesight, as one peeled off the layers of an onion, until now, finally, here stood life, *la vida,* in all its dreamlike glory and wonderment—alive with God's fire.

Jose must have fallen asleep. For the next thing he knew, he was cold and there were little birds making nervous sounds all about him. Mariposa was gone, but he could still smell her all over himself. He stretched. He was on a flat, smooth boulder at the edge of the water. Oh, yes, he now remembered that they'd come out of the stream and made love on this rock. He smiled. There was golden morning light all about him. Oh, life was an absolute marvel, the living proof of God's existence.

The little sparrows were making a terrible racket; it was as if they were trying to tell him something. Quickly, Jose got up, glanced about, and started back upstream through the brush. He got dressed. He didn't know what had startled the birds, but he wasn't going to wait around to find out. He saddled up and went to find his men. He now knew exactly what their next military move would be. And it was so easy, so obvious, he wondered why he hadn't seen it before. That night, Jose and his men gathered in the oaks north of town, and Jose told the young horsemen that he'd come up with a plan.

"But what is it?" asked several young men excitedly.

"You'll see," said Jose, "but I'll guarantee you that it's so terrible, that this act alone will be what eventually brings the colonel to his destruction." He grinned. "After this, even his fellow officers are going to start openly ridiculing him, and drive him into such wild behavior, that then we're going to be able to take him apart, limb by limb," he added.

The short, freckle-faced Juan Kelly gave a *grito de gusto,* loving it. And the other young men followed. They had absolute faith in Jose's judgment and were willing to take on the Devil himself if he just gave the word.

The next time the colonel came, Jose and his band of young men were waiting for him in a little gully at the foothills of the big mountain. And here came the colonel and his company of well over one hundred soldiers, and even from a distance of six or seven hundred meters, Jose and his men could see that the colonel and his soldiers hadn't learned their lesson yet. They still carried too many weapons, weighing their horses down, and their mounts were over-fed and were just no match for these little, quick mountain horses.

Jose and his men stayed put in a little gully and let the colonel and his men pass by them on their way up the mountain. Jose could now well see that he'd done the right thing years ago, when he'd developed his breed of horses for these mountains. He'd bred the original Four White Stockings to the toughest little mountain mares he could find, and being a large, well-muscled thoroughbred, Four White Stockings had given size and muscle and great intelligence to his offspring. But having been raised up in this mountainous terrain, the tough little mountain mares had given huge hearts and lungs to their foals and also a cunning sixth sense for survival that had been completely bred out of the thoroughbreds over the centuries.

Jose and his men now watched the colonel and his men go up the mountain in the early morning mist, and they could see that already their mounts were blowing hard and were so covered with sweat that their shiny coats glistened in the early morning light. A few of Jose's young men openly laughed at the colonel, wondering how this ignorant man ever expected to catch them.

"Don't be laughing too much," Jose cautioned his companions, "for we are few and they are many, and unless all of *Méjico* quickly joins us in this struggle, our days are numbered, no matter how good and capable we are."

When the last of the colonel's men had disappeared over the ridge, Jose gave his horse the spurs, and he and his young horsemen slipped out of the gully and rode down into the great valley of Guanajuato. They rode on the main road past the rich *haciendas* and fields of fat cattle. The people watched them pass by, looking so young and ragged that they couldn't figure out what they were about. Then, just this side of Leon, Guanajuato, Jose reined in and they stopped to water their horses in a little creek under some trees.

"All right," said Jose, "what we're going to do is this: we're going to take the military garrison."

All the young men were stunned. Even Felipe Juan Kelly was speechless.

"But, my God, we're only twelve!" said one young man. "They must be hundreds! And they have *cañones!*"

Jose wasn't ruffled the least bit. "Look," he said, "I had my brother-in-law, Jose-Luis, check for me on his last business trip down here. And lately, the colonel has been coming up with all his able-bodied men. He's only been leaving behind half a dozen old soldiers."

Several young men began to smile and talk excitedly among themselves.

"But just wait," said Manuel, Mateo and Pelon's other brother. "Maybe it's a trap."

"Good thinking, Manuel," said Jose, "and I've considered that. But, no, I'm sure it's not a trap this time. The colonel still thinks we're only stupid kids. Not even in his wildest dreams does he expect this," added Jose, grinning.

"Oh, I'm getting excited!" said short little muscular Juan Kelly. "I feel like screaming! Let's do it!" he added with a shout. "Let's do it!"

"All right," said Jose, "we're going to do it, but calmly. And from now on we'll be going in groups of two or three and, let's see, ah, about a half a kilometer apart. Kelly, you go with me; you, too, Jorge, and the three of us will make the first move, and then the rest of you swarm the garrison like cockroaches. But be very careful. These old soldiers didn't get old because they don't know how to fight. Believe me, they've killed many a young man who underestimated them."

Mounting back up, they rode in small groups. They weren't smiling young men anymore. No, they now wore serious faces. They were far from home, and what they were prepared to do was a feat even beyond their wildest dreams. My God, nobody in his right mind took on a military garrison.

Riding up to the military outpost that the colonel and his men called home, Jose and Kelly and Jorge dismounted at the little outdoor *mercado* across the way from the front gates. Jose went under the tarps and bought a little paper cone full of candied fruit. Juan Kelly and Jorge stayed outside by their horses, looking around at all the people and different little storefronts. There was only one guard at the entrance of the garrison. There were just a couple of dozen people and a few dogs in the dusty dirt street. Jose came back out and the three boys ate their candied fruit and waited for their friends.

As each group came in, they stopped at different places up and down the little way. No one had really noticed them yet.

"All right," said Jose, once he saw that everyone was present. "Now remember, no weapons for the three of us," he said to Juan Kelly and Jorge.

Reluctantly, Jorge left his rifle, and the three of them were just starting across the dusty little street when a huge second guard came up, kicking the first, who was half asleep in his chair. Jose took two steps back, handed the remaining candy to two passing little boys, and got the rope off his saddle. He winked at his two companions, and they continued across the street. The two little boys watched them as they ate the candy. It was just midmorning, but the sun was already blasting hot.

"I'll take the big one," said Juan Kelly with a vicious little grin. Jose was the smallest of all his brothers, but Juan Kelly was even shorter than he.

"All right, but nothing fancy," said Jose. And why it was that Juan Kelly liked taking on big men, Jose didn't know. But he'd seen this short, muscular friend of his work over many a big man.

"Get to your feet!" the big guard was saying to his fellow soldier. "And get us some cold beer! Damn this weather!"

"I'll get the beer for you," said Juan Kelly, acting very innocently. "Just give me the money, *señor.*"

The two guards turned to look at Kelly and in that moment, Kelly took two quick steps toward them with his right hand stretched out like he was expecting them to give him money, but then he leaped on the big, well-armed guard like a snarling alley cat. Jose roped the other one while he still sat in his chair. Jorge picked up a rock and jumped on the big guard, too, smashing his head with the stone. In seconds, the three boys had both guards down. Now the other young men swarmed the garrison with weapons drawn, searching for the other soldiers. They found two asleep and the other two in the outhouse. Jose and his men had hit the military outpost so quickly, so unexpectedly, that not one single shot was even fired.

People began to gather. The two little boys were devouring the candy that Jose had given them, with huge, staring eyes. Nobody, but nobody, could really believe what these wild, ragged-looking young men had just done.

Quickly, Jose had his men hitch up a set of mules to two wagons and load up all the weapons and ammunition. "Then set fire to the garrison!" he added.

"You do that," bellowed the huge old guard with blood running down his face, "and I swear that we'll hunt you down to the ends of the earth!"

Juan Kelly started laughing *con carcajadas.* "But for taking your guns and ammunition, you won't hunt us to the ends of the earth, eh?" He turned to Jose. "These *cabrones locos* always kill me with their *caca de toro!* Here, for months they've been trying to kill us with all they have, and now we're supposed to suddenly get scared." He pulled out his knife. "You bastards killed my beloved father Felipe!" raged Kelly, and he drove his huge crude Mexican knife into the man's groin and twisted up and in before Jose could stop him. The man screamed out in horror, eyes huge with disbelief. "Any of you others want to threaten us?" asked Kelly, jerking out his blade.

The other guards were silent. Not another single word was echoed. And Jose and his men set fire to the garrison.

A whole crowd of people had gathered. Some were now even helping Jose's men set torches to the outpost. For years, the whole area had lived in constant terror of this military garrison and now, in a matter of seconds, it had been captured and set on fire. And the huge old guard, who was well known for abusing young girls, was lying in a pool of blood, screaming in terror. A very pretty young woman still in her early teens ran up, wanting to know who had cut the old man's *tanates,* and when everyone pointed to Juan Kelly, she threw her arms around Kelly, kissing him in a frenzy. Kelly loved it and winked at Jose.

Before the ragged-looking young warriors had even gotten out of town, a ballad was being sung about them, calling them the wild mountain boys who had ridden into town one glorious day like the rising sun and freed the land of tyranny.

That evening right outside of Piedra Gorda, Jose and his men loaded the weapons and supplies that they wanted on four little sure-footed burros and left the remaining weapons for the townspeople to start arming themselves.

With his second daring stroke of military genius, Jose had elevated himself and his band of young men from local boys trying to avenge themselves to a troop of well-organized militia with the capacity of taking on and defeating the finest fighting men that Don Porfirio could put in the field. The heroic acts of Jose and his young men spread like wildfire. At every little *ranchita,* young men began to gather, thinking that they, too, could now organize and put an end to the abuses of the *Rurales* who patrolled their given area.

■t was said that the colonel and his men were in Guadalajara, the capital of Jalisco, when they got word of what had happened to their garrison. It was also said that several of the colonel's fellow officers began laughing at him, saying that maybe they'd be better off hiring this young man Jose to keep the peace in that area than to give the colonel any more weapons, which would surely just end up in Jose's hands anyway.

El Coronel, it was said, became so enraged that he crushed his brandy glass in his hand *a lo Victoriano Huerta* and walked out of the room, summoned his men, and then rode out. It was later said by those who watched the colonel ride out with his men that same night, that that night was the turning point of Colonel Montemayor de los Santos's military career. For his fellow officers had seen it in his eyes: he was no longer the happy, fun-loving man that he'd always been. No, he'd become a terror before their very eyes.

■t was just before daybreak when Colonel Montemayor hit the little mountain settlement. And he well knew that Jose and his young horsemen weren't present, but he didn't care. These cowardly imbeciles had killed one of his oldest and best friends. Why, that huge old guard that they'd knifed in his *tanates* had been with the colonel ever since he'd joined the military service of Don Porfirio's troops. Of course, there'd always been rumors of the old bull being a little abusive with young women when he'd had a little too much to drink, but that was to be expected when a man had given his life to fighting for the people's rights. What professional military man didn't get a little wild now and then? Oh, these cowardly fools were going to pay as they'd never paid before.

And so with the first glimpse of day, the colonel and his men came racing into the settlement, screaming and shooting at anything that moved. In the dark early light, they shot at the women who were drawing water from the well in the plaza. They shot the old blind woman as she came walking down the pathway to church. They ran over dogs and pigs and children who criss-crossed in front of them, trying to get away. And then, when they got to the Villaseñor house, they began shooting through the windows and doorways at anything that moved.

Don Juan had just been sitting down in the kitchen to have his first cup of hot chocolate when the shooting started up the street. Instantly, he was on his feet, seizing his rifle and yelling for his family to get to the back of the house. When the shooting started coming in their windows, Don Juan and his family were already down on the floor, crawling toward the back of the house as fast as they could. "Keep still," Don Juan was saying. "Not one single sound!"

Not getting any response from the home, the colonel and his men turned their attention to the animals in the corrals, killing anything that moved.

"I want them to starve this winter!" bellowed the colonel, like the Devil himself. "I want these bastards to be wishing that they'd never been born!" he screamed, shooting at the pigs in the pen.

Basilio and Agustin had been sleeping under the oak leaves alongside a rock fence when they awoke and saw their beautiful little goats being slaughtered for no reason whatsoever. They went crazy-*loco* and began picking up stones from the rock wall and hurling them at the soldiers.

The soldiers turned and shot at the two giants, but their bullets just seemed to make the two huge men angrier. Basilio leaped on one rider and tore him off his horse, broke his neck, and whirled his corpse over his head, throwing him at another horseman and knocking down the horse and rider. In moments, the two giants had half a dozen men and horses on the ground, but the colonel and his remaining soldiers just kept shooting at the two giants, the way hunters would shoot at wounded bears.

From behind the rock wall at the back of their home, Don Juan and his *familia* watched. Miraculously, not one of them had been shot when the colonel and his men had opened fire on their home. And little Juan now saw Basilio and Agustin being riddled with bullets and he screamed, wanting to go to them, but his mother and father held him down.

Laughing happily, one armed man now signaled his fellow soldiers back, and he brought out his *reata* and roped Basilio by the feet. He wanted to drag the gigantic *hombre* up the street and around the plaza like a prized kill. But, twisting and turning, Basilio was able to get hold of the rope with his massive, powerful hands, and he jerked the horseman and his saddle off his mount, dropping the horse.

The other soldiers laughed hysterically and now they, too, put away their weapons and pulled out their ropes. Four horsemen then roped Basilio by his legs and arms and began to pull at him in opposite directions. Agustin tried to get to his brother to help him, but they'd roped him, too. Basilio's screams of pain could be heard echoing throughout the entire settlement as the four horsemen gave their mounts the spurs, tearing his body into pieces.

Little Juan covered his ears, not wanting to hear. Oh, these two giants were his best friends, and all they'd been trying to do was save their little goats. Doña Margarita held her little son close to her heart, praying to God Almighty the whole while.

Then, just at that moment, when the terrible, snapping rips could be heard of Basilio's limbs being pulled from his body, a shot exploded and Basilio's head burst into pieces. And there stood the mighty Don Juan with his rifle in hand, out in midstreet.

Instantly, the soldiers were upon Don Juan, wanting to string him up for interfering with justice, but Colonel Montemayor de los Santos lunged his horse in between his soldiers.

"No! Let him go!" he bellowed with rage. "I want him to live, so he can see what's going to happen to his *familia* as we take them down, one by one!" He rode his large, well-fed horse right up close to Don Juan. "Did you really think that you could get away with this, my friend?" he said. "You sealed your fate the day you chose to marry into the likes of these backward, ignorant people, and you know it!" he added with a delicious scream. "For there's not one civilized nation in all of the Americas that's done well by keeping these cowardly lowlife savages in their midst!" And he spat into Don Juan's face. "I hope you burn in hell, you turncoat!"

Don Juan wiped the spit from his face, but he said nothing. He just stood there, staring at the colonel, as his men disarmed him. And now they had Agustin roped four ways and they began to pull him apart, too. But Agustin was even larger and stronger than his older brother, Basilio. And with a mighty jerk, he snapped one of their braided rawhide ropes in two, and then another. But the two men who had him by the legs bolted their horses before he could grab hold of their ropes, and they dragged him up the cobblestone street and around the well in the plaza, screaming joyfully, and then back down the cobblestone way. Agustin's huge, bellowing voice could be heard across the entire valley.

Little Juan ran to his father's side. There was just nothing that they could do. And Agustin wouldn't die or go unconscious, no matter how much his huge head banged against the rock-laid street. Finally the two horsemen tired of their fun, and they now turned their mounts in opposite directions and gave their horses the spurs. Agustin screamed to the heavens when the horses hit the end of their ropes, ripping his legs apart with loud, crackling sounds. And his body was split up the middle of his crotch, with his huge balls and cock going with his left leg.

"And this is what will happen to all of you every time Jose and his men so much as raise their hands at us!" yelled the colonel. "Did you fools really think that you could ridicule me and the forces of our great *Presidente* Don Porfirio and get away with it? We'll be back tenfold next time!"

The Father Sun hadn't even shown his huge bright face across the great central valley of Guanajuato when the colonel and his men rode off. The new day was only beginning, but already the entire little mountain settlement was in mourning. They just couldn't believe what had come to pass.

All that day, reports came in that the colonel and his terrible assassins had also hit other little outlying *rancheritas* in the area. In one swift, lightning attack, the colonel wanted to show all of the people of this mountainous area what became of them if they opposed authority.

When little Juan saw his brother Jose and his men ride in that afternoon, he could still hear Agustin's screams echoing inside his head. Never had he heard such screams of agony in all his life. Having been raised on a ranch, he'd heard a lot of animals scream when they were being castrated or slaughtered, but nothing had ever sounded like this. Oh, he was sure that Basilio and Agustin's screams would haunt him for the rest of his life.

Coming up the cobblestone street, Jose and his men saw the senseless slaughter of the livestock, and then they saw the bodies of Basilio and Agustin and the two women who'd been shot at the well, and the child who'd been trampled. Agustin's two legs had been put back by his body, but still the sight was so monstrous that it turned Jose's stomach. A couple of people began yelling at Jose, telling him that he was to blame for this disaster. Another said that they should shoot Jose for having started the whole problem.

"Shut your damned mouths!" yelled Juan Kelly, his hands becoming fists. "Here, he's the only Christian who stood up against the Devil himself and now you blame him! I'll kill the next one of you who badmouths him!"

"*Cálmate,* Juan," said Jose, putting his hand on Juan Kelly. "They're just upset and don't know what to do. Look," said Jose, glancing around at everyone, "we did wrong to leave you unguarded. I thought that he'd come after us in the woods, *mano-a-mano,* but I was wrong. This colonel isn't a military man who's going to fight with honor. No, he's a coward, a rapist, an assassin, a human monstrosity from hell itself! But we'll never let this happen again. From now on, we'll go on the attack!''

Most of the people stayed and listened and were reassured by Jose's words, but others just shook their head and walked away. They'd had enough and they were going to pack up and leave, thinking that it would be safer for them in some other part of Mexico. But what the people didn't realize was that this same thing was happening all over Mexico—in every valley, in every mountain. For the meek of the earth had risen up by the tens of thousands all across the land and the days of the privileged few were done. The Mother Earth loved all of her children equally, and no monstrous, two-headed snake of sick authority could keep *la gente* down for long.

It was almost dusk when someone came into the plaza, saying that he'd found the body of the old blind woman up on the little knoll right outside of town where she came down to church each day.

When Jose, who was at the cemetery visiting his true love, heard the news, he put on his *sombrero* and started up the pathway with all of the other people. Little Juan walked alongside his brother. The sun had just gone down, and everywhere people had fires burning. They were cooking up all the choice pieces of the livestock that had been slaughtered. A guitar could be heard playing in the distance. Among the crying and weeping, children could also be heard playing and laughing.

Getting to the old blind woman's body, Jose took off his hat and knelt down, taking her in his arms. "She was my teacher," he said, hugging her close. "She was the first one to teach me how to see with my heart, even in darkness."

Two men picked up the old *india*'s body to take her down the hill to the church, where they would place her with the other dead bodies. And what Jose did next, little Juan would never

forget. Why, his brother stood up and closed his eyes and began
to dance down the pathway to the church. And Jose didn't just
move a little here and there; oh, no, he was prancing and hop-
ping between the stones with wild abandon. Then he took off
his huge hat and was flying up and down the pathway as the
procession of people brought the old Indian woman's body
down the knoll. The man playing his guitar came up and he
began to play a fast one, matching Jose's movements, and soon
other people were dancing, too. And here came a procession *de
los muertos,* of the dead, and they were dancing, singing, laughing. The day had started out in disaster but here, only hours
later, fires were cooking up a feast, and the whole settlement
echoed of life and happiness.

People came with flowers, placing them over the old woman's
body. Others came with lit candles, joining the procession.
Opening his eyes, Jose saw the people dancing all about him,
and he took his little brother's hand and pulled him in to dance,
too. And little Juan was pretty fast-footed and agile, having
been raised with goats all of his life, but he wasn't able to keep
up with his older brother as Jose went down the knoll and
through the rocks with his eyes closed once more—dancing
with an abundance of love!

As they approached the church, there was Juan Kelly and
several of Jose's other men, and they began to clap. And at the
entrance of the church, Jose continued dancing with his eyes
closed, with such amazing grace that he was truly as beautiful as
an angel.

"Look!" yelled an old woman who also went to church every
day, "the spirit of our old *india* has entered Jose's body! Holy be
God's name!"

People made the sign of the cross over themselves and began
to pray. For they, too, could well see that the old woman had
spoken the truth. For there was no other earthly explanation for
how Jose was able to come down the rocky, twisting path with
his eyes closed, looking as graceful as the blind old *india.*

The Father Sun had just gone down, and the western night sky was lightly laced with a long *rebozo* of pale golden clouds. The whole mountain settlement looked so beautiful, so blessed with life, *la vida*. This was, indeed, another Holy moment here, upon the Mother Earth.

And then another old woman was heard to say, "Look, there go Basilio and Agustin's souls!"

La gente looked up at the sky to where she was pointing and they saw that, yes, indeed, it was true. There went two little silvery clouds, passing through the long lace of pale golden clouds.

"Oh, I just knew it!" said Doña Margarita, standing alongside her old church friend. "Basilio and Agustin truly were put here upon the earth to re-open Saint Peter's gates for all of us!"

"With their great keys!" added a lusty-looking old woman who'd just walked up. This old woman was the local midwife. Her name was Fatima, and she was known for her blunt, juicy words and her love of young, strong men.

"Oh, yes! And did you see the look on those soldiers' faces?" said another old lady. "Why, even as they tore Agustin apart, they went pale with fear and jealousy when they saw the great size of his manly jewels!"

"You filthy, disgusting old women!" yelled one very upset husband. "Don't you see that we're standing here before the Holy Church of God?!"

"Oh, yes!" said Doña Margarita, laughing. "And we're giving our respects to all the different jewels of life that God gave us to enjoy! Just look at those two little silvery clouds. Go, Basilio! Go, Agustin! And open up those Gates of Heaven for all of us!"

"Yes, and use those mighty keys!" shouted Fatima, laughing with her low, sensual-sounding roar of *carcajadas*.

Hearing this lecherous laugh, all the women joined the old midwife's laughter. And Jose continued dancing, and his young men were clapping. But many of the older men were feeling pissed, and so they began to curse and drink. But no matter, the celebration of life and death continued. For it wasn't enough that Christ had died on the cross for the sins of all humankind. Each village, each new generation, had the spiritual necessity inside of their very own God-given souls to relive the great pageantry of this Most Holy of Dances.

The two little silvery clouds of Basilio's and Agustin's souls passed through the golden lace, and then there went Mariposa, hand-in-hand with Jose's son. Jose stopped dancing and held there in absolute awe as he watched this most beautiful of all processions—the ascension of a soul returning to the heavens.

Doña Margarita came close and took her son Jose's hand. And Don Juan came close, too, but he just couldn't see what it was that they saw. All he saw were clouds and the beauty of the going sunlight, but nothing fantastic or miraculous. Little Juan, on the other hand, who stood beside his mother and brother, did see the great spectacle of yet another passing. For because he had been raised primarily by his mother, that's what all of life was for Juan: a great, miraculous passing, as all living life reached for the light of God.

"Well," said one of the old women who went to church daily with Doña Margarita and her group of spiritual friends, "I guess we got new friends up in heaven now, so we can start praying stronger than ever! But, damn, i sure never thought that it would be one so young as Mariposa to lead the way for us old ones."

"She was among our most innocent and pure of heart," said Doña Margarita, wiping the tears from her eyes. "She'd just barely begun to learn the true meaning of love." She took Jose in her arms, holding him close. "She's with God now, *mi hijito,*" she added. "She's returned home, and all is well."

"Yes, I know that now," said Jose, wiping his tears. "Love truly is a gift from God, and nothing can destroy a gift from God, especially not death."

"You've learned well, *mi hijito,*" said Doña Margarita, smiling. "Few mortal men, never having passed blood in childbirth, are able to know such wisdom."

She drew her son in with a big *abrazo*, holding him heart-to-heart.

"Let us hope, *mi hijito*, that we are as fortunate when our times come," added Doña Margarita. "Look at her great escorts as she ascends the steps of heaven. Why, the souls of those mighty giants have lit up the whole sky!"

And it was true, the whole sky was lit up in magnificent colors of pink and gold and silver, orange and red and lavender, and the people who had the eyes to see and the ears to hear now saw the Gates of Heaven open wide and they could hear the singing of ten thousand angels as Basilio and Agustin escorted Mariposa through. It was so beautiful that it brought tears to the eyes and an itching to the feet, for they, too, down here upon the earth, now wished to return home to God and all His glory.

So that night, all of *la gente* held a wondrous vigil there inside of the church for the six people who'd been killed. Hundreds of candles were lit and the people prayed long into the night. And then they began to feast and sing and dance, and it was another great celebration *para los muertos*, for the dead, Mexican-style, with laughter and happiness. And Doña Margarita and Don Juan were part of the celebration, kicking up their heels and having a wonderful time, too.

It was said that when the colonel heard of this great celebration, after he'd put such terror into these people, he almost went mad with rage and began screaming and breaking things, saying that these ignorant people were such filthy savages that they had no right to live, for they had no earthly respect, even for their own dead.

The colonel became sick and his stomach filled with gas, and he had a hard time eating, and every time he shot down a brandy, which was his favorite drink, he'd choke and cough and go into convulsions. For nearly a month, the colonel lay in bed, trying to regain his power so he could return to the mountain to finish off these people who just wouldn't stop ridiculing him every chance they had.

Hearing of the colonel's bedridden condition, little Juan would never forget how his father and mother started laughing and saying that maybe they should send the poor man a bottle of their finest tequila. Juan just couldn't understand what was going on, but now, even amid all of this death and destruction, his parents were happier and treating each other with more love than he'd ever remembered.

Love was in the air. *Amor del corazón* was choking the very atmosphere with good, wonderful, warm feelings.

TWO

GRANDMOTHER

(A TIME OF FEMALE CONSCIOUS-
NESS that began about 78,000 B.C., 32,000
years before language came to be. A time of
dreaming, of being in the womb of existence, a time of flux and possibilities; that
quiet, peaceful female-time of pregnancy before the volcano-like birth of present male
creation.)

Dreaming, dreaming, while the men and children still slept, the women now got up to go and pray with the early hours of the pre-dawn. And pray the women did, talking to the stars as they'd been doing since the beginning. For since the time of creation it had been the female whom God had entrusted with the task of carrying the seeds of life until it was their hour of fruition.

And the women of Los Altos could now well see that once more the whole world was going to pieces because of men's *caprichos,* and so it was time for them—the caretakers of the earth—to take over the leadership of their *familias.* And, also, they now had strong, new local champions up in high places, and so the entire heavens were alive with the buzzing of their earthly predicament.

And so each morning, little Juan Salvador Villaseñor would awake to watch his old mother, Doña Margarita, get out of bed where she'd been sleeping with him and put on her black shawl and go to the church in the dark to pray with her women friends. And pray they did, especially on the days that the priest wasn't there to interfere with their direct communications with the Almighty.

Then the Father Sun would just be coming up over the distant horizon and the whole house would be full of the aroma of fresh tortillas, when little Juan would see his mother coming back in the front door from the church. She'd be smiling and singing to herself, no matter how awful everything was going on all around them. And when he and his sisters would ask their mother what could possibly be so funny, she'd tell them that she'd just heard another good one at the church from Our Blessed Mother of God. Then her eyes would fill with mischief as she began to busy herself in the kitchen and she'd tell them a crazy, funny story, and soon they'd all be laughing. It was like they couldn't help themselves: laughter just erupted from their hearts, filling their starving souls with music of the heavens!

When the colonel got well, he immediately began coming back up the mountain with his troop of butchers, but they were never able to penetrate into this mountainous area of Los Altos far enough to attack another ranch or settlement again. Jose and his group of young riders had grown to a force of well over thirty, and they were now well armed and confident and so they'd attack the colonel and his soldiers as soon as they started up the mountain. Jose and his men would hit them here, then hit them there, killing two or three soldiers and then taking off and disappearing. Finally the colonel and his *Rurales* were shooting at every little rustle of leaves or any sound or movement that they heard.

Soon the colonel and his men came to understand that if they just passed through the area, not abusing anyone, they'd be left alone. But if they caused anyone harm, then Jose and his men would set up ambushes and kill them as they went out, even way past dark. Once, when they'd shot an old man just for the hell of it coming out of his outhouse, six of them were killed that night while they slept and human shit was stuffed in their mouths. The colonel's men began to think that Jose was either the Devil himself or the avenging angel of God. This was when the colonel and his men received word that they were to avoid the whole area of Los Altos where Jose and his armed young men patrolled. The colonel was told that he couldn't just keep on fighting his private little war; that he and his men were needed to help the other regiments with all these other uprisings that were starting up everywhere.

Then came word that Mexico City, the capital of the nation, had been taken back by the people, *la gente del pueblo,* and that Don Porfirio and his bunch of rich foreign friends had fled the country to Europe.

A great celebration broke out all across Mexico. They, the meek, the mud *gente,* who'd been made from the clay of the heart-center of the Mother Earth, had won! They'd beaten the no-good *Rurales,* and *Méjico,* the great, God-given land of *el mestizo,* once again belonged to those who truly loved and worked the mother-soil with their own two hands!

But the celebration didn't last for long; for then came word that the idealistic new little president, Francisco Madero, had been murdered by Victoriano Huerta, the nationally famous assassin who'd been the terrible right-hand man of the ex-president. And word also came that, now, a whole new war had started and this one was going to be worse than the previous one. For *la gente* were divided and didn't know whom to follow.

Just about this same time was when the great man, Don Pio, passed on in his sleep one night. It was said that his last words were "Oh, I thank *Dios* Almighty that I lived to see this great day! Once more *la gente de la tierra* are alive! And *Méjico es nuestra tierra madre!*" And he hugged his young full-blooded Indian bride in a big *abrazo* and went off to sleep with the angels.

Also, right about this time was when it became commonly known that a price of one thousand *pesos* in gold had been placed on Jose's head—the greatest sum ever placed on anyone in all the region. And this price was not to kill him, but to bring him in alive at all costs. For the authorities in Guadalajara wished to make Jose an offer that he couldn't refuse.

And, of course, the rumor that the authorities wanted Jose alive and not dead was exactly all it took to give Jose's Judas the *corazón* to come forward and betray him.

Little Juan was herding the last of their animals home the day that his twenty-three-year-old cousin-brother Agustin of reddish-brown hair and beautiful, even white teeth came racing by and yelled, "Your brother Jose has been arrested! And they're bringing him up the valley in chains!"

"But how did that happen?" asked Juanito, completely astounded.

"I don't know, but they're saying he was betrayed by one of his own men!" said Agustin, laughing a strange, nervous laugh, then racing off on his horse.

Leaving the animals in a hidden *arroyo,* Juan ran home as fast as his little legs could carry him. "Mama! Mama!" he yelled, bursting in under the *ramada*. But looking all around the house, little Juan found no one home, so he took off to the church. Lately his sisters Luisa and Emilia had also been going to church with their mother every chance they could.

In the last year, their whole life had been completely destroyed up here in Los Altos de Jalisco. Their father, Don Juan, was gone. He'd left two months before to go down to Del Mar, California, to find work with his sons Jesus and Teodoro, and their cousin-brother Everardo. Domingo was gone, too. He'd left the week before to go and find their father. Their whole settlement lay in waste, and they had nothing left to eat but roots and whatever else they could scavenge. Their only hope for survival was for Don Juan to return from the United States with some money so that they could buy food and supplies.

"Mama! Mama!" yelled Juan, racing up to the entrance of the little church. "Our cousin-brother Agustin says that Jose has been arrested and that he was betrayed by one of his own men! And that they're bringing him up the valley in chains right now!"

Doña Margarita never said one single word. No, she just motioned for her little son to come close and she snuggled him into her side as she continued praying. Juan's little heart was pounding wildly. He wanted his mother to jump up and do something to save his brother Jose. He wanted his mother to turn into a pack of vicious wolves, as he knew that she could do, and sweep down, out of the heavens, and destroy the colonel and his men once and for all. But she wasn't doing anything. No, she was just sitting here quietly and continuing with her prayers oh so calmly, as if he hadn't said a thing. And the other old women, all around her, what did they do? Why, they just continued praying, too.

Juan glanced around and he saw the huge statue of Jesus nailed on the cross and the big crown of long, terrible thorns on Jesus' head and the long, thick nails in his feet and hands. Blood dripped down from the thorns on Jesus' head to his chest, and more blood ran from the big open knife wound in his side where the soldier had stabbed him with his sword, and then even more blood ran from his hands and feet, too. Oh, it looked just awful. Juan had never been able to figure out why God had let this terrible thing happen to his Only Begotten Son. Then it hit Juan like a lightning bolt.

"Oh, Mama," whispered little Juan, trying hard not to talk too loudly in the house of God, "are they going to crucify Jose, too?"

Hearing this, a couple of the old women laughed, but Juan didn't think it was funny one little bit. For everyone knew how great a spirit Jose was, and so the *Rurales* were going to try to do as much harm to him as they possibly could.

"No," said Doña Margarita, finishing up with her prayers and making the sign of the cross over herself, "they will not harm your brother—so help me God!"

"But what will you do, Mama?" asked Juan. "Will you turn into a pack of wolves and kill all of the soldiers?"

The other old women, who'd also stopped their praying, heard this and laughed all the more. Juan turned and gave the old women a dirty look.

Smiling, Doña Margarita gave her hand to her youngest child and had him help her up, then together they went out of the dark, cool church toward the hot, bright, glaring-white outdoors. "We'll see, *mi hijito,*" she said very simply. "We'll see what comes, and then we'll do what we can."

"But you will save him, right? You won't let them do to him like God let happen to His Son with the cross, eh?"

Mindfully, Doña Margarita looked at her little son. They were at the door of the holy house of the Lord. Behind them it was cool and dark; a world full of statues and candles and fine wood and tile. In front of them was the dusty, bright, glaring-hot outdoors. "Listen, *mi hijito,* and listen very closely; ours is not to question, or to assume that we can understand; ours is to realize, that we do what we can with the help of God, but that ultimately . . . the destiny of our lives was written in the heavens and was rooted in the depths of the earth herself long ago. And so it isn't for us old souls to panic or hurry or lose faith, but —and this is a big 'but'—to go slow and easy, always realizing that all of life is but a dream, and *que será será en esta gran vida, con el favor de Dios!*" And, saying this, she kissed the crucifix of her well-worn rosary.

Juan heard his mother's words, he really did, but still he was upset. "But, oh, Mama!" said Juanito impatiently. "Didn't you hear me? They have Jose in chains and I'm sure that they've beaten him, too!" No, he wasn't calm inside, like his mother. He was crazy-*loco* with panic!

"And wasn't our Lord God the Savior also whipped and beaten and then forced to carry his own cross to Calvary? Oh, no, *mi hijito,* understand deep inside your soul that everything is going to be, not just all right, but wonderful, if only we keep *nuestra fe!*"

Juan didn't like hearing this one little bit. He wanted his mother to stop all this nonsense and do something like he knew that she could do. Oh, he'd never forget when she'd turned into a female-coyote and she'd saved him from that pack of mad dogs. Why, his mother was the force of the earth and of the heavens alike, and so he wanted her to do something, and do it right now!

"Come, *mi hijito,*" said the old woman, seeing how upset her little son was, "and remember that like the deep, true river waters that gently cut a lasting pathway through mountain and stone, we humans are to cut our way—not with ax and steel, but fearlessly with love and more love, if we are to survive for long." She kissed the fingertips of her right hand, gently touching herself on the forehead and then across the heart. "Jose is going to be just fine, *mi hijito.* I know, I can feel it here in *mi corazón,*" she said, massaging herself on her dried-up old breasts as they now went out the door of the dark, cool church into the bright-white hot outdoors.

And Juan could well see that his mother had spoken as if she really had no doubts or fears, and he wanted to believe in her, he really did, but he just couldn't.

Then, here came the colonel and his men between the burned fields of corn and alfalfa, and they were lifting a cloud of dust as they brought Jose down the dirt road. As they entered the plaza, *la gente* could see that Jose's face had been whipped and beaten, and he was all bent over like he was ready to drop from exhaustion. Two horsemen were jerking him along with the ropes that they had about his neck and chained hands.

The townspeople gathered, and they made the sign of the cross over themselves as Jose was brought past them. At the well in the middle of the plaza, a lovely, good-hearted young woman took an earthen cup and was going to give Jose some water when a handsome young soldier cut in front of her with his fine, well-fed horse, grabbing the cup of water for himself with a big, nasty grin.

Seeing this, Doña Margarita told Juan to quickly take water to the colonel and his men. "Then, once half of the men have received water," said Doña Margarita, "bring a cup to Jose."

And saying this, the old woman then went over to her son. "Oh, *mi hijito, mi hijito,* the love of my life," she said in agonizing pain. "We'll give you water as soon as we can!"

"*Gracias,* Mama," said Jose, mumbling his words. He could hardly speak. His eyes were rolling. His whole face was all swollen from the savage beating. "But be careful, I don't want anything to happen to you, Mama."

"Don't worry," she said simply. "We're with God."

And she stroked him, and was giving him love when Juanito came rushing over with a cup of water. "Half of the men have been given water," he said, completely out of breath. "Here's a cup for you, Jose."

Doña Margarita took the cup of water and put it to her son's mouth, but before he'd even gotten one good swallow, the colonel—who'd dismounted—stepped in, knocking the cup from her hand.

"He will have no water!" bellowed the big, powerful man.

And then, at that very moment, was when little Juan saw a miracle happen before his very eyes. His skinny little old mother didn't shy away from the colonel. No, she whirled about, facing him eye-to-eye, and in the bright-white glaring light of the day, she was suddenly *un tigre!* She was a great female jaguar, a rage-angry mother coyote, and she was huge! And he was sure that his mother could have easily lashed out with all her powers and ripped the heart out of this mere mortal who stood before her, but she didn't. No, instead, she just stood there glaring, giving him the full force of her female eye. And the powerful, well-fed man saw her stare, saw her look of absolute fearlessness, and he froze in his tracks in dead terror.

"NO!" shouted Doña Margarita. "In God's name, you will not stop me from giving water to my son!" she roared. "You might arrest him, beat him, and even execute him, *Coronel* Montemayor, but you will have respect for the life that your dear mother gave you! And you will not stop me from giving water to my own flesh and blood!"

And Juan could see that the colonel was stunned, that he didn't know what to do. He hadn't expected such power and commanding intelligence to come from such a filthy little rag-ged-looking old Indian woman. But then the big man caught his breath and smiled. So this was the fierce blood that Don Juan had decided to marry and have his children with. It was inter-esting, very interesting, but, still, completely out of place for a man of Don Juan's stature. He quit smiling and glanced around, saw that all his men were ready and heavily outnum-bered all these other old women who had their beady old eyes on him, too, and he spoke.

"All right, you can give the dirty little Indian coward some water," said the colonel graciously. "Or, otherwise, who knows, he might die on us before we can get him to the state capital for his proper execution!" he added with power, and then laughed. But it was a nervous laugh. He was still feeling very unsure.

"But I thought that your orders were that they wanted him alive so that they could make him an offer," said the mother of Jorge and Manuel, two of the best young men who rode with Jose.

Hearing this, the colonel laughed a big belly laugh. "And you really believed that?!" he said, laughing all the more. "Oh, you backward *indios* are such simple-minded imbeciles that it baffles the mind that you were ever able to survive before we came and began to civilize you! He's a killer, a traitor, a thief of government property. What did you think that we'd do? Make him an officer?"

"Exactly!" said Doña Margarita with all her power. "And if you were smart, that's exactly what you would do! For not once were you able to beat him in honest combat, and so without his cunning you are all destined to die and to come to *nada* once again, as you did before . . . way back, long ago, in your forgotten memories of *nuestra hermana planeta!*"

"Oh," said the colonel, not really hearing or understanding what the old woman had said, "so now I see that you must be the one that Jose gets his big fancy mouth from, that I've heard so much about." He laughed. "Well, it's all over now, you ugly old *india!* Because we got him, and he's dead!" bellowed the big, well-fed man.

"Not in the eyes of God Almighty!" said Doña Margarita calmly. "For Jose, my son, knows love, and his soul will live for all eternity! But you—who's never known love or respect of life here or anywhere else—are destined to burn in your own fires of hell forever! Not once knowing peace or love here on *nuestra sagrada madre,* much less in heaven!"

The colonel had had enough. Quickly, he took off his gloves, rolled them together tightly, pulled them long and straight, and then, staring Doña Margarita in the eyes, he slapped her across the face with his gloves as hard as he could. Instantly, Jose's whole body rose up as if from the dead, and even though he was in chains and had a rope about his neck and hands, he was ready to kill. Juan was ready to leap on the colonel, too.

"No!" said Doña Margarita to both of her dark, small sons. "Let the colonel have his way today! For down deep inside he knows that his days, and the days of his privileged few, are numbered. The heavens above do not forget what it is that we plant here upon our Sacred Mother Earth! God forgive you, my dear *Coronel,*" she added, "for you did not know enough to plant even a little bit of compassion or love here on earth for you to later harvest up in heaven!"

"Why, you stupid, ugly, insulting old *india!*" bellowed the colonel with rage. "Those are the very words we brought to your God-forsaken, savage shores! Do you really think that you can intimidate me with our own religion, you old goat-smelling sow?!" And he suddenly grabbed her by the throat, jerking her close. "Don't mince words with me, you old witch! I've seen your kind before! Twisting everything decent that we've tried so hard to do for you in the name of God-given Christianity into something treacherous and evil!"

Juan leaped on him, but was slapped away with such force that he saw red and his mind went blank.

"No, no, I'm not going to kill her," he said to Juan and Jose. "Oh, God, no!" he added. "I want this old Indian witch to live so that she can die a thousand deaths as we kill off each one of her children and burn all your dreams to the ground!

"Don't think that I don't know who you are!" he shouted at Doña Margarita. "I knew Jose was too good for a boy his age, so I investigated and found that his advisor was the sly old fox of the mountains himself, his grandfather Colonel Pio Castro, but the old man is dead now! He died before we could get to him and kill the old traitor! But you others aren't old!" he yelled, trembling with rage as he turned to the crowd as a whole. "So, hopefully, you're not going to die before we get to each and every one of you *indios sin razón* and exterminate you like the no-good rodents that you are! And you, old woman, I swear that you will come to hate the day you put a spell on Don Juan and forced him to marry out of his stature and bring into this world a bunch of sick, diseased half-breed *mestizos* to ruin our sacred Catholic land!"

And saying this, he shoved Doña Margarita away with such force that he knocked her to the ground. Quickly, he turned and mounted his horse. "On to the state capital," he yelled to his men, "so we can celebrate this execution among civilized people!"

Getting to her feet, Doña Margarita—short and tiny and all

wrinkled up like the *madre tierra* herself—tried to hug Jose just one last time, but he was jerked out of her hands before she could take him in her arms. "Go with God, my son," she called after him, tears streaming down her earthen-looking old face. "Go with God! And know that the sacred will of the Almighty will be done, *mi amor!* I promise you! The sacred will of God will be done!"

Juan took his mother in his arms, holding her as the tears continued running down her face. The armed men were pulling and yanking at Jose's throat and hands as they went up the cobblestone street and out of town. Oh, Juan felt so helpless, so useless. But he was only going on seven or eight years of age, so what could he do?

"Oh, Mama," he said in frustration, "if God is really with us, then why is He letting all this happen to us?! Why doesn't He just come down from the heavens with ten thousand angels and kill all those no-good *Rurales* right now?"

"Quiet!" said an old woman to Juan as she came up, putting her arms about his mother. "Why, she just performed a God-given miracle! Didn't you see that colonel go pale with fear every time your mother spoke? Why, the heavens are with us at this very moment," she added, making the sign of the cross over herself. "Just open your eyes and see all the glorious angels singing about us, *malcriado!*"

Juan didn't know what to say. He couldn't see any singing angels, and he certainly hadn't expected one of his mother's old, useless church friends to get so mad at him. He was shocked.

"It's all right," said Doña Margarita to her old woman friend, "it's all right. He's still young and doesn't know the ways of the heavens."

"Yes, and soon he'll have hair between his legs and still have no idea how life goes, if we don't speak up to him now!" snapped the old woman.

"And you're right," said Doña Margarita. "Absolutely right.

For it's not just the colonel who's such a lost human being, but so many of our own men who now think that guns and violence are the only means with which to settle matters here upon our sacred earth." She made the sign of the cross over herself, thanking God for having given her such a wealth of understanding. Then she said to her little son, "Come, let's go home and eat. Remember, as I've told you time and again, *mi hijito,* even God needs help in performing miracles here upon the earth. And tomorrow is another day, another gift from the Almighty, and so everything is possible *mañana,* if only we—the people of the earth—keep the faith that all will be well, once we've finally rooted these last lost-souls that God has sent to us from the stars to educate in the matters *del corazón!* For they have been lost for so long that they really don't know what it is that they do. God forgive them."

"Well, yeah, I'm sure you're right," said Juan, hearing his mother speak some more of her useless talk, "but right now I need to go and attend to the animals. I'll be back by dark, Mama."

"Be careful, *mi hijito,* very careful," she said, hugging him. "You are my love! My very special *angelito!*"

And she tried to kiss him, but he jerked away and took off running as fast as he could go. Oh, he was all confused and as mad as hell and wanted to get away from his mother and God. Here, his brother was being taken off in chains to his execution, and neither God nor his mother was doing a damn thing about it. His father, Don Juan, now, he would've done something. At least he would've shot a soldier or two before getting killed.

"Women just don't know how to do a damn thing but pray and hide," he said to himself, "and so I don't want anything more to do with them! What I want right now is a gun! Yes, a big, shiny black Colt .45!"

"Bang! Bang!" yelled Juan, picking up a stick and pretending to shoot every little clump of rock or brush that he saw. They were all soldiers, and so he'd shoot them dead, right in their heart. He killed well over a thousand soldiers before he got back home that night with Chivo and the other animals who'd survived the slaughter of the *Rurales*. And he killed the colonel himself well over a hundred times, too. Oh, his mother was talking such *loco*-crazy nonsense. Nothing was ever going to be all right again! Their whole village lay in waste, and their livestock had all been slaughtered, except for these few animals, and there was hardly anyone left of their once-large, strong *familia*. Just Luisa, Emilia, and Juan and their mother. Even Lucha and Maria had been smart enough to take off last week to be with their cousin-brother Agustin.

Then, that's when it hit Juan. It hit him right between the eyes like a lightning bolt. And he suddenly remembered that people had been saying that Agustin had come into some money and he'd bought new clothes and he and Lucha and Maria were planning to go to the United States.

Now Juan very carefully recalled how Agustin had looked as he'd come racing up the valley with the news of Jose's arrest. He'd been all dressed up in his new clothes and, yes, he'd laughed a nervous laugh, just like a frightened, guilty human being. Juan's eyes went huge with disbelief as he now wondered . . . if, in fact, it was, maybe, even their own cousin-brother who'd—oh, my God—betrayed Jose and collected the thousand *pesos* in gold!

Then that evening as the sun was going down, a strange thing happened. First a neighbor woman came by and gave them a pot of soup made with roots and armadillo meat, saying that this was the food of the underground. Then two other old women brought over a few tortillas and some cooked sweet squash and beans, saying that this was food of the middle world. Then each woman took Doña Margarita in her arms and hugged her in a big, tight *abrazo*, with such *amor*, saying that love, and only love, was the food of the upper world.

Then, after they'd eaten, the foul-mouthed old midwife Fatima showed up with a chicken, and she told them to follow her. Quickly, Juan and his sisters and mother followed the midwife and the other old women out of the *ramada* and into an opening in the oak trees behind their home. Then there, out of sight of the town, Fatima had them build a huge fire, then she slit the chicken's throat, tossing the bird—feathers and all—into the burning flames.

Little Juan didn't know what to think. He'd never seen a chicken cooked in this manner. And, glancing around, he could see that his sisters didn't know what to think, either. But their mother just winked at them and said nothing, and her old church friends now began to chant.

And as the smell of the blazing chicken filled the air with a terrible burning-feather odor and the old women continued chanting, Juan would later swear that he began to feel eerie-feelings creeping all about him. Then Juan realized what it was that these old women were doing. They weren't cooking the chicken to eat. No, they'd sacrificed the chicken and now they were calling upon the spirits of their ancestry to come forth and assist them in their hour of need.

Juan took hold of his mother's hand. He was getting pretty nervous. The light of the day was going quickly and the night was approaching. Juan just didn't feel comfortable with what these old women were doing. Why, it was beginning to feel to him as if the earth itself was really opening up and all the local spirits of the past were coming forth.

And, also, Juan well knew that if the priest found out what his mother's old church friends were doing, he'd be furious. For these women weren't just praying to the Sacred Father, God of the Holy Catholic Church, anymore; no, they were now going back to their old Indian ways, before the Europeans had ever come upon their shores, and they were also praying to the Holy Mother God of all creation. They were acknowledging the three sacred worlds of existence—not just the holiness of the heavens

—and they were summoning all the spirits, male and female alike, and particularly the ones who'd last gone over to the other side of the great beyond: Don Pio, Agustin, Basilio, Mariposa, and the others who'd been killed by the colonel and his gang of assassins.

Cold chills snaked up and down little Juan's spine as he watched the fire snapping and burning. He knew that what these old women were doing was very dangerous and strictly forbidden, and if his father Don Juan had been home, it would never have been allowed. But Don Juan was gone, and the priest hadn't been here in more than six months, either; and so now here was Juan, along with his mother and sisters, watching these old women chanting freely and bringing forth all the spirits of the heavens and the earth alike.

And now the old women began to dance, swaying with their old bodies in strange ways and chanting in soft, eerie sounds. They were talking to the stars. They were asking the approaching Mother Night to bless their beloved friend Doña Margarita among all women and give her the power to bring forth miracles.

Then, Juan couldn't believe it: his own mother suddenly got so excited, that she picked up two stones and began to clap them together as she jumped in, joining the dancers. And his mother was swift of foot as a young cat as she moved in and out of the other women, making music by banging the two stones together.

And so bang, bang went the stones as Doña Margarita danced. Then Juan's sisters picked up rocks and joined in, too. And they were moving their arms like birds in flight; first banging the stones in front of themselves and then behind themselves. Juan had never seen such a thing, and he'd always thought that his mother and family were totally against these old ways of *los indios,* but he could now see that he'd been wrong. For his mother and sisters were dancing so gracefully that he was sure that they'd done this many times before.

The Father Sun was gone, and the Mother Moon was out, and the old midwife began to speak, telling the moon in a clipped sing-song-voice to always remember that they, the women, came from the night, and so she, the moon, was their special friend. "For, before light, there was darkness," said Fatima to the heavens, "and darkness is female and eterrr-nal!"

Fatima swayed her head from side to side, tossing her long, wild grey-white hair like the wings of a bird. Then she raised her arms, floating her hands to each side like rippling water, as if they had no bones. The old woman looked like she was in a trance, and her whole face and body seemed to be getting younger and younger as Juan watched her move with such grace and dignity.

Then Fatima approached their mother, Doña Margarita, giving her her blessing, and Juan would later swear that he'd actually felt *la tierra* tremble beneath him. "Remember, always remember, *amiga mía* Margarita," said the midwife, as if talking in a dream-like language, "that women, like water, are forever; and men, like fire, are only temporary. And so, of course, it was destined to come to this, once more. And so we women mustn't panic, but instead open up our eyes and ask the spirits what it is that is being asked of us, *las mujeres,* this time. For the waters of the universe are infinite, and this is what always happens to men and their little male fires when life gets too difficult," she said, laughing. "They either go crazy-*loco* or just run off to their games of war or empire-making, and it's left to us, the women, as always, to come forth and balance the forces of the earth and the heavens with our great, open thighs," she said, spreading her legs apart and leaning way back, "giving love and more love, so that the river of life can go on and on forever!"

And, saying this, the youngish-looking old midwife now came close to little Juan, thighs still open, and laughed right in his face, startling him. "And don't you ever forget, *muchacho,* no matter how much hair you grow between your legs," she said with power, "that it was me, a woman, who first saw your little cock and *tanates* come into this world! And if you're lucky, it will be a woman's gentle touch who will see you out of life, *la vida,* too!"

And she then reached for little Juan's crotch to jerk him close, showing him that she really meant business, but Doña Margarita took the old midwife by the arm just in time and danced away with her.

"But he must be taught," the old woman shouted back over her shoulder to Juan as Doña Margarita led her away, "that all men must be impregnated by an older woman and given a second birth if they are to have respect for life!"

"Yes, you're absolutely right," said Doña Margarita, holding on tightly to her old friend. "But you leave my little son alone! I will be the one to teach him how to respect life. Not you!"

"Good, then," said the old midwife, laughing in the low-sounding rumbling voice of hers. "As long as it is done before he gets too big for his *tanates!*"

Hearing this, Juan's eyes were huge as he watched his mother and Fatima dance away. He had absolutely no idea what it was that they were talking about. All he knew was that the midwife had smelled so foul when she'd come close to him, trying to grab him, that he would have gotten sick if his mother hadn't taken her away.

"Oh, we all saw you, my angel Margarita, suffering so much over the years," the midwife was now saying to Doña Margarita. "You should have listened to your beloved father and never married such a heavy burden!"

"Shhhhhhh!" said Doña Margarita, not letting herself get caught up with the crude woman's talk. "Just keep dancing, *amiga mía!* For it isn't for us to question or belittle, but to accept with love and understanding . . . that anytime we women want, we can arise like the great waters of the earth and put out all these little fires of men's self-importance as we've done so many times before!"

"Yes, that's true," said Fatima, laughing. "Just like our

Mother Moon moves the tides of the seas of *nuestra tierra madre,* so can we women flood the lands *de los pueblos* anytime we wish! Our spiritual powers are as infinite as the stars above, for we come from the darkness! And we come from the silence! And we are eternal! Having existed since the pregnancy of time, way before male light and male song ever even thought of becoming."

"Glory be to God, my friend!" said Doña Margarita. "But, now, ssshhh, no more, and let's just keep dancing. Oh, it feels so good to be wild, free women once more, dancing with substance, just as our coyote sisters sing and dance with substance to the stars each night!"

"¡Aaaaaiiiii Chihuahua!" yelled the old midwife, laughing *con carcajadas.* "It's been a long time, hasn't it?"

"Oh, yes!" said Doña Margarita. "Way too long!"

And, hand in hand, they now picked up the pace, dancing around and around the fire, and Juan's sisters began to bang their rocks together, faster and faster. Then the midwife let go of their mother's hand and went into a tight spin, her eyes getting larger and larger with concentration. And suddenly she let go of a blood-curdling screaming-*grito del alma,* and she jumped right into the middle of the burning-hot fire.

Gasping in terrible fear, Juan watched as the crazy woman now began to spread out the hot-burning coals with her bare feet, just like a mother hen scratching the earth to find earthworms for her chicks. And it was strange, but her feet didn't smell like they were getting burned.

Then, Juan couldn't believe it, but he now heard the other old women screech to the high heavens and they leaped into the fire with Fatima, too. All the women were now dancing among the burning-hot coals, spreading them into the formation of a circle. Juan had never seen such a thing in all of his life. Oh, my God, why, these old women were now stomping on the hottest coals, grinding them into the earth, and they didn't seem to be burning themselves or to be in any pain, either.

Then, to further his astonishment, little Juan now saw his own mother leap into the glowing, red-hot coals. Then went Emilia, then Luisa, too, and now they were all dancing, shouting, and flying about like birds, like human-angels, and they were in ecstasy. And he could have sworn that he heard laughter, and he glanced up at the heavens and he saw that, yes, there were Basilio and Agustin, laughing *con carcajadas* as they kept watch over them from the Gates of Heaven.

The dancing went on and on, faster and faster, until the women finally began to drop from exhaustion. All of the glowing coals had been stomped into black ashes by their naked feet. The women were all laughing, grinning, and looking so young and very happy and . . . and then each woman came over to Doña Margarita and threw her arms about her in a big *abrazo*, telling her, *"Todo* the whole universe is now open to you, sacred woman, and the world of making miracles is all yours, as it has been for awakened women since the beginning."

And they made the sign of the cross over themselves, raising their arms to the heavens, and calling in all the help of God and Christ and all of the other ancestors of the spiritual universe!

Juan couldn't figure out what was going on. Did these women really think that, by killing a chicken and dancing on fire, they'd turned his old mother into some great warrior-woman, and now she had magic powers and she was going to be able to save his brother Jose? Juan felt like laughing, but he didn't. He could see that these women truly meant business. Why, they had a strange look in their eyes, and they weren't that old anymore. No, they'd actually, somehow, gotten ageless and as powerful looking as a pack of starving wolves.

Emilia came over and took Juan by the hand. "Come on, Juan, and join us," she said, grinning ear-to-ear. None of the women could stop grinning and hugging one another. "You, too, can do it. Most of the coals are gone. And I promise you, the fire has become our *amiga*. Truly, she won't burn you, she's not male anymore. She's become our loving mother."

But Juan only shook his head. There was no way on earth that he was going to try it. The coals were still smoking and didn't feel friendly or female to him. No, even from a distance, they felt burning-hot.

The ageless young women were now searching through the ashes with their bare feet, locating the chicken bones. And they were doing it so naturally, gripping the little bones with their naked toes and lifting them out of the smoking ashes. Then they took the bones in hand and began assembling them into a little altar at the head of the fire circle. Each woman cut some of her hair and tied it with a colorful piece of cloth, placing it about the chicken bones. The rocks that they'd used for making music were brought up and put in place, too. Their most cherished pieces of jewelry were taken off their ears and wrists and carefully placed among the bones and human hair. Cornmeal was taken and made into a triangle inside of the fire circle. Then two sticks were tied together with a piece of rawhide to make a simple cross, and the cross was placed at the head of the altar. The women now positioned themselves about the Holy Circle of the Blessed Trinity, and silently they bowed their heads and began to pray.

Coming to the edge of the circle where his mother was standing in the ashes, Juan took her hand. Strangely enough, after giving witness to all this crazy-*loquería,* Juan didn't feel scared anymore. No, it was as if a great peace had come over all of them.

He listened to the women praying and, no, these weren't the memorized prayers of the Holy Catholic Church, but heartfelt chants and word-repetitions that sounded like they came straight from these women's souls. And they were saying that, like the great old trees of the world, they were now finally deeply rooted into the Mother Earth three times once more, and so they could reach for the Father Sky with substance in their God-given souls.

Then he heard his mother saying over and over again that, no, she would not hate; she would not hate. But, instead, she'd plant her two feet the-needed-three-sacred-times into *la tierra sagrada,* creating a Holy Six-Pointed Star-Flower, then reach for the all-forgiving light of God to illuminate her way. "The colonel and his deeds will not overcome my love and fill *mi corazón* with hate," she said. "For I bless the colonel and his men and their mothers who brought them into our wondrous world, and I will continue on my own path of truth and beauty, so help me God!"

Juan couldn't believe what his mother was saying; for how could she possibly be blessing the colonel and his men after all that they'd done? He glanced up at the heavens, taking a big breath, and he saw that the sky was full of stars and the quarter moon was grinning down upon them like the smile of God Himself. Oh, this had been such a terrifying, confusing night for him. But, on the other hand, he did feel kind of good and happy inside.

He smiled back at the stars and the moon and, lo and behold, they smiled right back at him, winking *con gusto!*

5

And so **la gente**—*the meek, the mud people of the earth
—had been reborn along with this new Baby Shooting
Sun, and theirs was now a time to dance with wild abandon, relearning the long-lost origins of all song!*

For three nights, Doña Margarita visited the
site of the fire dance; then on the third day, she awoke and
called all of *la familia* together and announced that she was
going to Guadalajara to get Jose released to her custody.

They were all stunned—Juan and Luisa and Emilia. They
didn't know what to think. Luisa was the first one to speak. She
was the oldest, and she was a married woman now, and so she
had substance.

"But, Mama," said Luisa, "what in God's name makes you
think that they will release him to you?!"

"Because for the past three nights, *mi hijita,* I've prayed and
the powers of heaven and earth have come to me, giving me the
same dream," their mother said calmly. "And each time in this
dream, the little she-fox comes to me, and with all her great
cunning, she explains to me so clearly that now is the time for

me to go alone on a long voyage. My shadow and I are complete."

"All right, I understand," said Luisa. "You and your shadow were reunited at the fire dance. But, oh, Mama, you could get lost, or worse, killed! I don't want you going alone!"

Doña Margarita laughed. "Woman of such little faith, stop being so *escandalosa* and get hold of yourself. I will not be going alone, you know that, I'll be going with God walking as my shadow, every step."

Hearing these words, Juan shook his head. Couldn't his mother stop talking all this nonsense and see that God had abandoned them?

"Oh, Mama, be reasonable!" continued Luisa. "Wait till my husband, Jose-Luis, comes back, and take him with you, if need be. But don't be telling us that you'll be going with God. Don't you see what's become of us in the last year? The truth is that God has forsaken us, Mama!"

"Exactly," Juan mumbled under his breath, completely agreeing with his sister Luisa.

Doña Margarita glanced at Juan, then turned back to Luisa. "Don't be saying that, *mi hijita,*" said their mother softly, gently. "For you are planting the dangerous seed of our destruction."

"Oh, Mama, stop telling me what to say or not to say! I'm a grown woman, and I can say what I wish!" said Luisa in frustration.

In a flash, their mother leaped out of her chair and had Luisa by the ear. "But not grown enough for me to not grab you by the ear and put you on your knees!" said Doña Margarita, twisting Luisa down to the floor. "I will not permit you or anyone else in this *familia* to speak like that! Yes, we've lost many loved ones, and Jose was taken away in chains, but look at you, Luisa; as we speak, you are big with child! Don't you see that the miracle of life goes on and on? Why, there's no stopping the flow of God's love! And you should know that! You danced on fire! You helped us call in the spirits! You are a woman, *mi hijita,* not a man—who's lost from the miracle of giving birth!"

"Oh, Mama, please," said Luisa, tears pouring from her eyes as she squirmed in pain. "You're all we have left! I don't even know anymore if I want to bring my child into this terrible world!"

Hearing this, Doña Margarita was stunned. She released Luisa's ear. "Oh, *mi hijita, mi hijita,* you just don't know what it is that you say. Good God, where have you been all these years when I've been training you? Haven't you learned yet that this world isn't terrible? Just look around you and feast your eyes; it's absolutely beautiful, and it will always be beautiful. It's only the affairs of men that are in such a terrible state!"

"But, Mama, there's been so much death and suffering! And we have nothing to eat half of the time anymore! Truly, I just don't know if this is a world to bring a child into!"

With tears in her old eyes, Doña Margarita took her big, stout daughter by her arms. *"Cálmate,* my child," she said gently. "Calm yourself and open your *corazón;* look at me in the eyes with your heart of hearts and see that all is well, has always been well, and will always be well. Didn't you see the sunrise this morning? Why, it was as wondrous as I've ever seen. Why this is, indeed, a beautiful world to bring a child into. For we will give your child love, *querida,* and we will teach your child how to grow strong with faith in God, and soon these *caprichos* of men will be over once more, and life, *la vida,* will go on as always. For, remember, as the midwife said the night of the fire dance, we, women—like water—are eternal, and so it isn't ours to panic or question, but to go on and on wide-open with our flow of love and more love. This is why God in His infinite wisdom entrusted us and not men to carry the seeds of *la vida.* "

"Oh, God, I hope so," said Luisa, wiping her eyes. "But, Mama, I sometimes get so scared and confused."

"We all do, *mi hijita;* we all do. And that's why it was important that we danced in the old ways. Everything is going to be fine, *con el favor de Dios.*"

Juan and Emilia came close and they hugged Luisa and their mother, too. Luisa had truly spoken the truth for all of them; their mother was all that they had left, and they didn't want her going off alone, either. But they could also see that their mother was as confident as the earth herself.

After breakfast Doña Margarita got her shawl and was ready to go. One of the old women who'd danced on the fire with them brought her a gourd full of water. Another fire dancer bought her some *huaraches* that she'd just made. Everyone was coming to see Doña Margarita off. Then, there was the grand old skinny Indian woman, walking up the little cobblestone street by herself with nothing but rags and bare feet. She was saving the new sandals that she'd been given until she got into town. Fatima was the only one who wasn't here to see their mother off. The indestructible old midwife was at a *ranchita,* half a day's walk away, attending to another birth—another gift from God.

Juan and his sisters Emilia and Luisa followed their mother to the edge of the little settlement, where she waved them back, saying that she had to go on alone.

"But, Mama!" said Luisa, suddenly looking sick with fear again. "What will happen to us?"

"You will live. That's what will happen to you," said their mother calmly. "Now go home with your brother and sister and await your father's return from the United States. I prayed for him last night. He should have heard me and is on his way home as we speak." She made the sign of the cross over herself. "God is watching over all of us. Everything is fine," she added, smiling.

"Of course," said Emilia, putting her long, slender arm around the shoulders of her shorter, wider sister Luisa. "And don't worry. I'll take care of everything, Mama." It was surprising everyone, but the beautiful, tall Emilia was becoming more and more confident as their daily struggle for survival continued.

Their mother turned and started down the red-earth road— the road that left their settlement and went across the valley, passing near Doña Josefina's house, and then went up a little slope and into the oaks. Juan's whole body began to tremble. Oh, my God, never before in all his life had he ever been apart from his mother. He began to weep uncontrollably. Emilia came close to hug her little brother, too, but Juan's pet bull Chivo stepped between them, taking up ground alongside Juan. The great all-black bull could feel Juan's anguish, and he began to plow the earth, bellowing to the high heavens.

"Don't," said Emilia, watching her little brother and the bull getting more and more worked up. "I know that you've never been apart from Mama before, but she clearly told us not to—"

Juan's trembling stopped, and he shouted to the heavens and took off racing after their mother. "Mama! Mama!" he screamed, as he went running up the road as fast as his little legs could carry him.

Chivo trotted after him, swinging his mighty horns from side to side, bellowing with heart-felt anguish, too. And no one, but no one, dared to try to stop Juan or his huge monstrous bull.

Doña Margarita never lessened her stride or turned to look back at her screaming little son or the bellowing bull. No, she just kept going at a good, easy coyote-trot-walk. She was almost sixty years old, had given birth to Juan, her nineteenth child, at the age of fifty; but she was still an excellent walker, just as everyone else was an excellent walker all over these mountains.

Little Juan kept crying and crying, and soon the little settlement was left far behind in the distance. They'd come to the end of the valley. Here the main road led around a series of small lakes and to the town of Arandas, thirty-some kilometers away. Doña Margarita took pity on her little son and stopped to rest in the shade of a large oak. She called Juan to her side.

"Mi hijito," she said, "look, I don't want you to be following me with Chivo anymore. From here on, I'm going to have to go alone. Believe me, what I am about to do . . . is going to take all the cunning and strength I have, and so I cannot have you tagging along with me."

The bull had settled down and was grazing alongside the first pond.

"But I want to help you, Mama," said Juan Salvador, tears pouring down his little face. Oh, his heart was breaking. He just didn't know if he could even live one single day without his mother.

"You can't help me," she said, taking him by his little shoulders. "No one can help me. Don't you remember how you went across those fields all alone the night you went to Josefina's house to summon the Devil?"

"Well, yes," said Juan, wiping his tears, "but I was so scared being alone, Mama!"

"Yes, you were scared, *mi hijito,* as you had every right to be. But, also, you were all-alive to every little sound and thought and movement. You will never forget that night as long as you live; for you were open with a naked heart to all the heavens above. And . . . and this is exactly what I need to do now, *mi hijito.* I need to be so frightened that I'm aware of every little thing. I need to be so open to the heavens with all my heart, that no little whisper of the stars eludes these old coyote ears of mine. Do you understand? A person alone is an army, especially when the stars above are speaking to them."

"But, Mama, how will I live without you?" he asked.

The old woman laughed. "And this is the very same question that was asked of God when we left the Garden of Eden and . . . every child has asked their parents ever since." She smiled. "Look, *mi hijito,* you will live just fine without me. Why, before I'm even out of sight, I guarantee you that Chivo and you will find some mischief to get into, and I'll be forgotten." She kissed him. "And this is the way it should be. For life just keeps going and going, repeating itself over and over, like a sacred circle." She made the sign of the cross over herself, kissing her thumb that was crossed over her index finger.

He dried his eyes. "Then I'm not going to die?" he asked.

She hugged him. "Of course not, *mi hijito,* you're going to live. Just like I lived when my father left home and I thought I'd die, but I didn't.

"Take my hand, *mi hijito,*" she added, "and know that I am your mother, your *madre,* and I will be here for you and your sisters forever, especially at night when you say your prayers and you go to sleep, returning to heaven with *Papito Dios.* For, remember, Juanito, the soul knows no distance. And all *madres* come from the heart of the earth and are for all time, just like the ground you walk on. Do you now know why we did that fire dance the other night, *mi hijito?*"

He shook his head. "No, I don't."

"It was to re-unite us to *nuestra tierra madre.* Ashes to ashes . . . to show us what it is that we humans can do once we get beyond our earthly fears. For a fearless person is an open vessel for the stars to flow through, giving us the powers to do the impossible here on earth! You see, fire dances are only to remind us of our own greatness. That's all."

"And the chicken, why was she killed?"

"To help remind us, too," she said. "But the chicken is no more necessary than the offering of Christ's blood and flesh at the church. What is really necessary is only for us to open ourselves up fearlessly, *con todo nuestro corazón,* to the light of God's love."

"But I got so scared, seeing the chicken thrown into the blazing fire and then all of you jumping into it, too," said Juan.

"Good," she said. "That's only natural the first time. But now go back and visit that fire altar while I'm gone. It will speak to you, *mi hijito.*"

"Speak?"

"Yes."

"Ghosts?"

She laughed. "A few, maybe, but mostly only the spirits of the highest order. For none of us carried hate in our souls that night. But now no more of this, for I must hurry to go bring your brother Jose back home with us before anything more happens to him!" She got to her feet, taking up ground. "And always remember, *mi hijito,* that when we earth-people plant our feet into *la tierra madre,* like we did on the night of the fire, then we are like a well-planted flower on the hill of eternal love, and we are indestructible! No wind, or rain, or storm can uproot a flower planted in love.

"So, now, do as I do and plant your two feet with me, one-two, one-two, and feel the powers of the earth coming up through your naked soles, impregnating you with all the spirits of the ground that we stand on." Juan got to his feet, doing as told. "Good. One-two, one-two; for, I tell you, each and every piece of *tierra* is sacred, indeed; each tree, each blade of grass has been painted with human blood and sweat and love over the ages, and it is for us to re-paint, too. For we, *los niños de la tierra,* have been here on earth in full partnership with the Almighty in making miracles since the beginning. In fact, that is why we are here: to help God do the Sacred Good.

"And so now stomp your feet strong and hard, one-two, one-two, and grind the soles of your feet into the earth as we did that night with the hot coals, and realize to the core of your being that I go with God, *mi hijito,* accepting with all *mi corazón* this immediate challenge that life, *la vida,* has bestowed upon me!"

And having said this, the old ragged woman now kissed her little son one last time and then she turned and started up the road once again—alone, single-minded, and terrible in her absolute calmness. For each step she now took was rooted with complete confidence in the sacredness of the very ground she walked on. She was not alone. Her shadow was full.

Little Juan stood there and watched her go, and he had huge tears running down his face. He really hadn't understood in words everything that his mother had said. All he knew was that his heart was broken forever, and yet . . . well, he was beginning to feel a little hungry as he watched his mother go around the first little lake, step by step. And looking across the shallow water covered with white lilies, his mother seemed to get smaller and smaller as she now went into the oaks beyond the flat pond covered with flowers, and then . . . she was gone. Just like that, she'd disappeared into the trees, and Juan almost let out a bloodcurdling scream of agonizing pain, but he didn't. For suddenly he realized that he wasn't just hungry; he was starving!

And so, feeling this powerful yearning for food, Juan forgot all about his mother and glanced around for something to eat. He saw Chivo over there in hip-deep water, eating the lilies in the lake and truly enjoying himself. Juan picked up a stone to throw at his big, lucky bull, but then he stopped. A huge flock of red-headed ducks were circling overhead, going toward the second little lake just beyond them.

Immediately, Juan got an idea. What if he could get Chivo to leave his present feast and go to the next little lake? Then he, Juan, could crawl along Chivo's side, hiding from the ducks, then slip down under the carpet of lilies and, yes, yes, he'd go underwater like a frog and catch himself a big, fat duck by the feet!

His mouth began to water. Oh, yes, that's what he would do! He'd catch a duck, or maybe even two, and take them home to his sisters—the only remaining people of their once-*gran familia* —and they'd have a huge, wonderful feast.

"And then I'll be a hero!" he said aloud. "I'll be the new Jose, the great, of all our mountains!"

But then Juan remembered that he didn't know how to swim.

"Damnit!" he said, throwing the rock at Chivo, but missing him. "I don't know how to swim!"

And saying this, Juan was just about ready to give up and go home, but then he got another idea. "Just wait," he said to himself, feeling the pains of hunger driving him on, "what makes me think that I can't swim, just because I've never done it before? Eh, that makes no sense. Does a goat say to himself that he can't swim just because he's never done it? Does a duck say to itself that it can't fly just because it's never flown? Hell, no! And, besides, I'm starving!"

And so with his mouth watering, Juan now approached Chivo. There were hundreds of ducks coming into the second pond just beyond them now. But what Juan didn't see was that a huge old snake had also seen the ducks and was now coming up over a fallen log and going into the thick grass, approaching the second lake, too.

"Come on, Chivo!" Juan was yelling. "Help me get a duck, and I'll feed you some peaches when we pass Josefina's house!"

Hearing the word *peaches*, the bull brought up his mighty head, which was all covered with white flowers and green vines tangled about his horns and ears.

"Chivo," yelled Juan, "let's go! I'm going to feast on the fat of the land tonight, just like you!"

The huge bull looked at his little friend, but, no, he didn't want to go anywhere. He was perfectly content just where he was, feasting on a *paraíso* of flowers and greenery.

"Damnit, Chivo, come on, I'm hungry, too!"

Then, three weeks later to the day, there came Doña Margarita back down the very road on which she'd left, and she had Jose in tow. They were walking slowly, and the old woman had her shoulder under her son's armpit, helping him along. They'd beaten Jose, they'd starved him, they'd tried to break him in every inhumane way they could.

The news of Doña Margarita's incredible miracle passed through the whole valley like wildfire. A wagon was brought up. The old woman and her son were taken the last few miles into the settlement in the back of the wagon. Pelon, Juan's young friend, found Juan tending to the livestock way up in the high *barrancas.*

"Juan! Juan!" screamed little, skinny Pelon. "Your mother has returned! And she's brought your brother Jose back from the dead!"

Juan was digging up roots and eating with *gusto* when he first heard Pelon's shouts. Oh, he and his sisters had hardly had anything to eat for weeks. No, he hadn't been able to get a duck that day. The lake had turned out to be much deeper than he'd expected. And then there'd been that huge, monstrous snake in the water, stalking Juan as he'd stalked the ducks.

"What is it?" yelled Juan, climbing up on some rocks to shout back at Pelon.

"Your mama!" screamed Pelon. "She's returned from the dead and she has Jose with her!"

Hearing this, Juan stopped chewing the roots that he'd dug up. "Mama!" he screamed, leaping off the rocks and racing through the trees and underbrush. "My mama has come home! *Mi mamá* has returned! Oh, my God! This is *un milagro!*" screamed Juan, quickly making the cross over himself as he came rushing up to Pelon.

"Yes, it is a miracle," said Pelon, making the sign of the cross over himself, too.

Both boys looked at each other, really looked at each other, and were so overwhelmed with joy that they hugged each other in a big *abrazo.* Then they quickly rounded up the animals as fast as they could and started the odd little herd of livestock home, singing as they went. And this odd little herd consisted of Chivo, two cows, a mother pig with babies, three goats, and an old white-faced burro who was so old that he was having trouble just keeping up with the little piglets, who were dodging in and out of rocks and tree roots.

Getting to the village, the two little boys left the livestock at the edge of town, and they found that *la gente* had come in from all the area. They'd come in from their burned-out ranches, they'd come in from their hiding places in the forest, they'd come in from the deep crevices in the tall *barrancas,* and they'd all come so that they could give witness to this joyous miracle of a mother having returned with her son from the state capital, the depths of sin and devastation! For so many of their loved ones had been killed or had just disappeared in the last few years that *la gente* had all but given up hope. In fact, all that was left of their once-rich valley of well over a hundred and fifty people were these people now assembled in the burned-out Villaseñor house. And this force of people comprised of seven ragged women, three crippled old men, nine children, two babies and, of course, Doña Margarita and her own *familia.*

Jose was nowhere to be seen when Juan and Pelon came running inside the ruins of Juan's family's once-grand house. Jose had asked to be left by the cemetery at the entrance of the town so he could visit with his true love and his grandfather.

"So go on! Go on!" said one of Doña Margarita's old church friends, as Juan and Pelon came rushing in.

Oh, *la gente* were so excited that it was hard for them to keep still. Doña Margarita had been in the middle of her story when Juan and Pelon had come inside. She'd been sitting down on the floor, leaning back on a half-crumbled adobe wall, having her feet massaged by Emilia with herbs and warm oil and talking excitedly to everyone, when she'd seen her youngest gift from God come rushing in. She'd stopped her words and her heart had come bursting up into her throat. "Oh, *mi amor! ¡Mi amor!"* she said, and her old, wrinkled-up face had lit up like the sun himself.

"Mama, Mama!" screamed Juan, tumbling into his mother's arms, knocking her over.

"Juan!" shouted Emilia, trying to jerk Juan off their mother. "Watch what you do! You're not little anymore!"

"Oh, let him be," said Doña Margarita, tears of joy coming to her eyes. "He's still my little baby!"

"No, Mama!" said Luisa. "Emilia is right! He's big and he has to start learning how to behave, or he could hurt you!"

"All right, all right," said Doña Margarita, holding Juan to her *corazón* as she continued to lie there on the floor. "Oh, I missed you so much, *mi hijito!* But I see that you lived. Did you and Chivo get into mischief as soon as I was out of sight?" she added.

Juan turned all red, flashing on the monstrous snake. "Yes," he said. He could still see in his mind's eye how the snake had pulled him underwater, thrashing and kicking. Oh, he had to thank Chivo for his life.

She laughed. "All right, I can see the whole thing in your eyes, *travieso,* but we'll talk later. Right now I wish to go on with my story. For, as always, God was once more all-wise and merciful, if only we have the eyes to see.

"All right, now, where was I?" she asked, sitting up and leaning back on the crumbled adobe wall as Emilia went back to massaging the soles of her feet, the gateway to all healing. "Oh, that feels so good, *mi hijita.* Just keep rubbing—ooooh, yes! That's heaven!"

"Thank you, Mama," said Emilia, glowing with happiness as she continued to give pleasure to their mother.

"You'd just gotten into Arandas and were so tired that you didn't know what to do," said one huge, dark Indian woman who had a scar across her left cheek. She was one of Doña Margarita's oldest and dearest church *amigas,* but she hadn't been invited to the fire dance. A cruel side sometimes came out of this old woman, and so they hadn't wanted to take any chances and have her turn their fire dance into a ritual of vengeance.

"Oh, that's right! Arriving in Arandas, I was so tired that I decided to go to the church to rest my feet. For I really had no idea where I was going, or what I was going to do." She laughed, glancing around at everyone. "But also, as all we women well know, when we don't know what to do—different than men—we often do our very greatest service for God here on earth. For the unknown has never been a woman's enemy, but instead, her strength!"

The seven old women, plus Luisa and Emilia, all nodded their heads in agreement.

"Of course," said Fatima, coming in at this moment, "since the first passage of blood, we women, different than men, are forced to recognize the very simple fact that, when it's all said and done, we humans really aren't in control of life, *la vida.*"

"Nor can we just run away when we have tits full of milk and hungry mouths to feed," said another.

"Exactly!" said Doña Margarita. "And so, feeling tired and not knowing what to do, I went into the church to pray for guidance."

"Oh, food," said the midwife, seeing the soup in a large earthen *olla* that Luisa was cooking on a little burning fire in the middle of the group. "I'm starving! But, hell, soup is about all we eat anymore! Soup of weeds, soup of snails and quail, soup of whatever the hell we can find!"

Serving herself, Fatima sat down on the ground with the soup and some tortillas, leaning back on a crumbled wall. No, the Villaseñor house was no longer a fine, large home. It was now just a crumbled little lean-to with missing walls and a half-burned-off roof. But the smells of the cooking soup, the smells of herbs and oil that Emilia was using on her mother's feet, and the hum of the excited people made the place a real *casa,* in every sense of the holy word.

"The church was empty, so I sat down and began to pray," continued Doña Margarita as Fatima began to eat like a starving she-wolf. "Little by little, I began to see very clearly . . . that not only didn't I know anyone in Arandas anymore, but that you can't squeeze water out of stone or money for passage to Guadalajara from another poor, unfortunate person like myself. Oh, I truly saw that my situation was very grave. For I now knew that I needed help from someone who had money and power. And of course, I knew no such animal.

"Well, with this feeling of helplessness, I turned to Our Great lady *de* Guadalupe as we always do and said, 'My Great Lady, I need Your help. I need for You to please ask Your Dear Husband God to give me light in my hour of darkness.'

"But, you know," she added, glancing at her old church friends, "how Our Lady always insists on a proper visit with a few good dirty jokes before she'll listen. But I was just too tired this time, and so I guess that, well, I must've fallen asleep. For the next thing I knew, I awoke and there was this light all around me. And then I remembered that those had been my very last words, 'to give me light,' and so now, of course, here was all this light, brighter than I'd ever seen in all my life, and yet it didn't blind the eyes. No, it was gentle in its brilliance.

"Excuse me," said Doña Margarita, stopping and licking her lips, "but does anyone happen to have a little tequila or *mescal?* I'm a little thirsty from the long walk."

Everyone roared with laughter. My God, she'd seen miracles, and she'd done miracles, and she'd just walked in from hell itself and all she was was a little thirsty? *La gente* laughed *con carcajadas!*

"I have a very special bottle," said one of the old Indian women who'd been to the fire dance. Her wrinkled-up ancient eyes were full of mischief. "I'll go get it. I've been saving it for a special day, hidden in the church for nearly five years!"

"Five years!" said Doña Margarita incredulously.

"Of course, my husband would have drunk it, if I hadn't hidden it." And she got to her feet and took off. All of the people continued laughing. The old woman was an absolute genius. Their little church was the only structure that was still standing in their settlement.

Luisa continued to serve bowls of soup. When it was Doña Margarita's turn, the old woman shook her head, saying that she'd wait for her drink of tequila first. She began to roll herself one of her little homemade *cigarritos*. Oh, this good weed was truly a sacred herb for old bones. No wonder that *la yerbita* was considered by many to be one of the first cultivated plants of hunter-gatherers.

When the old woman came back with the jug of tequila, she took the bottle straight to Doña Margarita. "To our own lady of significance!" she said. "To our very own inspiration of the ages, *una india hermana de corazón,* I give this bottle of our sacred cactus, and may the spirit of the *agave* relax your flesh and empower your hollow bones with youth and vitality!"

"Thank you," said Doña Margarita, bowing respectfully. "And I accept. Now let's drink *a toda madre!*"

And so these two old, dried-up Indian women now looked so young and full of mischief as they uncorked the large earthen jug and each took a swig, just like a man—with their heads thrown back and a shout, *un grito de gusto!* Everyone applauded and the two old women drank again, face to face, and then one more time for the heavens, too! A magic glow began to warm the entire sacred place.

"Well," said Doña Margarita, feeling much better now and wiping her mouth with the back of her hand, "there I was, sitting inside the house of God, circled by all this wondrous light, and I breathed and breathed, three times, until I could feel the life-power of God coming into me. And then suddenly I was full and good and strong, and—you know, that crystal-clear clarity of mind that we all get just before we leap into the fire, knowing that we won't be burned—it came flying into me, and I was suddenly as calm and confident as a big fat cow lying down and chewing her cud."

She laughed. "Oh, what the hell! Pass the jug again! I think I'm going to get *borracha a toda madre!*" she said, winking her left eye.

Everyone loved it, telling her to do it, for she was truly deserving.

She took another long pull, using two hands, then let out a

scream of *"¡Aaaaaaiiiiii-yyyyyaaaaiiii! Carrr-ammmba! ¡Como son las mujeres!* I mean, only an hour earlier, I, a woman, had come into that church knowing *nada*—nothing except that I loved my son Jose *con todo mi corazón"*—tears sprang to her old eyes—"and now, here I was, surrounded by heavenly light and seeing it all so clearly, everything! And I knew exactly what to do! It was just that I'd been too *pendeja* scared to think of it before. Because, well, I did know someone in town who was rich and powerful, but he was the sworn enemy of my *familia,* so I hadn't dared to think of him."

"That's it!" yelled one of the old women who'd dance on the fire. "The unthinkable becomes so obvious!"

"Exactly," said Doña Margarita, continuing. "You see, years ago in a fit of anger, my dear husband had roped this business-man off his horse and beat him with his fists for a deal that they'd had over some goats. But now, here in this new light, in this new way of seeing everything in brilliance, I didn't see this well-to-do businessman as the enemy of my family anymore. No, now I just saw him very clearly for what he really was: a man, just a man, another fellow human being with his own needs and sorrows and *pinche* destiny to live!" She grinned. Oh, she was truly drunk on thought, drunk on tequila, drunk on the juices of life, *la vida!* "For I now saw so clearly," she said, "that there are no enemies upon the earth or, for that matter, any-where else in all the universe! If—and this is a big 'if'—we stay rooted in our love of God, forgiving them their trespasses as we wished ours to be forgiven, too!"

Hearing this, several people made the sign of the cross over themselves. This was a Holy moment, indeed. For here was this great old lady, holding in ecstasy, drunk out of her ever-loving-wild-mind, rooted in the heart-twisting realities of life, *la vida.*

Luisa handed her a bowl of soup. "Mama, your eyes look a little wild. I think you better eat."

"Wild, eh? Hell, you haven't seen wild yet, *mi hijita!* No woman sees wild until the age of fifty! For I was never able to

really, really see the Gateway to Heaven—until I was grey between the legs—and these steps, I tell you, they are wild, indeed!''

And saying this, she let go of a big *pedo*-fart. "For not one
step was ever gained by the safe or frightened," she said, letting
go of another tremendous *pedo*-fart. "But by the bold! Who go
forth with the big *pedos* and the wet-hungry *nalgas* of life, *la
vida!*''

La gente were rolling on the floor with *carcajadas*. They just
couldn't believe what they were hearing. But the old midwife
and other fire dancers who well-knew Doña Margarita—especially when she got like this—weren't surprised. For they knew
that this was the very reason why the Virgin Mary and Doña
Margarita were able to pass it by the hours, trading dirty,
raunchy jokes. For who else but a juicy full woman would have
God chosen for his wife and mother?! Eh, God wasn't shy. He
liked *viejas con nalgas a toda madre!*

Seeing all this female raucousness, one old crippled man
couldn't stand it anymore and he screamed out, "Now these old
women tell us this, eh, now that I'm too old to take advantage of
the lustful situation! May the timid Devil—who led me all my
life—go straight to hell! *Nalgitas de mi corazón,* to you I now
pray alone! Thighs of the heavens, take me home!''

The laughter, the *carcajadas,* that erupted from all those present, now filled the burned-out, roofless ruins of the once-grand
home with such *gusto,* such joy, that now even the heavens
above began to sing.

Seeing that her soup was still too hot, Doña Margarita blew
on it, then continued, "Well, anyway, after that, I rose up with
the power of a legion of angels and went out of the church with
such conviction of soul that no earthly force could've stopped
me! For this is exactly what happens to each and every one of us
when we finally see the light and understand that love, and love
alone, is the greatest power of all the universe! And especially so

with our enemies. For all our enemies ever really wanted was our love and, yes, respect!''

She made the sign of the cross over her bowl of soup, blessing it, and began to eat. The other people did, too. They were all hungry. And high above, the stars smiled down upon them.

Finishing her soup, Doña Margarita wiped her mouth with the back of her hand, took a big, deep breath, burped, then glanced up at the heavens, giving a little wink, and went on. ''And so I then got up to go and see this enemy of *mi familia,* while I still had it all straight in my head, but you know how God sometimes gets with *nuestra gente,* once He starts talking. He just wouldn't shut up! So I finally had to turn to God's light and say, 'Enough! I don't have time for any more enlightenment right now, God! Remember, I'm still a soul in an earthly body, and now, I need to go to do my motherly duty, and so I don't want to hear anything more. And, lo and behold, I'd no more than said this, and the light left the church, just like that—boom —and there was no more bright, heavenly light. I turned and thanked the Virgin for Her help, telling her that she could accompany me if she wished, or I could go alone, for I was full of grace, and like this, I went out of the church and across town to see my husband's enemy—the very same man who'd tricked my husband out of our goats years before.

''I went into this man's place of business and waited my turn in line to see him, and when I introduced myself, telling him who I was, he, of course, got very angry. But, no, I didn't shy away, having the Mother of God at my side, who'd decided to tag along because of her boredom in the heavens. 'Look,' I told him, 'I've come for your help, so that I can get my son out of prison.' '' She laughed. ''Oh, he was shocked, I tell you!

'' 'But don't you realize that I have bad blood with your husband?' he said to me.

'' 'Yes, of course, I do,' I said.

'' 'So, then, why in God's name did you come to me?'

'' 'Because I don't know anyone else in town who has money

or power, and you do,' I said, keeping myself rooted in my own power. And he was so stunned, so astonished by my bluntness, that he just stared at me in disbelief.

" 'Look,' he said, beginning to get red faced with anger, 'let me make things perfectly clear to you. I want absolutely nothing to do with you or any of your family for as long as I live!'

" 'I couldn't agree with you more,' I said, still refusing to take insult. 'I often feel the very same way. Now, as I was saying, my son Jose is in prison, and I need your help.'

"The man sat back. He was astonished. *'Señora,'* he said, 'a revolution is going on! We all have our problems! Now, no more of this! I have work to do! Get out! Get out! I have no time for you!'

" 'But I do have time for us,' I said, 'all the time in the world,' I repeated. 'Look, I brought food and water, so I'll just settle down in this corner until you have time for me.'

"He looked at me as if I were crazy. 'Lady,' he said, raising his voice, 'either you don't understand Spanish, or something is very wrong with you! I hate your husband and all his offspring for all eternity! I would do nothing to help you and your son, even if I could!' And he turned his back to me, returning to his work. But I had God on my side, so I had no worries, and I just sat down on the floor and began to eat my *frijoles* and tortillas and sip my water, feeling very good. For at least he'd noticed me.''

The people shook their heads in astonishment. From the bottom of their souls, they just loved Doña Margarita's tenacity. Not God in heaven or man on earth could keep this powerful, tiny woman from accomplishing her motherly duty!

They again passed around the jug of tequila made from the sacred *agave* cactus. Oh, life, *la vida,* truly was a great adventure —even in the darkest of times—when you had the heavens walking at your side, filling your shadow with power.

"The poor man," she continued, having taken another drink, "he had absolutely no idea what to do with me. But I knew what to do, just as *nuestra gente* have been knowing what to do since the beginning of time, ever since the armadillo came up from the center of the world and gave birth to our ancient female city *Alas del Amor,* the Wings of Love, I just sat there with all the cunning of the armadillo . . . for hours, until I finally became invisible, until I was part of the furnishings, and people could no longer see me.

"And that's when the second miracle happened," she said, smiling. "For, once they'd forgotten about me, then my husband's enemy began to speak to his customers and employees as if I wasn't there. And he told them about what had happened between him and my husband. And, suddenly, I understood *todo,* everything! So I now made the sign of the cross over myself and stood up, fully armed with God, and in one swift, terrible attack, I gave that businessman what it was that he'd been wanting all these years. I gave him honor—yes, honor—by saying, 'Don Ernesto, I fully realize that what happened between my husband and you was terrible! And I further agree with you that my dear husband was a fool, and you are a man of honor!'

"Everyone in the place stopped what they were doing and turned to stare at me. Especially the men. For no woman, I'm sure, had ever spoken of her husband like this and lived. But, well, I've never been a woman who was impressed with men's habits—not even of the Pope himself—so I had no such scruples! I closed my eyes in concentration and continued.

" 'I've been here for nearly three fists of the sun, Don Ernesto, and I've seen you handle situation after situation like a man of great cunning and intelligence,' I said. 'And, sad to say, I know my good husband only too well and fully realize how he always prides himself in being able to settle matters of life with his fists or a gun.

" 'And I further realize that he should never have sold you those goats in the first place, but—and this is a powerful "but" —he still had no right to later rope you off your horse and beat

you with his fists like a fool! For he'd accepted your deal; and
mad he was, but at himself!

" 'For, I swear to you, like my father the great Don Pio always
told me, fists and guns are only for fools and children. The real
battles of *la vida* are always fought here inside of our own hearts
and souls, having the confidence not to panic into external violence, but, instead, to hold steady as a stone, and keep working
day after day, as you yourself have done here in your business,
Don Ernesto!'

"And then I opened my eyes, looking at this businessman
fully in the face, and I saw that I had him. I'd given him what
he'd wanted and with conviction! But now I needed more—
much more. I needed his love. So I closed my eyes again, drawing up from my deepest powers that God had given me, and
said, 'And, furthermore, I'd like to apologize for my husband's
foolish behavior, and salute you, Don Ernesto, who's done so
well! For, yes, I fully know that your father left you money, and I
know that fools talk and they say that this is how you got to
where you are today in this fine office but . . . they're wrong!
Wrong a thousand times! For, give money to a fool, and that
fool will lose it by sunset, especially with this war going on all
around us.

" 'The truth is, Don Ernesto, that it takes a greater cunning
to keep what's been given to you than to build up from nothing.
For when you have nothing, you have nothing to lose, and so
then you can afford to be brave. But . . . but to be brave when
you had much to lose, oh, this takes *tanates* of the highest order!
And so I salute you! For you have done wonders with what your
father left you. And, therefore, you are a man to respect! And I
do!' "

All the people in the little burned-out house applauded. Oh,
this old Indian woman, Doña Margarita, was their hero! Their
inspiration! Their God-given gift here upon the Mother Earth!

"And so I had him good now," continued the wise old she-
fox, "because he just sat there, as if he himself had truly seen

the light, as if he was seeing me for the very first time. For, you see, I had, in fact, brought with me the light of God. I'd brought within my being, the brilliance of that light, that I'd witnessed inside of the church. For this is what we humans really are when it's all said and done: the brilliant reflection of God's own majestic light—if only we open up *nuestros corazones!*

" '*Señora,*' he said, standing up and coming around his desk to take my hand, 'you can have whatever you want within my capacity! You are an inspiration! You are a living tribute to your father, the great Don Pio, who came into this region and drove the bands of bandits out of our mountains, so honest men could live! I bow my head in deepest respect to you, my great lady.' "

Doña Margarita was crying. "Oh, he'd become so beautiful!" she said. "He—the sworn enemy of *mi familia*—was now my greatest lover! For God had, indeed, come down upon the earth and touched us, Holy Be His Name!" And she made the sign of the cross over herself, and there wasn't a dry eye in the whole burned-out place.

" 'Thank you,' I said to him, 'thank you. But all I need from you is train fare to Guadalajara. God will provide me with the rest.'

" 'I'm sure He will,' he said to me, taking me in his arms with tears flowing from his eyes, 'for you are a woman of power, just like my own beloved mother, God rest her Indian soul!' And he gave me kisses, there on my dirty face and dirty clothes, and then he gave me the money I needed, plus some extra cash— which, of course, I gave to the first beggar I saw on the street. For we came into this world with nothing in our hands, and so only with nothing in our naked hands are we then forced to create each moment with all the power of God's glory! And he then had one of this best men drive me to the train depot over the mountains, two hours away.

"And that was the beginning," said the old woman, "the beginning of my God-given days of living miracles! For this is what life truly is: a miracle, an opportunity for each and every one of us to make our earthly existence into a land of paradise, once we've seen the light!"

And here, Doña Margarita stopped, not saying another single word. She was done, finished, spent—and oh, so happy.

"But you can't stop here!" screamed one old, crippled man. "Go on! Please, go on, *señora nuestra,* go on! You feed our starving souls!"

"Yes," said one of her old church friends. "Show us the way! For, truly, we've been cold and lost and hungry for so long, that I'd all but given up hope, until now!" The tears filled this old woman's eyes. "You have given us the breath of God, *señora!*"

"Well, all right, I'll go on," said the wrinkled-up old warrior-woman. "But first you must pass that bottle one more time." She grinned. And everyone laughed, and this time she took a small gulp. "Ah, tequila, tequila! How you make me young and strong! But, of course, if I'm not careful, then you always double-cross me and make me older than ever before!" She farted a good one, laughing *con carcajadas,* gave a big burp, then continued.

"Well, then, getting on the train, I decided to find the richest, most powerful-looking man I could. As I said earlier, you can't squeeze money out of the poor any more than you can squeeze water out of stone. So I finally found this well-dressed European-looking man in a private car reading *Don Quixote de la Mancha,* and I sat down next to him and told him that was a fine book, that I'd read it many times myself.

"Well, the poor man looked at my ragged clothes and he didn't know what to think of me, so he got up and moved away. But I stuck to him like a tick up a dog's ass, saying to him, 'Don't you realize you can't get away from me? For you were put on this train by God, *señor,* to be of service to me!' "

"You really said that?" asked a younger woman, completely astonished.

"Of course," she said. "How could I not, when it is the absolute truth? Why do you think that God, in all His wisdom, sent these people from Europe to us here in *Méjico,* if not for us, *la gente,* who come straight from the earth's center, to teach them *del corazón?* Eh, you tell me. For once you are in this state of pure light, then, simply, all of life is a living miracle. Every person you meet is, indeed, Holy and was sent to you personally by God, so you may share together for the glory of His name! There is no more free-will or resistance in this state of being; for you are one with God, and so, hence, all of your life is blessed.

"But I'll tell you," she continued, "this rich, European-looking man was still resisting, still trying to get away from me, so finally I just grabbed him and said, 'Sit down! I can't keep chasing you up and down the train! I'm too old for that! And besides, I'm no prostitute making advances at you!' "

Everyone roared with wild laughter, loving Doña Margarita's audacity. Especially her old church friends who'd danced on the fire with her.

"Oh, but you can never tell, *señora,*" said Fatima, who'd eaten and drunk her fill, "in riding hundreds of young stallions, I've found that these old ones of mine are sometimes the very thing a young man needs! For we old ones do know the moves of *la coo-coo-coo-cooo-oooo* and *con ganas!*"

Some laughed, but others didn't and grew embarrassed. Not only had this old midwife brought many a child into this world, but she was also famous for making it her sworn duty to saddle up many a young man later in life and be the first woman to bring him forth into the art of love-making—her second midwifing, the old woman always called it.

"Yes, I'm sure you're right," said Doña Margarita. She was one of the few women in the settlement who didn't make any moral judgments over the midwife's behavior. She could still recall that before Christianity had come upon their shores, for thousands and thousands of years this was, in fact, what midwives had done: given birth to their male charges twice; once from their mother's thighs and a second time from their own thighs. For this was, indeed, what all males needed: two birthings before they could become impregnated with respect for life.

"And, to continue, I then said, 'I'm a mother that's here before you because my son is in prison and doesn't deserve to be! And the story I'm about to tell you makes that book you read pale in comparison! Because what I'm about to tell you is absolutely true, and it comes straight from a mother's burning heart!'

"And at that moment, the train jerked in its tracks as if by the mighty hand of God, and the man was thrown back into his seat; and I knew that I had him now."

And so, closing her eyes, Doña Margarita continued speaking, telling everyone of how she'd given this man what he wanted, too—a spellbinding story of how her son Jose, the great, the protector of their mountains, had kept the Revolution off their mountains for years with only a handful of boys.

"And I explained to him that Jose was short and dark like myself," said the old lady, "but that such a man isn't measured of height from his feet to his head, as is done by European standards, but by the *indio* way of measuring a human being from their head to the heavens above! For a man such as Jose gives proof to all the living world that God still lives, and will always live here upon the Mother Earth as long as each new generation paints for themselves the spirit of God with their own blood and sweat and, yes, of course, love!

"Then I explained to him how my son had gotten arrested, not because he'd destroyed army after army, but because he'd put to shame the local federal marshal who'd tried to force himself on a beautiful young widow. And now he was sentenced to be executed in Guadalajara for such an act of chivalry! And so, the short of it was, that he, Jose, was the new Don Quixote de la Mancha of all the Americas, and I was his Sancho Panza, but a woman Sancho of the greatest of female cunning!

"And, oh, I tell you, I kept that rich man on the edge of his seat with Jose's great feats and daring examples of greatness until we reached Guadalajara. Getting there, the rich man took me to his home, showered me with money, and introduced me to all the important people that he knew. Then armed with his money and the names of these rich, influential people, I went to their homes and I petitioned them day and night until I got a dozen of them to go with me to the prison to get my son released to me in my custody.

"The general in charge of the prison was outraged, saying that no one, but no one, had ever been set free from his prison before. He told me that I was either the Devil himself or I was the most cunning, determined woman he'd ever had the misfortune of encountering.

" 'If my soldiers had half of your *tanates, señora,'* said the general to me, 'there'd be no Revolution!'

" 'No, you're wrong!' I told him, 'for my *tanates* are the breasts that give milk to every child in every village in all of *Méjico*—no matter how poor—and that's why you will lose! Now! And for all eternity! For we are *los niños de la tierra,* and it was never Our Sacred Mother Earth's intention to just give support to you prestigious few who live life, *la vida,* with your heads up your social asshole so far that you can't see up from down!'

"Well, that general got so mad that he threw me out, along with my son Jose, but only on the condition that I myself promised that Jose would never fight against them again. And so, well, this is why—" tears came to her eyes once more "—Jose must leave tomorrow, as soon as he can!"

And here she stopped, taking a deep breath; and at that moment, Jose himself entered, walking with the help of a staff. He looked so weak, so worn, that even in the fire's dim light, his cheeks seemed yellowish as death. He was coughing and kept a rag over his mouth. Oh, he looked awful. He truly wasn't that beautiful, dark, small fighting cock of a man who'd been taken off in chains that day.

Little Juan leaped up, rushing to his big brother, shouting, "Jose! Jose!"

And as she watched her two small dark sons hugging each other heart-to-heart, there in the flickering light of the little fire, tears of *gusto* streamed down Doña Margarita's face. Oh, she'd had so many children; she and her dear husband had given birth to so many fine, wondrous souls here upon this good earth, and yet it seemed that these two were all the maleness that was left of their once-*gran familia*.

She began to cry in anguish, in sorrow, tears running down her old, wrinkled-up face—a face so brown and worn that it looked like the very skin of Mother Earth herself.

That night Juan and his older brother slept together, and when one awoke, the other did, too. For their dreams were speaking to each other, and their souls were becoming as one.

"Jose," said Juan, waking up once and looking at the stars past the burned-out roof of their home, "tell me, did you know that Mama and her old church friends danced on fire before she went to get you?"

"No," said Jose, "but it doesn't surprise me."

Hearing this, little Juan took a deep breath and continued looking up at the heavens. "Then you know about fire dancing?"

"Of course," said Jose. "Women do it all over Mexico in secret. Some men do it, too."

"Why?"

"Why in secret or why do people do it?"

"Both."

Now it was Jose's turn to take a breath and glance up at the vastness of the heavens. But, oh, he had to be so careful not to breathe deeply. They'd truly beaten him, crushed him; they'd done everything they could possibly think of doing to him, short of killing him. "One, they do it in secret," he said, "because if

the Church or priests find out, they can legally have them perse-
cuted, even burned at the stake like witches. Two, they do it
because to pray to God, the Father, is like, well, admitting to
only one parent, and what child can go far in life without loving
their mother, too?"

"Oh, I see," said Juan. "Then God is both male and female?"

"Exactly. And it's only in the last six or seven thousand years
that the maleness of God alone has been worshiped."

"I see, I see," said Juan, and he once more drifted off, dreaming of his brother's words as he went in and out of sleep, of
dream, of wonderment.

The heavens above smiled, and the earth turned, whispering
to their earthly children in quiet-tones of endearment.

"Tell me something else," said Juan, waking up once again,
"did you really love Mariposa? I mean, really, really?"

Jose breathed lightly. "Well, yes, of course," he said. He was
well aware that the earth and the heavens were speaking
through them. "I loved her very much. But why do you ask? Do
you have your eye on someone?"

"Oh, no!" said Juan, taken completely aback. "Not at all!
The reason I ask is because, well, in all truthfulness, I really
only love our mama, and so I don't see how anyone can love
anyone else, but their own mother."

Jose nodded, giving a small smile. "How old are you?" he
asked.

"I don't really know," said Juan. "I think eight, or maybe
nine. Mama told me that when I came, I came so unexpectedly
that she forgot to write down the year. But for sure, she remem-
bers that I was born on the eighteenth of *agosto.*"

"I see," said Jose, "well, then, let's just say that you're nine,
okay? This way I can talk to you as *un hombrecito a todo dar.* All
right?"

"Why, of course!" said Juan, suddenly feeling older and
stronger. He really thought he was maybe closer to seven or

eight, and so being considered nine—the second step into man-hood—was wonderful!

They could hear all the others sleeping on the ground around them. The little fire had died down, and they could see that the whole sky was full of stars above the ruins of the thick adobe walls of their once-*gran casa*.

"See those stars up there?" said Jose. "See how they give light to each other and light up the entire sky?"

"Yes," said Juan, looking skyward.

"Well, when I was visiting our grandfather a few nights before his death, he told me that's what we all are: passing stars giving a little light to each other for our few short days here on earth." He breathed. Oh, how he'd loved his *abuelito*. "And this light that we give each other, it's love, he said."

"Then all that light we see in the sky is love?" asked Juan, looking up at the stars and moon and all the heavens in a whole new way.

"Exactly," said Jose. "You see, it's like, well, after you leave your mother's womb, all of life feels dark and lost and empty until you finally find your own special love, and then—boom—you're found!" Tears of joy came to Jose's eyes. "It's magical, I tell you; you suddenly find yourself surrounded by light, just like those stars above us."

"Really? That's what happens to you when you fall in love? It must be wonderful!"

"It is, and if you're lucky, very lucky, one day you'll also know what it feels like when a man and a woman finally find each other . . . and . . . and make love. Oh, the touch of Mariposa, the smell, the feel, it was heaven, I tell you!"

Juan was dumbfounded. He'd never heard such talk. But then, he thought of Jose-Luis and his sister Luisa and how they'd behaved so ridiculously before they'd married. And he thought of his parents and how he'd never thought that they loved each other, until that day when his father had given his Colt .45 to Jose—and Jose had ridden off with his band of young men—and his parents had put their arms about each other and they'd looked so beautiful together.

"Well, at least I'll never feel like that," said Juan. "Because the only one I want to feel such love for is our own mother!"

Jose almost laughed aloud. But he didn't and said, "Good, I'm glad you feel that way right now, because you're only nine; and until you're a grown man and you find your own true love, all of life is just training."

"But my love for Mama isn't 'just training'!" said Juan angrily. "My love for Mama is real!" He wiped the tears from his eyes.

Jose breathed gently. And, yes, he fully knew that maybe he was pushing his little brother too far and that they might awaken people, but he also knew that they didn't have much time. At daybreak he was going to have to leave. As it was, the colonel and his men might already be on their way to intercept him before he left for the United States. The colonel had been gone when they'd released him, and he'd be raging mad when he found out. Oh, he didn't know what had gotten into that *coronel,* but the poor man had gone insane when he hadn't been able to break him.

Jose now flashed on Prince Cuauhtemoc, the nephew of the Aztec Emperor Montezuma, and how the Spaniards had tortured him for weeks on end, even burning off his feet, but they still hadn't been able to subdue him. What was it with these Europeans who had come upon their shores? It just seemed like their whole life was one of frustrated conquest in their mad search for gold. Had they no understanding or faith in their own God?

"Juan," he now said, "listen carefully, because I'm going to have to tell you a few hard truths." He breathed. "Our father is gone, and Domingo left, and maybe they'll all come back healthy and strong; but, well, maybe they won't." He breathed easy again, very easy. The pain was terrible. His whole chest felt like it was going to burst every time he inhaled even lightly. If it hadn't been for the foul-tasting roots that his mother had forced him to chew on their way home, he could never have made it back to their mountains. The roots had numbed his pain and given him strength.

"Yes, I know that your love for our mother is real," he continued. "But, also, I know that as you grow older, and are forced to do things you never thought you'd do, you will come to see, Juan, that all of life—until we find our own true love—is preparation.

"Why do you think the colonel went so crazy-*loco* seeing the love that Mariposa and I had together, eh? The poor man even ended up killing that which he loved, God forgive him." The tears streamed down Jose's face. "And why do you think our parents have stayed together, even after so much heartache? Because love—real adult love—is the biggest yearning hunger of all of our years of preparation that we got from our mother's womb and our youth—all those dreams and secret thoughts, all that gnawing hunger. And so our love either ends up being our ultimate joy in life, or our crucifixion."

Jose had to stop talking, and he began to cough and gag. Quickly, he put the rag to his mouth that he'd used earlier, spitting into it. Juan could smell whatever it was that his brother had spat. And it smelled foul, just like when you first opened up the stomach of a pig and all that sweet-repulsive gas hit your face.

"Oh, believe me, *hermanito*," continued Jose between coughs, "I was scheduled to be hanged the next day, and I was so scared until . . . I realized that love is indestructible, just like our *papagrande* told me. And so, no, I wasn't going to really die when they hanged me; no, I was going to be free at last and able to go up into the heavens and be with God and Mariposa for all eternity! And that's when the fear left me, Juan, and I was powerful! They could beat me, they could kill me, they could destroy my manhood, or even burn off my feet and legs, as they'd done to our beloved hero Cuauhtemoc; but, still, I would

keep strong, I tell you, for I had all this love here inside of my
God-given soul!''

The tears streamed down Jose's face, and Juan could well-see
that his brother had meant every word that he'd just said to the
core of his entire being. "Then you mean that loving Mariposa
helped you to be powerful and brave?" asked Juan, thinking that
this was the craziest thing he'd ever heard.

"Oh, God, yes!" said Jose. "With Mariposa's love, I became
the bravest and most powerful human being I'd ever been!"

"But, then, why do I always hear the *muchachos* say that so-
and-so has gotten soft-in-the-head because he's in love? And
why do men always laugh at someone who's going to get married?"

"Because they're scared, Juan."

"But Domingo says that he doesn't even know the word
fear."

Jose took a big breath. "Domingo—I'm sorry to say—is a liar.
Why do you think he isn't here, and our father isn't here, also?"
And saying this, Jose well-knew that he'd trespassed, that he'd
stepped over the line and he should never have said this to his
little brother; but, well, there wasn't much time. "And don't
think I don't love Domingo and our father very much," continued Jose, "but God help me, most men are liars! And they lie
about that which they fear most! And that's love! Because, believe me, it takes guts to love, Juan. It takes real *tanates* to open
up your heart and soul and admit that you're in love.

"I was twelve years old, Juan, twelve, when I was banned
from our *casa* by the man I loved most!" The tears continued
pouring down Jose's face. "It was like God Himself had dis-
owned me! But, no, I didn't let myself fall into that age-old trap
of hating or abandoning *nuestro padre*. No, Juan, I held strong,
as strong as you held on to Four White Stockings that day you
hugged his hoof. And I forgave our father, again and again, and
it hurt!" he said. "But I just kept forgiving and forgiving! I
wasn't going to hate and . . . and end up like our father!

"So don't you ever think that love is weak, or believe some stupid, ignorant boy or man who ridicules love or laughs at someone when they get married. Oh, I would've loved to marry Mariposa! I proposed to her almost every day. But she thought I was too young for her." He wiped his eyes, glancing up at the sky. "Oh, my God, and I'm sure that she was coming to tell me that she'd marry me the night the colonel and his men—"

He stopped his words and closed his eyes. He just couldn't go on. He could still hear her screams inside of his head as they'd abused their eternal souls with her earthly body.

And Juan continued giving witness to the tears running down his brother's wide, dark cheeks, and he could now well-see that all this love business did make sense and was very powerful, indeed.

"I love you, Jose," said Juan. "And I promise you, that I will love, too, just like you; I don't want to hate like our father, either."

Two little white clouds passed by high overhead. Both brothers looked at each other and they smiled. Then they drew in close together in a big *abrazo,* giving comfort to each other, and little by little, they drifted back off to sleep. The two little white clouds—guardians of their souls—smiled and blessed them.

And behind the jagged, half-destroyed adobe wall was their beloved old mother and Emilia and Luisa, all wrapped in blankets, too. But Doña Margarita wasn't sleeping. No, she was wide awake and looking up at the heavens, as the tears streamed down her old, wrinkled face. Her two sons had spoken like angels, and she was so proud of them. And, yet, oh, my God, she also felt so terrible that they'd had to inherit the seeds of their parents' torment. For Jose had, indeed, spoken the truth when he'd said that a person's love was either their greatest joy in life or their crucifixion. And her father, Don Pio, had warned her. He'd told her that Juan Jesus didn't walk in the grace of God's beauty, but, instead, in the mad-imbalance of *el Diablo,* and so he'd bring war between their very own blood.

The old woman wiped her eyes, still looking up at the heavens. And, yes, she truly knew that she was totally responsible for her children's suffering; but, oh, *Dios mío* up in heaven, if she had it all over to do, she'd marry Juan Jesus again—for she'd loved him and, God help her, she still did!

With trembling hands, she took her rosary and began to finger the beads as she prayed, speaking to God and letting go of all her earthly fears. She well-knew that her son had spoken the truth when he'd said that love, and love alone, was what every human being was, indeed, searching for here on earth. And to think that fine horses or big ranches or piles of gold would take this growing hunger away, was to completely not understand the true blessings of God.

For ever since the beginning when God made the heavens and the earth, making everything in twos—including the original Twin Sister *Planetas*—there'd been a great spiritual design to the whole plan, and that had been that all the halves of being —all the male and female parts of existence—would finally, at long last, come together in peace and harmony, reuniting with God in a glorious celebration! And on this day, called Judgment Day, no humans would pass judgment on one another, for their souls would be at one with the Almighty!

But, oh, it had taken such a heavy hand for her to finally find this out for herself, just as it had taken such a heavy hand for Jose, and now it would probably take just as heavy a hand for Juan. Poor boys; her decision to marry Don Juan had truly cost her sons dearly. Seven sons she'd had who had grown to adulthood—seven sons and seven daughters—and all that was left of her fourteen glorious children were these two boys and Luisa and Emilia.

"God forgive me," she said to herself, tears streaming down her dark, worn Indian face. "God forgive us all for the seeds we pass on to our children in the name of love!"

6

Dancing, dancing, the Holy Spirit of the Mother Earth and of the Father Sky now made love with such white-hot fever, that fever would reign until the age of gold came raining forth, with God's abundance of diamond-studded unconditional love!

Juan must have gone into a deep, deep sleep, for the next thing he knew was that he awoke with a start. And there was his brother Jose, up on his elbows, coughing uncontrollably—gagging, spitting, his whole body jerking in convulsions. And the gobs that Jose spat up smelled so foul that they turned Juan's stomach.

"What is it, Jose?" asked Juan. "It smells awful!"

"It's nothing," said Jose, holding a rag to his mouth.

"Are you dying?" asked Juan.

And from behind the wall, their mother heard the question, too. She gripped her breast.

Jose swallowed. "Yes," he said, "but no one must know; no one. Do you understand? I don't want Mama or our sisters worrying."

Juan almost cried out. He had to cover his mouth. "Yes," he said, nodding. "I understand."

"Good," said Jose. "Now come on, help me up; it's almost daybreak and there are still a few things I need to tell you." His eyes rolled over in horrible pain. "Damn, it looks like you—the baby of our family—is maybe all we got left, Juan . . . so, well, you're going to have to be *el hombre de nuestra casa.*"

Tears burst from Doña Margarita's old eyes, and she covered her mouth in anguish. Oh, God, no! She really didn't want her youngest to now feel like he was responsible for their home, too. Why, this was exactly what had driven their father Don Juan into working himself into a panic over and over again, and was also now driving Jose! Men could be such damned fools, wanting to be heroes, and yet entrusting so little to God and thinking that they needed to do everything themselves!

But no, she wasn't going to make a sound. She wiped her eyes. She was going to honor her son Jose's decision and keep still. But, oh, she was pissed. How dare God just use her and her children to do His grand designs, putting them through such heart-wrenching misery! She was going to talk to the Virgin Mary, Mother of God, today and give Her a good piece of her mind! Enough was enough, damnit!

Getting to his feet, Jose could hardly walk. Juan had to give his brother his shoulder as they went out of the ruins of the house and across the cobblestones. Juan could feel his brother's body contract with terrible pain every time he breathed.

And in the darkness of the pre-dawn, the colonel and his men were coming up a little wooded draw, leading their horses quietly. There were only a dozen men with the colonel this time, and they had some huge dogs with them. They were coming in a small, well-organized force of specially selected men, hoping to sneak up on these people who had been giving the colonel such a difficult time, destroying them once and for all.

The large beautiful dogs had brass-studded leather muzzles over their snouts. They were pure-bred hounds that had been given to the colonel by one of the visiting military advisors from Germany. These German military advisors had come into Mexico with the high hopes of building Mexico's revolutionary armies into a fighting force that could eventually attack the United States, and that way the U.S. wouldn't be able to come into the war that was brewing in Europe.

Coming to a flat little meadow, the colonel had his men stop to water their horses. Holding his stomach, he walked off to a private distance and found a good log to take a morning crap. The break of day was just beginning to come up on the distant horizon. Hearing his men and their horses moving about gave the colonel a great sense of peace as he undid his gunbelt and pulled down his pants.

But, unbeknownst to the colonel, two little dark eyes were watching him. The little boy, Pelon—Juan's boyhood friend— had buried himself under the oak leaves when he'd heard the colonel and his men coming, and he was now watching the colonel from a distance of no more than five meters. And as Pelon watched the colonel pull down his pants and put his big white ass over the fallen log, he noticed that part of his own right leg was exposed. Pelon was filled with horror. What if the colonel turned and saw him? And then, to make matters worse, now came one of the colonel's men walking right past Pelon, up to the colonel.

"Mi coronel," said the soldier in the dim early morning light, "I think you should know that one of our Indian guides has discovered some—"

"Can't it wait?" shouted the colonel. It was obvious that he didn't feel well and was in a foul mood. "Damnit, a man needs to take his crap in private! Get the hell away from here! Get! Get! Learn how to handle some things by yourself, god-damnit!"

The man saluted, did an about-face, and briskly walked

away. Pelon breathed easy once again. And here came the colonel's farts and *caca,* and they were huge and numerous, indeed —and so terrible-smelling that Pelon almost gagged.

Jose and little Juan were by the corrals now. Jose had had to stop to catch his breath. Juan turned his face away as his brother breathed. Jose really did smell of death.

"So, Juan, you're going to have to be smart and strong," Jose was saying between bouts of pain, "and quickly learn how to be *un macho de los buenos,* just like our *abuelito* Don Pio, and not do anything stupid to endanger yourself or what's left of *nuestra familia.* Do you understand, eh? I'm depending on you." Tears ran down Juan's little face, but still Jose went on. "Why do you think that a beautiful young Indian girl like Herlinda fell madly in love with our grandfather, sixty years her senior, and wanted his seed deep inside of herself, instead of the seeds of all those young men who were after her? Because, I tell you, a good, smart woman wants a warrior of the highest order; a man who has the guts to love, Juan, *con todo su corazón,* and, hence, he can bring warmth and safety to her nest. And this is what you now got to become: a warrior of the highest and bring safety and warmth to *nuestra familia.*

"Most men, you see, aren't really that sure of their manhood, Juan," Jose continued as the light of the new day began to come up behind them, "and so that's why they seek danger and can be so destructive. But when a man like Don Pio comes along, his genius is that he's so sure of his manly love that he's able to bring honor and responsibility out of his men, even in the middle of battle, and they then become the holy instruments of life, supporting *la familia,* and not the wild beasts of hate and death, like has happened to this colonel and his gang of murderers!"

A breeze came up. The last stars of the night were winking goodnight to them. The stars above and the earth below well-knew that Jose had earned his wisdom, as true and real as any woman's birthing.

"Men are fire, Juan, and so with guidance they can be as great and brilliant as Jesus Christ Himself, who, remember, had one hell of a strong mama! But men also like *el barr-ullo,* the trouble, the *chinga-chinga,* and so if they are not given rein by a strong, steady hand early in their life, then they don't know how to lend their warmth and light for the good of *la familia,* and they become arrogant and imposing, caring more about their damned *caprichos* and dreams than their loved ones. This is exactly what happened with Camacho, a good man, who got so wrapped up in his wood-making dreams of fortune that he began to blame Mariposa for everything, instead of simply loving her." Tears now ran down Jose's face, too. "Promise me that you'll always love, Juan, that you'll always be a lover first, no matter what!"

"Te juro," said Juan, wiping his eyes, smearing his face with dirt and tears, "with all my *corazón.* "

They hugged each other in a big *abrazo*—heart to heart, soul to soul.

Wiping himself, the colonel tossed the piece of white cloth away, and the piece of rag went flying in the air, almost landing on Pelon's half-exposed right leg. Pelon lay there watching in terror as the big man now pulled up his pants and strapped on his gunbelt. His men had already mounted up and were ready to go. One soldier brought the colonel's horse over to him. Pelon prayed to God that they didn't trample him. The colonel had a hard time getting onto his horse. And in the coming light of the new day, Pelon could see that the colonel didn't look well at all. No, he'd aged terribly and looked all bloated like a sick old bull.

"**W**hy do you think that it was you who summoned the Devil that night of the full moon and that you're now the last male left," said Jose to his little brother. "And why do you think that I was the one who suffered our father's wrath and got thrown out of our home, and then it was I who brought peace between us. Because, Juan, there are no accidents in life. In our native tongue the word *accident* does not even exist. This is how our mother's people see life. That no matter how life turns you and twists you, the stars above are always with you, and so a person never abandons love or gets bitter or hateful. And so that's why we must forgive our father and these colonels, because they just don't know. Do you understand?"

"Well, yes, I kind of do," said Juan, his little heart going crazy. "But don't you sometimes just want to get even, Jose? Eh, I'd like to forgive the colonel and his men, but only after they're all dead and burning in hell!"

Jose grinned and started laughing, but it hurt him so much that he doubled over in pain. "Yes, of course, I feel like that often, Juan," he said, gripping his groin. "I would've loved to rush out and do battle head-to-head with the colonel in vengeance after he killed Mariposa, but our grandfather talked me out of it, explaining to me that this was exactly what the colonel wanted me to do, so he could destroy me.

"No, Juan," he said, "you and me, we need to be smarter—much smarter, like the jaguar—and measure our battles of life, *la vida*, very carefully. That's why I was able to come up with the idea of attacking the colonel's outpost and arming our people. Only when we're free of hate and vengeance are we able to really think. Do we kill the coyote because we hate him? No, we don't, *hermanito*. We know that he was put here on earth by God, just as we were put on earth, too. So, yes, we might destroy a coyote or the colonel, but we must do it with respect and understanding—never hatred.

"Do you understand," continued Jose, "our father could have learned a great deal from the wolves on that cold winter, if he had respected the wolves and understood that they also were the children of God, instead of killing the wolves with such hate and blind-vengeance."

Juan nodded. "All right, I see what you mean, but, oh, sometimes it's just so much easier to hate and want revenge!" he said.

"Of course," said Jose. "Hate is easy. Love is the hard one, especially during difficult times."

Tears came to Juan's eyes and he reached out, putting his right hand on his brother's right. "Oh, I do love you and respect you, Jose; so, yes, I promise that I'll try not to hate, and I'll love and take good care of *nuestra familia.*"

Eye-to-eye, Jose looked at his little brother, then slowly took him in his arms. "I believe you, Juan, I believe in you completely. Oh, you were no accident! Believe-you-me, you were no accident!" he added with power.

"Did anyone ever think I was?"

Jose just smiled. "No, of course not," said Jose, lying. "When you were born, we were all there watching, and you came out looking so dark and beautiful and all wrinkled! We all loved you instantly!"

Jose held his little brother in his arms, and Juan well-knew that his brother had lied, but . . . he said nothing, *nada, nada,* as they continued hugging in an *abrazo.*

Pelon could hear that the colonel and his men were leaving. He could hear the horses' hooves swishing through the grass and the saddle leather moaning. He was sure that they were out of the meadow now and going into the trees, so he glanced around, but only with his eyes. He was very careful not to move his head. And listening oh-so intently as the horsemen rode farther and farther away, Pelon now began to slowly rise up, little by little, out of the oak leaves. But then, there—not more than a few meters from him—he saw an Indian sitting perfectly still on his little brown horse.

Pelon froze, heart in his throat with terror, looking at the Indian eye-to-eye, not moving, not breathing. Then the Indian grinned, nodded, and turned his horse, riding off to join the others.

Pelon fell back in the leaves, realizing that he'd been caught by a very patient hand. He saw the coming of the early morning light, and he hoped to God that the Indian didn't turn him in to the colonel.

Getting up, he knelt down in the leaves and began to pray. And here came the new day, beams of golden light through the trees, and it was wondrous.

Jose was still hugging his little brother Juan, when they heard the call of a strange-sounding bird. Instantly, both brothers froze, listening closely. The strange-sounding bird called once again.

Jose relaxed. "Answer them," he said. "I can't do it."

Filling his chest with air, Juan called back, imitating the birdcall that they'd just heard. The strange-sounding bird answered back and then there came two of Jose's men out of the trees, leading Two White Stockings. The two riders were Jorge and Manuel, Pelon's two older brothers. They dismounted and gave Jose and Juan greeting, but then quickly added that the colonel had been spotted.

"And this time, *el coronel* comes with just a dozen men, but they have dogs with them," said Jorge. "Big ones, really huge, like we've never seen before. But don't worry, we've got a surprise already set up for them with some hornet nests, like we used to do for the wolves when we were kids."

The two brothers burst out laughing. Over the last few years, they'd been using all the tricks that they learned as kids on the colonel.

"Come on," said Jorge to Jose, "they'll be easy shooting when they're fighting off the hornets."

Jose shook his head. "I can't join you," he said.

"What do you mean you can't join us?" asked Jorge.

"My mother gave her word that I'd never fight them again; and, besides, I don't know if I can even ride anymore."

"But, Jose, we've been waiting for you," said Manuel.

Jose pursed his lips together and turned to Juan. "You better go back now, Juan. And tell Mama and everyone *a'Dios* for me. Go now, go."

"But—"

"No 'buts,' Juan. We've talked, and you have a destiny to live far beyond our wildest dreams. You don't need me anymore, Juan, like these men don't need me anymore, either. In fact, remember, it's us who now need you, Juan, to live on for all of us, blood for blood, heart for heart."

"But, oh, Jose!" said Juan, his eyes suddenly filling with tears. "I don't want you to leave us!"

"Juan, I am not leaving you," said Jose quietly but firmly. "Look, you go to the place where Mama and her friends had the fire dance and sit there quietly; and I promise you that the earth will speak to you and you'll see the true miracle of all living life, and that is that no one ever leaves you, *hermanito;* we're all right here with you forever, if you just have the ears to hear and the eyes to see.

"Now, no more. Go, Juan, please, turn and go. I need to leave with Jorge and his brother right now!"

And having said this, Jose now turned back around to his two childhood friends and said, "Help me on my horse, but very carefully, please." And Jose approached Two White Stockings, letting the stallion smell him, and he smelled the great horse, too, kissing him and giving him words of endearment.

"But what is this?" said Manuel, the younger of the two brothers, grinning as he now watched Jose move his horse over to a large rock. "Why do you need a rock to mount up? You move *como que te caparón*—as if they castrated you!"

"Shut your damned mouth!" yelled Juan.

"It's all right," said Jose. "They don't know, Juan."

Hearing this, both brothers went pale.

"Oh, my God!" said Manuel. "We didn't know, Jose! Those bastards! Those son-of-a-bitches!"

"We'll get them for you, Jose!" said Jorge, making the sign of the cross over himself. "We'll get that colonel, if it's the last dying thing we do!"

"No," said Jose calmly. "Don't talk like that. For you must live; not die. You and your brother must be careful and take good care of yourselves, Jorge. There's been too much death for *nuestra gente de la tierra* already."

"But we can't let them get away with this!"

"Come on, just help me up on my horse and let's see if I can ride," said Jose.

Jose then crawled up on the boulder as best as he could, looking like an old crippled spider. But from on top of the rock, he still couldn't lift his foot to the stirrup—he was in so much pain in trying to spread his legs.

Instantly, both brothers stepped forward to help him. It took every fiber of Jose's entire being just to put his foot in the stirrup and get his other leg over the saddle without passing out or screaming with pain. Tears and sweat were running down Jose's face as he settled himself on the horse. Manuel was holding the stallion's reins, making sure that the animal didn't move until Jose was ready. Manuel had tears in his eyes, too. Oh, the idea of castration was a thousand times worse than death.

"Well, at least this isn't a *gringo* saddle," said Jose, trying to make light of it. "And there's an open crack behind the saddle horn, giving me a little room so—ooooh, sweet Jesus, help me!" His whole body was vibrating with terrible pain. "All right, let's go!" he said.

And Juan watched the other two leap upon their horses and

then they were off, going through the trees. Tears were streaming down Juan's face. Over the years, he'd helped cut many young pigs and bull calves, so he could well imagine the pain that his brother was feeling with every step that his horse took. But there went Jose, so brave, so powerful, holding on as best he could. Juan wiped his eyes, making the sign of the cross over himself.

"Oh, Lord God," said Juan, "please help my brother. Please, I beg of You, help my dear brother, God! He's the best! And he loves You so!"

And with tears streaming down his little face, Juan now knelt down to pray, to ask God for guidance. For he could feel his little heart filling with the want of vengeance, the very thing that his brother had warned him against, and he didn't want to get hateful and disappoint his brother. But then Juan suddenly remembered that he'd forgotten to warn Jose that it might be their very own cousin-brother Agustin who'd betrayed him and that Agustin was also headed for the United States.

"Jose!" shouted Juan, leaping to his feet and racing through the trees. "Jose! Jose! It was maybe our own cousin-brother Agustin who betrayed you! Jose! Jose! I love you, please come back! Please, Jose! We all love you so much!"

But as he ran through the woods, echoing with sound, Juan couldn't find hide nor hair of them. Then, coming to an outcropping of rocks, Juan saw that his brother was already well out of the forest and way down below, moving quickly across an open meadow. And Jorge and Manuel were racing head-long to the right, toward the breaks and gullies where they no doubt knew that the colonel was headed.

"Jose!" yelled Juan. "Jose!" He cupped both of his hands to his mouth and called to his brother with all his might, his little voice echoing out over the land. "Jose! Jose! I love you! Come back, Jo-oooo-sssseee!"

Hearing his little brother's echoing call, Jose reined in his horse, turning about, and he saw the tiny speck of his brother up on the high *barrancas* behind him. But he was in too much pain to call back or to even wave, so he simply just sent his love to his little brother, heart-to-heart with tears streaming down his face, then turned his horse, going off quickly. Oh, my God, he didn't want to go, either. He was only twenty and had never been away from his home.

Seeing his brother disappearing into the breaks beyond the meadow, Juan dropped to the ground and began to cry, feeling terrible, because he'd failed to warn his brother whom he loved so much. And he was just going to cry, wallowing in self-pity, when he suddenly remembered the colonel. He leaped up, racing for home. Oh, my God, he had to warn his mother and sisters and everyone else about *el coronel* as quickly as he could. He had no time for feeling terrible right now. Right now he had to get back up the mountain and get everyone out of the settlement and back to their hiding places so that there wouldn't be another slaughter.

"*El coronel* is coming!" shouted Juan, as he ran back up the mountainside toward home. "*El coronel* is coming!" Oh, he'd failed to warn Jose of their cousin-brother, but he wasn't going to fail again. And so he ran up through the trees toward home, shouting with all his might!

Doña Margarita was sitting in her outhouse, looking to the east as the sun, the right eye of God, *el ojo derecho de Dios*, began to come up over the distant horizon, when she first heard her youngest son Juan shouting, "*El coronel* is coming! *El coronel* is coming! We got to get into hiding!"

And a few weeks back, hearing this man's name would have brought terror into Doña Margarita's old heart. But now, having come back from the state capital and knowing fully well how they'd abused themselves with her beloved son Jose, she had no such fear. For what more could they possibly do to her and her loved ones? Eh, nothing, *nada, nada.*

So the wrinkled-up old woman now sat here on the smooth wooden planks of her outhouse, and she had no fears. And so, having no fear, she could truly see that she should have always known it would all come to this when she'd married Juan Jesus. For no one, but no one, could interfere with another's destiny. Why, the great mother serpent herself—who'd guided her since she'd been a child—had even given her own life to Don Juan, trying to show him the milky-way from the stars to the earth. The great female serpent had come down from her home in the heavens in all her star-studded glory, impregnating the Mother Earth with deep shafts of diamonds. Then she'd surfaced, showing herself to Juan Jesus, but he'd mistaken her love-dance —of midwifing the earth—for a challenge of war, and so he'd attacked, and she'd allowed herself to be killed, instead of taking his life.

Looking at the coming of the new day, the old woman sat there smoking and crapping, truly wondering if she'd maybe done wrong to have married her husband. For the story of her husband was really the story of all of Mexico, ever since the Spaniards had first come upon their shores, and the second son, unable to inherit his father's wealth back in Spain, would come to this new land to make his fortune with a vengeance, hoping to someday show up his father and the first son. But, still, she'd never dreamed that day would come when Juan Jesus would befriend a man like the colonel and that he'd only introduce to the colonel his light-colored sons. And so, of course, the colonel had then gone crazy-mad at Luisa's wedding when he'd found out that the dark Indian boy, whom Mariposa was with, was also his good friend's son.

Not having been able to raise up his arm to wave goodbye to his little brother, Jose now rode his horse out of the open meadow and into one of the little breaks leading down into the great central valley of Guanajuato. Jose was holding onto the large wooden horn of his Mexican saddle and trying hard not to pass out. But, oh, it was difficult.

They'd cut him, they'd cut him like a rancher cuts a pig, laughing *con carcajadas* as they'd showed him his manhood. But no, he hadn't turned away. He'd held there, hanging off the stone wall, hands and feet in chains, and he'd watched them watching him as they'd thrown his *tanates* to the dogs; and he'd seen the fear in their eyes, no matter how much they pretended to be fearless.

And he'd been able to do this, not because he was inhumanly brave, but because he'd been in that place of peace where the rabbit goes to just as the coyote grabs him up in his mouth and the rabbit knows that he's breathed his last. And so he relaxes, letting go of all earthly fears, realizing deep within his ancient soul that this isn't bad or terrible, but the inevitable of all living life, so that he, the rabbit, can die, giving nourishment to his brother the coyote, and then the coyote can die, too, and become part of the earth, returning as new green grass for the rabbit's young to enjoy. The Mother Earth gave birth and the Father Sky gave death, and both were miracles of the never-ending cycle of life as we all reached for the Holy Spirit of ourselves in our voyage back to God.

And so Jose now once more relaxed like the rabbit, as he'd done when they'd cut him, and he rode north on Two White Stockings—son of Four White Stockings—and each step his horse took sent pains shooting up from his crotch, throughout his whole body. But, no, he wouldn't give in to his pain, nor into hatred or fear. For he had to keep going. He had to live and not go crazy-*loco*. He had to survive and not get bitter or hateful. He had to keep strong *con su fe en Dios*, so he could send for his *familia* once he'd gotten situated across the border and had a place for them. He had no time for false male pride or stupid, ignorant rage. After all, he wasn't just his father's son. In his veins also ran his mother's blood—the blood of the very heart-center of the earth that was destined to root these long-lost souls who'd come from their destroyed Twin Sister *Planeta* and had forgotten how to trust their *corazones,* and that's why they were always getting so bitter and angry when life didn't go as they envisioned. Poor fools, they'd been lost for so long that they just didn't know anymore.

Hearing her little son Juan still shouting that the colonel was coming, Doña Margarita took a corncob husk from the shelf and began to work it with her hands, softening it so she could wipe herself. The dawn was coming, a whole new day would soon be upon them, and she knew that everything looked disastrous at the moment, but, still, down deep inside herself, she just knew that everything was going to turn out for the sacred good, if only she could keep hold of her faith.

Oh, since the night of the fire dance, she'd returned to the site three times and she'd talked to the stars, praying for guidance. For to pray, to truly pray with all your heart and soul, moved the heavens and earth alike, getting down into the very guts of all existence, cleansing the old and making room for new life. And so on the third night, praying with her old church friends, the heavens had sung to them and the earth had trembled and water had begun bubbling up out of the very ground beneath them. The universe had blessed them, and the site of their fire dance had become a Holy place, a Holy entrance for them to travel back down into the heart-center of the Mother Earth—a gateway to the lower world, the place that Jesus had visited for three days before His ascension into the great beyond, the place where we all had to go to impregnate ourselves with life before we could travel to the stars.

The old woman wiped herself, tossing the corn husk down the hole of the outhouse, then stepped out into the coming light of the new day. She kissed the crucifix of her rosary, sending all of her love to her son Jose as he rode north to make a new life of himself, and now she was ready. She was rooted. Her shadow was complete. For she'd prayed to God, smoked for herself, crapped for the Devil, and now she was fully prepared to deal with this poor lost little colonel once and for all!

Jorge and Manuel had just come riding up through the trees and thick chaparral when they spotted their two friends. Each young man had a hornet's nest in hand and was being oh-so careful in handling it as they crawled out on some rocks, preparing to whirl the nests down on the unsuspecting colonel and his men. Quickly, Jorge and his brother dismounted, got their rifles, and went quietly through the trees and thick underbrush up on the outcropping of rocks where their *compadres* in arms were crouched behind the brush, looking down at the approaching colonel and his men. The two hornets' nests were huge ones. The evening before, Jorge and Manuel had helped these two young friends of theirs smoke and wrap these yellow jackets' paper-like nests. Smoking a hornet's nest was an art, and it was done best—they'd painfully found out over the years —by burning semiwet cow pies that got especially hot and smoky.

The colonel and his small group of men and six purebred dogs were coming up the little wooded draw. The colonel and one other man were the only ones on their horses. Jorge and the other boy well-knew that this was going to be an especially wonderful ambush. When they got one of the nests to burst directly underneath the colonel's horse's belly, his big horse was going to go crazy-*loco!*

Jorge and his brother and the other two young men could hardly keep from laughing—they were so excited with anticipation. Why, it seemed like every little trick that they'd learned as kids, in playing war-games among themselves, was now being used to torment these *Rurales.*

The two teenage boys were getting ready to leap up and fling the nests down. They didn't want the colonel and his men getting any closer, but Jorge—the oldest, at twenty—held up his hand, shaking his head no, and took one nest, wanting to get in closer.

"These bastard-cowards cut Jose!" whispered Jorge under his breath. The two boys were mortified. "I don't want the colonel getting away this time! I want to make sure we kill *el cabrón!*"

"*¡Órale!*" whispered one of the two boys. They were also brothers, but they were new. They hadn't been with Jose from the beginning; still, they well-knew of Jose's incredible reputation as a man among men.

The youngest boy—fifteen years old—made the sign of the cross over himself, and all four boys now crawled down between the rocks and chaparral, hearts pounding against the earth, as they got in closer and closer. When the colonel and his men got up to the head of the little draw, they'd be able to whirl the hornets' nests at them with ease, then cut them to pieces with their weapons as the men and dogs and horses all dodged about in pain from the terrible sting of these huge yellow-jackets. And, best of all, these yellow jackets could sting again and again, not dying after their first sting like their cousins, the honey-producing bees. Oh, this was going to be wonderful! An absolute ambush of pure genius, just as Jose, the great, had always taught them to do.

Then all four boys were ready. The colonel was now so close that they could actually see the breath blowing out of the round, dark nostrils of his horse's nose. On Jorge's signal, all four boys leaped up, screaming and throwing the nests of the yellow jackets. But, incredibly, the little black-and-yellow stinging beasts didn't come exploding out of their nests by the thousands, as the boys had seen happen so many times before. No, this time just a few yellow jackets came dribbling out in a confused flight of *nada, nada,* nothing, and the four boys were left standing there, shooting as best they could while the colonel and his dozen men returned their fire.

And among the colonel's men we could now see, in the early

morning light, that the other man who was mounted on his horse was very blond. And this man had a pistol in his hand, but he wasn't shooting. No, he was simply watching as he kept near the huge dogs, talking to them in a calm tone of voice. The man's name was Captain Hans Kayser, and he was the German military advisor who had volunteered to accompany the colonel and his men this morning.

The four young boys were cut to ribbons, sinking to their knees with surprised terror etched across their faces. The colonel began laughing *con carcajadas*. None of the boys' bullets had even touched him or his horse. And he'd seen two of them taking deliberate aim on him, but they'd miraculously missed him somehow.

"¡Qué desmadre a todo dar!" yelled the colonel with joy, still laughing as he rode his horse over to his drinking friend Captain Hans Kayser. "Did you see, we got them all! And their little trick of the hornets didn't work this time for these backward savages! Come, let's have a drink, Captain, while my man-servant prepares us a little breakfast! Ah, the hunger a man gets after a good battle!"

But the German didn't seem very impressed. By having read the colonel's reports very carefully, and also knowing how soldiers always lied—exaggerating either the power of their enemies or the size of their victories—he well-knew that this was probably the first ambush in which the colonel and his men had won against these mountain youths who had gained such fame for themselves.

The colonel brought out his flask and began to drink as his manservant built a little fire for the cooking. Dismounting, the German took the dogs—whose huge square heads almost came to his chest—over to smell their fallen prey. The German found that one of the young men was still alive, so he pulled the dogs back and took aim with his pistol at the boy's head to finish him off.

"Oh, no! Don't!" shouted the colonel, seeing what the captain was about to do. "Don't shoot him!"

"But he's too far gone. You're not going to be able to save him," said the captain.

"Who said anything about saving him?" said the colonel, grinning as he walked over. "Here, now it's my turn to teach you a little something, Captain, and you'll then appreciate the true genius of the Spaniards when it comes to dealing with native people."

And the well-fed colonel handed his flask to his German friend, who took a small drink, then the colonel took another good, long pull himself.

"Give some water to this one," said the colonel to his sergeant, indicating the boy who was still breathing, "and bring him to, so he can watch us castrate him and his friends and—" he laughed "—feed our magnificent dogs breakfast!"

Hearing this, the German looked at the colonel with disgust.

"Come, now, *amigo,*" said the colonel, seeing the captain's look, "what have our people in Europe been doing to each other for centuries . . . hanging and quartering? Then in England, they even perfected the art of disemboweling their prisoners and keeping them alive, so they could boil their intestines in front of them and the prisoners could then watch them feed their innards to their dogs.

"Oh, no, this isn't Mexican, Captain, this is strictly European! The only element we've added is that we also poke out their eyes, so that they can't find their way on the other side. Remember, after all, we're dealing with a very primitive people who, like women and children, still believe in an afterlife."

Calmly, the colonel now brought out his knife, approaching Jorge, whom the soldiers had revived. The two Indian guides moved away, going over to where the colonel's manservant was starting to cook a little meat over the open fire.

"*Mira, mira,*" said the colonel, seeing his two guides' reaction. "And who had their temples full of human skulls when we

Europeans first came upon your shores?" He laughed, winking at Captain Hans Kayser. "But, yes, we all know it was *los azte-cas,* and you two, of course, aren't *azteca.* Because the *aztecas* were civilized people who knew how to face reality," he said, laughing again, "instead of running away and hiding behind all this spiritual *caca* you *indios* got!"

When the colonel's men spread Jorge's legs apart and Jorge saw what they were going to do to him, he screamed out in terror, fully realizing in a split second of total clarity that he was totally to blame for this entire disaster. If only he hadn't gotten cocky and tried to get in closer. From up above, they could've shot at the colonel and his men, even without the hornet's nests working, and still have gotten away. Jose had warned them time and again to never get too greedy in combat.

Jorge continued screaming as they ripped open his pants, and the colonel personally took the boy's manhood in hand. And even though he hadn't wanted to, the German now watched with complete fascination, eyes huge, as the colonel pulled the boy's testicles away from his curly-haired groin and began to cut. But one of the Indian guides couldn't stand it, and he drew his knife and came racing forward, jerking Jorge's head back by the hair, slitting his throat.

The colonel, who'd been grinning ear-to-ear, wanting so much to impress his German friend with his ruthlessness, now drew his handgun, shooting the Indian in his stomach. "There! Now die a slow, painful death, you son-of-a-witch's big tit!"

The other Indian guide—the one who had seen Pelon hiding beneath the leaves—took off running on foot.

"Shoot him, too!" yelled the colonel. "I don't want him warning the village!"

Racing through the trees and brush, the soldiers chased the other Indian, but he'd already reached the rocks and chaparral and was gone.

Reholstering his handgun, the colonel said to his German friend, "I know what you're thinking. If the damn fool had just let me shoot the boy in the first place, we wouldn't have any of these problems now.

"But you're wrong!" shouted the colonel. "We got no problems! When that Indian fool tells the people what we have done to these boys, they'll fear us even more! I've worked with the Texas Rangers at our border to the north! I know what I'm doing; you'll see! But now let's eat! Killing, like making love, always gives a man a good appetite!"

The colonel brought out his flask again, but it was empty. He was so worked up that he looked like a man possessed. "Turn the dogs loose on that *cabrón* Indian! Damnit, how I've hated needing to depend on these no-good *indios sin razón* all these years! We feed them, train them, and see how quickly the ungrateful *cabrones* turn on us, after we've done so much for them! As the Texans always used to say, the only Indian you can trust is a dead Indian. I'll tell you, as a young lieutenant I really enjoyed working the border with those ruthless Rangers, hunting down the Apaches! Oh, those *indios* were game!"

Seeing the sweat run down the colonel's face—he was so worked up—Captain Hans Kayser said, "I think that we'd do better not to turn the dogs loose, Colonel, and just trail the Indian with the dogs in hand. As I've told you, these are highly disciplined hounds, and we don't want to ruin them."

"All right, we'll do as you suggest," said the colonel, giving his flask to his manservant so he could refill it. He really wasn't feeling all that well.

And that day when the colonel and his men got into the little mountainous settlement, they found no one. Juan had managed to warn *la gente* in time for all of them to get away. The colonel had a couple of his men begin to shout, telling the whole world what they'd done to the four boys. "We castrated them! We poked their eyes out! And now they're lost for all eternity!"

Juan and his *familia* had to cover their ears so they wouldn't hear the shouting. They were hiding up in the rock crevices on the tall *barrancas* just above the oak trees north of town. Along with Juan and his family were Jorge's mother, Prieta, and several of the other townspeople.

"Don't listen to them," said Doña Margarita, making the sign of the cross over herself. "They're just trying to trick us. We must keep strong *con nuestra fe en Dios!*"

Jorge's mother, along with the other people, made the sign of the cross over herself, too, and they tried their best to hold on to Doña Margarita's words, but it was difficult.

For the colonel and his men well-knew what they were doing. The colonel's men now began to chant, to dance, and wave the clothes that they'd taken from the dead boys' bodies, crying out, pretending that this was their way of summoning the powers of the supernatural. Smiling, the German watched in total captivation as he continued to stroke the dogs lovingly.

Finally, Manuel and Jorge's mother couldn't stand it anymore, and she cried out, "Oh, *Dios mío,* those are the *trapos* I made for my boys with my own two hands!"

And screaming out in terror, the short, wide Indian woman leaped to her feet, wanting to attack her tormentors. But before she could get out of the pocket in which they were hiding, Luisa and Juan grabbed her, pulling her back down.

"No, Prieta!" Doña Margarita whispered to her. "Keep still! It's a trick, I tell you, so they can kill us all!"

But the dogs and soldiers had heard the old woman's cry, and now they all knew that the people were hiding somewhere up in the tall *barrancas,* just above the oaks.

"Keep yelling, keep waving those clothes," said the colonel, grinning. "They'll crack, and come running to us just like rabbits. This, too, is a little trick I learned from an old *gringo* Indian scout at the border. Oh, I tell you, those *americanos* knew the tricks when it came to dealing with their *indios!*"

The soldiers drew closer to the base of the *barrancas* from where they'd heard the scream. They began to cry out in eerie, high-pitched screeches, waving the clothes and repeating over and over again how they'd mutilated the boys in this life. "And now their souls are lost! And destined to wander for all eternity, unless you clothe 'em and send 'em with your blessing!"

Finally, the powerful full-blooded Indian woman Prieta couldn't stand it anymore. And crying out with a tormented soul, she tossed off Juan and Luisa—who'd been holding her down—like they were so much nothing, and she went screaming out of the rocks, racing down toward the soldiers. "Please," she begged, "see it in your hearts to give me my boys' clothes back! They need to have a proper Christian burial!"

"Ah, didn't I tell you?!" said the colonel, loving it. "Indians are such simple-minded, loyal people; that's why they'll crack every time. Turn the dogs loose on her!" he added. He was in ecstasy. He brought out his flask and drank as he watched the dogs yelping to the heavens. And the well-trained hounds quickly closed in on Prieta as she stood there on the steep hillside, begging for her sons' clothes. "You see, she wouldn't even run," continued the colonel. "You can count on it. She'd rather stand there like a fool, letting the dogs tear her apart, than abandon the possibility of us returning her sons' clothes to her. Incredible, eh?"

The German nodded. "Yes, and if such loyalty cannot be broken, you will never beat these people in ten thousand years."

This was not what the colonel had wanted to hear. This was, in fact, the very truth that had been driving him crazy ever since he'd taken to the field more than twenty years before. And this was also what he'd seen drive the Texas Rangers into rage, causing many of them terrible deaths in their old age, even years after their retirement. These damned *indios* just had no respect! He gripped his stomach in pain. The dogs were now tearing the old woman to pieces, but still she kept begging for the children's clothes.

"Oh, my God," said Juan to his *familia* up in the rocks of the *barranca,* as they watched in horror the dogs devouring Prieta. "Quick, we've got to run!"

"But I can't run," said Luisa.

"What do you mean you can't run?" asked Juan.

"She's too big with child," said Doña Margarita, trying her best to keep calm.

Juan didn't know what to do. The soldiers were now coming up the hill, too. And little Juan tried to think, to figure out what his brother Jose, the great, would do, but he was so scared that he couldn't think straight.

Then, oh, my God, there came the dogs. The soldiers had gotten the dogs off Prieta's body, and they were now coming up the steep hillside—dogs and soldiers, both sounding so eerie and unworldly and crazy with want of blood. The dogs had devoured Pelon's poor old mother, and they were now foaming at the mouth, wanting more. They sounded like *diablos* from hell, howling, barking, each dog looking even larger than Doña Josefina's legendary dog *El Diablo.* Oh, it was a nightmare of sound!

"Well," said Juan, getting to his feet, having decided what it was that his brother would've done, "I guess I'll just have to run out and lead them away from us."

"Oh, no, you don't!" said their mother. "We need you with us, Juan! You're the only man we have left!"

"But those dogs," said Juan, "are going to smell us out, Mama! We can't just stay here!"

And suddenly, without even speaking one single word, Emilia leaped up and went racing out of the pocket, around the rocks, and down the hill toward the approaching monster dogs and crazed soldiers, yelling as she went. "Run, Luisa! Run, Mama! Lead them to safety, Juan! *Córrale,* Juan! Lead them away!"

Instantly, Juan leaped up to go after his sister, but Luisa tripped him with an outstretched leg. "No!" she said. "Don't!" And she grabbed hold of him, pinning him to *la tierra madre.* "There's nothing you can do!"

And coming out of the rocks, Emilia looked so tall and beautiful and totally European as she came flying down the hillside with long, shapely legs and flying reddish-blond hair. The soldiers, the colonel, and the German all stopped and stared as if they were seeing a vision. Why, this young woman was absolutely breathtakingly gorgeous, and yet, here she came in all her angel-like presence, ready to give her life for these dirty, no-good Indian people. And she was yelling, shouting, "Run, Luisa, run, and save your child! Run, Mama, and save Juanito!"

Seeing this spectacle of such unselfish bravery, the colonel couldn't stand it anymore, and he went into a fit of rage, forgetting about the German advisor whom he'd been so intent on impressing. He tore off his military cap and threw it down, stomping it into the ground. Here were these damned people trying to embarrass him again! For not once in his whole damned life had anyone ever cared for him this much—not since the Indian woman who'd breast-fed him, but then his mother had fired her when he'd started calling her his mama. Oh, his own mother—the queen of Guadalajara's high society and a close friend of one of Don Juan's aunts—had never shown him this type of ridiculous love. Why, this kind of devotion made him want to puke, and was also what caused him to detest his good friend Don Juan so much, for being the turncoat that he was.

The German watched the colonel tear off his military hat and throw it on the ground, jumping up and down on it like a child gone berserk, and then rage on in anger, yelling at his men as this tall, beautiful young woman continued coming down the hill toward them.

"GET HER!" bellowed the colonel to his soldiers as he watched Emilia coming closer and closer in all her tall, long-legged, blue-eyed beauty. "Catch her before the dogs kill her," he screamed with all his might. "I don't want her to die! Oh, no, I want her to live, so we can show her what women were really put on earth for!"

And little Juan was kicking and trying to get up to go after his sister Emilia—whom he'd always loved so much—wanting to be the protector of his *familia,* as he'd promised his brother he would do. But Luisa kept him pinned down to *la tierra* with her great mass, saying, "No, Juan! You know these *barrancas!* You're the only chance that Mama and me have of escaping!"

"Luisa is right," said Doña Margarita, making the sign of the cross over herself as she watched the dogs and soldiers closing in upon her daughter. "You and your sister and the others go now. I will handle this matter."

"No, Mama!" screamed Luisa. "Not you, either!"

But before Luisa could let go of her brother and grab her mother, the crafty old woman was up and gone. One moment she'd been here beside them, and the next—like magic—Doña Margarita was over there, out of the pocket and racing down the hillside, too. "May your beloved mothers see all you young men now!" she yelled as she came flying like a deer down the hill toward the soldiers and the dogs. "May your own blessed mothers see how you are behaving and forgive you, for even God up in heaven is having trouble forgiving you now!"

Seeing the old *bruja* herself now running down the hill after her daughter, the colonel went even crazier with rage. Oh, how he'd truly wished that someone had loved him like this just once in his damned, miserable life. Why, this girl was an angel and her mother looked like a wrinkled-up old rat; and, yet, here they both came, so willing to die horrible deaths to save one another. To the depths of his soul, the colonel fully realized that if he'd just once had this kind of love in all his *pinche vida,* he, too, would now be kind and loving to all these simple-minded, loyal *gente de la tierra.* Oh, if only Mariposa, in all her wonder, had just loved him, as she should have, he'd be all different. But, no, she hadn't loved him, and instead, she'd gone *con un indio cabrón,* and so right was might, and he was now going to destroy all these stupid peasant fools once and for all! Yes, he wanted them all dead and gone off the face of the earth, forever!

"Get them both!" yelled the colonel. "Quick, turn all the dogs loose on them! Before they get us!"

Hearing these words, *before they get us,* the German now realized that something else was going on, something that he had absolutely no idea about. But, then, what he saw happen next, with his two very own eyes was soooo extraordinary that he began to wonder if he'd left his senses.

Just as the huge, well-disciplined purebred dogs were about to tear the two women apart, the old woman suddenly lifted up her skirt and squatted down, pissing on the ground like a female dog. Rushing up, the dogs didn't maul her or the young woman. No, they began to smell the place where the old Indian woman had pissed, then they began circling the two women, wagging their tails as they continued sniffing.

Some soldiers started laughing. The people, who'd been hiding in the pockets of rock, came out in plain sight, and they were laughing, too. And now these big, well-trained German-bred dogs were prancing about the two women in a courtship of love, getting wonderful erections. Everyone was laughing. Even the colonel was grinning, looking on with total childlike fascination. And the old Indian woman now took the beautiful young woman in hand, and they both began to pet the dancing dogs.

Captain Hans Kayser went berserk. He just couldn't believe what was happening to his dogs who had been bred for generations to be the finest killers of all the earth! Why, in just moments, they were turning into a pathetic pack of ballet lovers. In a mad rage, the German officer now drew his pistol. "Shoot!" he yelled. "Quick, we need to shoot those two women before they ruin our dogs!"

"No," said the sergeant who was standing alongside the German, laughing *con carcajadas.* "Don't you see? Their spirits are dancing with your dogs' spirits. We can't interrupt *los espíritus.*"

Hearing this, Captain Hans Kayser thought that they'd all gone crazy. "No, you fool! I will not permit this! All of Germany cannot permit this!" And the German raised up his own pistol, taking aim on Doña Margarita.

But before he could shoot, the sergeant knocked the captain's arm away, leveling his own rifle at the German's gut. "No," repeated the sergeant. "As I said, their spirits are dancing together and we will not interrupt!"

And then the colonel—who'd been watching with such out-of-his-mind joy—quit grinning, got hold of himself, and he started raging once again, screaming and yelling. Then he was rushing up the hillside and kicking the hell out of the dogs for not mauling the two women as they should be doing. The soldiers and the people laughed all the more. For it was now plain to see that the colonel's spirit had taken up the dance, too. The colonel wasn't thinking rationally anymore; oh, no, he was all caught up in the magic splendor of the moment, going crazy-*loco,* dancing up the wild steps of heaven with the dogs and the two women.

Finally, not being able to stop the excited dogs from prancing about in courtship, the colonel drew his own pistol in a last attempt of being rational. And—over the screaming protests of horror from Captain Hans Kayser—he began shooting the dogs.

All the laughter stopped. All the dancing ceased. And *la gente* made the sign of the cross over themselves. The colonel had panicked in fear and quit dancing this greatest of all dances of the human soul, and he was now shooting the dogs, who were rushing up to Doña Margarita in terrible pain, wanting to die by her feet.

And the souls of the dying dogs came up out of their earthly bodies and drew close to Doña Margarita, wanting to make peace with themselves before they went over to the other side. The old woman raised up her hands, giving each dog her blessing.

The colonel, still unable to see or comprehend what was happening, kept raging and shooting. But *la gente*—who could see—gave witness to this miracle of miracles, and their eyes filled with tears. For these poor German dogs had looked so beautiful, so angel-like, as they'd finally been able to shed their ancestry of being bred killers, and their spirit of love had arisen up from out of their long-forgotten souls.

Then it hit Juan. It hit him like a thunderbolt. Why, this was the site of the fire dance. This place that he and Luisa were looking down upon, where his mother and Emilia were with the dogs, was the exact location that he'd witnessed his old mother and her friends dancing on fire that night. And realizing this, suddenly Juan had eyes that saw and ears that heard, and he could now see that his mother was, indeed, a great big, beautiful, thousand-pound she-wolf, towering like a great horse over this pack of mere dogs; and the hounds were madly in love with her, adoring the very ground that she'd pissed on.

Juan rubbed his eyes, wondering if he'd gone crazy or what; but, no, he could see that he saw what he saw, and his mother truly was this great black she-wolf and the dogs were begging her for her blessing. And he could now also see that his sister Emilia was a gorgeous she-fox, and the hounds were crazy about her, too. Then he saw that there were angels by the dozens all about them, singing in harmony; and there was a pool of golden-white light raining down upon his mother and sister and the dying dogs as God, the Father, breathed down on them with an abundance of warmth and love. Everything at the fire site was ablaze with love, aflame with the Almighty's passion.

"Oh, my God, I can see!" exclaimed Juan. "I can see the fire of God's love, and I can hear the earth breathing—she's alive!"

Luisa hugged him close, kissing him. "Do you smell our *tierra madre,* too, and feel her trembling with her birth?"

"Oh, yes, I do, and it's glorious!" continued Juan, feeling the earth beneath him tremble as he spoke. "We're surrounded by angels and all of the heavens!" He began to cry. "The Mother Earth loves us, Luisa, and the Father Sky loves us, too!"

"Exactly!" said Luisa, tears of joy running down her cheeks.

But then, getting over his initial shock of being able to see *la vida* in all of its natural splendor of unconditional love, Juan could now also see that the situation was far from over. For the well-fed colonel himself was now lunging at Emilia, bellowing like a mad bull as he tried grabbing her.

"Come on, finish off these damned dogs for me!" he yelled to his men. "Then let's show this girl and her old witch-mother what women are for!"

But his men weren't obeying his orders. Even the ones who didn't have the eyes to see or the ears to hear, they could still feel deep inside of themselves that something Holy had, indeed, come to pass.

"Damn your stupid souls!" screamed the colonel. "Don't you see what this *bruja* has done to all of you?!"

But his men weren't moving.

"They must obey orders!" yelled the German, rushing in, looking completely mad, too. "Disobedience cannot be tolerated!"

"Tell it to your dogs," said one very handsome young soldier, laughing *con gusto*.

"What did you say to me?" bellowed the German, rushing up to the young soldier.

The soldier was taken aback, but only for a moment. Then laughing, he turned about and bent over, farting on the German a long, glorious huge *pedo*-fart. Captain Hans Kayser's eyes exploded! Never in all his life had he ever been farted on. He started to go for his gun, but then he saw that all the other soldiers were going crazy with laughter, too, and were watching him very closely, with their rifles ready. He decided to leave his weapon alone.

Suddenly, the colonel—who had Emilia down on the ground and had unbuckled his gunbelt and opened his pants to rape her —screamed out in pain and fell to the earth, going into convulsions. *La gente* went into hysteria, laughing even more. But the

soldiers quit laughing; and yet, not one of them moved forward
to help their leader.

Doña Margarita was the first to come close to the fallen man
and her daughter. And it would have surprised no one if she'd
picked up a stone and crushed his skull. But, instead, the old
she-wolf took her daughter in her arms and said, "Easy, *mi
hijita,* everything is going to be all right."

"Get away from here before I kill you! You hateful old witch!"
shouted the colonel.

"Come now, hasn't there been enough hatred and killing
already?" asked the old woman, refusing to be intimidated as
she continued giving comfort to her daughter. "It's all over, *mi
coronel,* just lie back and rest, my son."

"Don't call me your son, you smelly old witch!" screamed
out the colonel, trembling with all the power of his being.

The sergeant started laughing. Oh, this was really good; the
old *bruja* was made of iron. A few of the other soldiers began
laughing once again, too. They could all see that the colonel's
spirit had come out of his body and was starting to dance with
the old woman's spirit.

"I'm not of your blood!" continued the colonel. "I'm of civilized people, so don't you ever call me your son again!"

"But we're all God's children," she said, reaching out to
touch him, "so how can you not be my son, *mi hijito?*"

And hearing these most endearing of all words, *mi hijito,*
spoken to him so calmly as she now gently stroked his forehead
—just as the Indian woman with the huge, warm tits had
soothed his forehead when she'd nursed him—the man began
to melt, to soften, and everyone watched in total fascination.
Why, the big man was actually starting to cry, to have feelings
that he hadn't allowed himself since his childhood. And he was
just on the verge of bursting forth, through the needle's eye of
unconditional love and blossom like a flower—a rose—into the
whole new world of God's living *paraíso* on earth, when suddenly he got hold of himself. And trembling with rage, he didn't

cry. No, instead, he shoved the old Indian woman's hand away and he was suddenly screaming rape and murder once again!

The sergeant started clapping his hands in complete approval, laughing *con carcajadas.* For his colonel had just about gone over to the other side, as the old sergeant had seen so many good men do, going over to the enemy after so many years of fighting these stupid Indian peasants, that they'd lost their senses, not knowing what was real and what wasn't real anymore.

But the colonel hadn't let himself go over. No, he'd held on to his hatred with real guts, not allowing the *bruja* to trick him with her ridiculous love, and now he was screaming, "I'm going to do your daughter, just as I did Mariposa, you dirty, sneaky old Indian woman!" And he was good once again. He was powerful and confident. But, oh, for one dangerous moment there, it had really looked like the colonel had dropped his guard and his spirit was going to take flight from his body and start dancing with the old woman's spirit of the Holy Ghost, just as the dogs' had done.

The sergeant began to unbuckle his own gunbelt. His colonel was having trouble getting himself erect to rape the girl. But he knew that he'd have no such problem. After all, these damned people were the ones who'd killed his best friend—the giant old sergeant—when they'd raided their outpost, and so he wanted a piece of this damned *familia!*

"With your permission, *mi Coronel,*" said the sergeant politely, "but this one's mine!"

"By all means," said the colonel, feeling relieved that at least one of his men had come to his senses and was willing to behave like a real *hombre* once again.

For this old witch's powers were infinite and he'd thought that he might have lost all of his men, as had happened to him once before when these Indians had bewitched his entire force of soldiers down in Oaxaca and then in Chiapas. Oh, a civilized man could never be too careful when it came to dealing with these damned native people *de la tierra madre.*

And all this time the German watched, completely engrossed in how this rape now seemed to be bringing all the soldiers out of the trance that they'd been in and once more they were becoming a fighting force with lust and hate and purpose. But, oh, that old woman had almost won! Why, he'd never seen such a thing in all of his military career. And when he wrote up his report, it would be difficult for his superiors to understand what it was that had really taken place.

And up above, the heavens opened, and the angels sang. They all well-knew that this was just the beginning. For this dance of love and hate had been going on for tens of thousands upon tens of thousands of years.

The handsome young soldier who'd farted on the German couldn't stand it anymore. So he now leaped forward, grabbing his wiry old sergeant and throwing him off the breathtakingly-beautiful girl—whom he'd fallen madly in love with since the moment he'd first seen her coming down the hill. He ripped open his own pants and mounted her himself, whispering in her ear to please not be afraid, for he really loved her and meant her no harm.

Hearing his words, Emilia stopped screaming and she looked him in the eyes and she saw that he'd spoken the truth. And he was so handsome!

"No, don't stop screaming," he whispered, "or they'll know that I love you and—"

But he wasn't able to finish his words. Seeing what was really going on, the skinny old sergeant drew his sword, shoving it up the boy's ass with a vengeance, all the way to his heart.

Emilia's screams filled the entire valley, as she felt the boy's cock explode deep inside her and he kicked and jerked his last.

7

And so the last would be the first, and the youngest, the oldest; and out of these children of the earth and of the stars would now come a glorious new **gente** *in all their wonder and fire—willing to live, to die, but never to quit dancing for the love of God!*

And over the mountains in the state of Guanajuato, Jose was holding on to the large wooden horn of his Mexican saddle, trying to keep conscious as his horse continued taking him northward toward the United States. And, yes, he could feel the torment, the anguish, of his *familia,* but he was also feeling so much pain with each step that his horse took, that his brain was numb. But he well-knew that he had to keep strong and brave and not lose faith. For this day of anguish would also come to pass, *con el favor de Dios!*

That night, Jose sat alone before a little fire, resting. Flashes of cannons were exploding all around him as the armies of Francisco Villa and Venustiano Carranza tore at each other like two huge serpents in twisting, thrashing mortal combat. But Jose paid no attention to these cannons as he hid there in the chaparral with his horse, Two White Stockings. Jose had two small round rocks in his right hand, and he was rolling them back and forth, back and forth, as he spoke to the stars, asking God to send love and peace to his family. For Jose missed his mother and his *familia* more than life itself, and he was tempted to just turn around and go back.

The tears streamed down his face, and his horse came over, nudging him. He spoke to his horse and his horse spoke to him, and he just lay there, rolling the two little round rocks in his right hand, knowing deep within himself that all life here on earth was but a dream, and we were all in full partnership with the heavens when we swam gently, gently down the stream of life, *la vida*.

So Jose now took the two stones in his left hand, and he prayed, staying calm and relaxed in his love of God as he sent his *amor* to his loved ones back home, feeling stronger and stronger as he prayed. The two little stones rooted him to the earth, and his prayers rooted him to the heavens. No, he wasn't going to let the Devil tempt him or break him just because he'd been cut. He was going to get well and strong and keep traveling north, and life, *la vida*, was going to be good once more, for his *tanates* had never been what had made him a man. Oh, the two little round rocks, which he'd picked up from the river where he'd washed his groin, felt so good in his palm. They were of the earth, and he was of the earth, too; and they were giving him nourishment.

That night after the soldiers had left, the people came in from everywhere, giving honor to the survivors of the colonel's last *desmadre!* They ate roots and smoked the good weed, and held each other close, licking one another's wounds like dogs.

Little Pelon came up to Juan. They hadn't been able to stop him from seeing the remains of what had once been his mother's body. "I need to speak to you, Juan."

Juan Salvador was chewing a handful of weeds to ease his hunger. "Go on," said Juan.

"Well, I got a plan," said Pelon, picking up a stick and poking at the *tierra madre* with it. "And I need your help."

Juan nodded. He could see that his childhood friend had aged twenty years since he'd seen his mother's mutilated body. He would never be young again. "All right," said Juan, "I'm listening."

The quarter moon was out, looking like the thumbnail of God's right hand. The two boys sat down, facing each other like stones. Pelon explained his whole plan to Juan.

"So you see, Juan, I was there this morning, buried in the oak leaves, when the colonel and his men came up the mountain," he said oh so calmly. "I'll tell you, if only I'd had a gun, I could've killed him so easily, and then none of this would've happened, and *mi mamá* and *mis hermanos,* they would all be alive right now." Tears came to his eyes.

Nodding, Juan also picked up a stick to poke the earth. "It's hard, I tell you," he said, struggling to keep calm. "I, too, failed my brother Jose, and now, well, I failed my mother and sister, too." He poked the earth harder.

"Then you'll come in with me?" said Pelon.

"I'm in with you," said Juan.

"Good," said Pelon. "Because, you know, the colonel is going to keep coming back as long as we still breathe."

"Yes, I know; that's why I want that son-of-a-bitch dead!" said Juan.

"Exactly," said Pelon, taking a big breath. "If only I'd had a gun; my mother, my brother, they'd all be . . ." He began to weep uncontrollably. "I got no one, Juan. I'm all that's left of my whole *familia!"*

And he drew in close to Juan Salvador, hugging him. The stars above wept. The Mother Earth trembled.

One fine morning a few days later, Emilia awoke, humming to herself. She got up and went out to midfield and began digging in the *tierra madre* with a stick. And when she was asked what she was doing, she simply said that she was pregnant and that soon she and her child would be needing food.

And so all week, Emilia continued humming to herself as she worked the earth and planted *maíz*, knowing that women had been doing this since time began. Down deep inside of her young bones, Emilia well-knew that the abuses of men were nothing new, and so life—*la vida*—had to go on being made Holy by woman's sacred love, if there was to be any future for humankind.

And the tears flowed from her eyes as she once more saw that handsome young man's face inside of her mind's eye, and he told her that he loved her and he wasn't really raping her. Oh, if only she'd had the wisdom to have kept screaming, maybe they wouldn't have killed him and she and he could have gotten married someday in the most beautiful white-dress wedding in all the world.

Some people thought that Emilia had lost her mind. Others —as they saw her working the soil—thought she was perfectly sane and that maybe this incredible story that she kept telling herself could've become true, if they hadn't killed the boy for showing her tenderness. But, either way, it didn't matter. The truth was that Emilia had the power of mind to get up each morning with song in her heart, and the seed of life, *la vida,* that was deep inside of her was growing larger and larger with each new day.

Then one day, there came Don Juan and Jose-Luis on foot, leading two burros full of supplies. And they were so happy, so proud that they'd been able to get through the lines of the war and up the mountain. Villa and Carranza were now tearing at each other with armies of twenty-five thousand men each. In every gully, the streams were foaming with orange-red blood. Oh, the people were once more truly painting the earth with their dead bodies by the tens of thousands, just as Don Pio had said that they would.

"We're here!" yelled Jose-Luis, leading the first little burro up the cobblestone street of the burned-out ruins. "I've come with supplies once again!" he yelled proudly. "And look who I found on my way up the mountain! Don Juan is with me, too!"

With a big, happy grin, Jose-Luis pushed back his large straw hat and glanced around at this place that had once been such a beautiful, picturesque little mountain village; but there seemed to be no one around.

Don Juan came up with his burro and he glanced about, too. He wore new Levi's from the United States and American cowboy boots, shirt, and hat, and he looked well-fed. Both men were smiling, looking forward to seeing their families.

Seeing no one, Don Juan shrugged and went over to the well in the center of town and pulled the bell, calling, "Domingo! Margarita!" But still no one came. It was a bright, hot day. Don Juan took off his beautiful new American cowboy hat, wiped the sweat off the inside brim, then put his hat back on and got hold of the rope, pulling up the *olla* for some fresh, cool water. But what came up in the bucket wasn't just water, but Jorge's eyeless head, with his big, gumless teeth grinning up at the sky. Screaming, Don Juan let go of the rope. He pulled out his brand new Colt .45, shooting the well.

Jose-Luis rushed over, asking what had happened. But Don Juan was bellowing like a mad bull, new Colt .45 smoking in hand, and the veins of his powerful old neck were up like ropes. "Domingo!" shouted the big, strong man with all his might. "Domingo! Oh, God, please, no! Please!" Don Juan had never been able to locate his two other fair-haired sons nor their cousin-brother Everardo in California, and so Domingo—his last red-headed son—was now his only hope.

Jose-Luis got hold of the rope and pulled up the *olla*. He

could see that Jorge's head had been in the well so long, the boy was hardly recognizable. Jose-Luis grabbed the head by the hair, yanking it out of the bucket. He was furious.

"Those son-of-a-bitches, they don't just kill us, but they ruin our water, too! Luisa!" he screamed. "Luisa! What in the name of God drives these men?!"

"*El Diablo!*" said Don Juan, shooting his new .45 into the air once, twice, three times. "Please, dear God, don't tell me that they killed everybody! Oh, please, dear God, I beg You to have mercy on *mi familia,* if not on me!"

Jose-Luis continued screaming, too, "Luisa! Luisa! LUISA!" so full of fear for his pregnant wife, whom he loved more than life itself, especially since she was all he had left in all the world. Two months back some dirty little bastard soldiers had raped his poor old mother, then tied her to a cross and burned her and their house to the ground in the name of God-given Christianity, leaving the mark *de los Cristeros* around her corpse, calling her a witch and themselves the right hand of the Almighty. Luisa and their child-to-be was Jose-Luis's only hope for sanity left in all the world. "Luisa! Luisa! LUISA!" he called like a crazy-*loco* fool. "Juan! Emilia! Doña Margarita! Anybody! *¡Por el favor de Dios!*"

But all their fears, all the disasters that they'd given witness to for the last two years, still didn't prepare Jose-Luis and Don Juan for what they saw next: small rat-like creatures began to materialize out of the rocks to the north of their settlement. And when Don Juan realized that among these sick-looking creatures were, in fact, his very own *familia,* he turned his face away in disgust, not able to look them in the eyes. Oh, my God! He'd just come back from working on a horse ranch in Pasadena, California, where the people were all so well-fed and beautiful; why, even the dogs had been showcases of beauty and grooming.

But Jose-Luis, on the other hand, hadn't been raised by people who called themselves the sons of kings, and so he was able to face his *familia* with love and compassion. Jose-Luis had been raised by a powerful single mother, and so he knew how to endure pain and disappointment. With tears rolling down his huge, powerful face, Jose-Luis now took his wife, Luisa, into his arms, and he took Juan and Doña Margarita and Emilia, too, and wept like a child, but never once did he turn his male, needful face away from his loved ones.

And when Doña Margarita drew close to her husband's side, needing his fire, his strength, so that they could go on, his male fears just couldn't accept her. No, he pushed her away from himself, asking for Domingo once again.

"But didn't Domingo find you?" asked Doña Margarita, tears streaming down her dirty, old wrinkled-up face as she still tried to get close to her husband. "He left shortly after you left, to join you in California."

"Oh, my God, no!" screamed Don Juan. "But I didn't get to California until the spring! I worked in Albuquerque most of the time! How could you have let him go? You've ruined *nuestra familia,* you stupid Indian woman!"

"Papa," said Emilia, "don't talk to Mama like that! Why, she has performed miracles just to keep us alive while you've been gone!"

"Oh, now it's my fault!" he said, backing away, needing to protect himself. "Damn the day I ever married into this wretched tribe of imbeciles! I told you not to let anything happen to our family until I returned with money! And I came back! I kept my word! I didn't run away, staying in the United States!" he bellowed, yanking out the tails of his new shirt and exposing a row of money sewn in a cloth band about his waist. "I worked so hard! Sixteen hours a day, and all for nothing once again! Oh, my God! My God! Why have You forsaken me?!"

"But God hasn't forsaken us," said Doña Margarita. "Here, let me hold you, *mi amor,* and we can overcome!"

"No! Don't touch me, you filthy rat!"

"Papa!" cried Luisa. "Please, don't be like this! Hold us! We need you now more than ever! Both Emilia and I are with child!"

"With child?" said Don Juan, his whole face filling with horror. "But what shameful acts have been going on?! Emilia, my most beautiful child, you're . . . oh, my God, you're ruined!"

"Oh, no, Papa, I'm not ruined!" said Emilia. "He loved me! Please don't say that I'm ruined! I want us all to love my child!"

"But how can we love a monstrosity?! You never married," he said, turning his face away from his daughter.

Emilia's eyes closed, her head rolled, and she fell to the ground as if she'd been struck by a lightning bolt.

"Juan!" screamed Doña Margarita. "You stop this instantly! And take your two fine daughters in your arms and give them your love! You have absolutely no idea what we've been through!"

"But I can't," he said, refusing to even look at his *familia,* and instead, he turned to the heavens and with all his power he bellowed, "I have no more family! I have no more *familia!*" And he started back down the cobblestones from where he'd come.

"JUAN JESUS, for the love of GOD don't do this!" begged Doña Margarita, running after him. "Salvation isn't up in the heavens! And it never was! It's always been here with your *familia!*" But he just kept walking away from them, praying to God as he went. "Juan, please come back! No matter how far we've fallen, we can arise again, *con el favor de Dios!* We love you! We need you! You are our fire! Our strength! Please, come back!" she screamed, running, limping, crawling after him, grabbing hold of the back of his left leg, but he just kept going, dragging her as he kept trying to get away from them. "Do not forsake us, *mi esposo;* do not forsake us, for the love of God, look at me, my love!"

Hearing these last words, he stopped. He held. He closed his eyes and began to tremble, but he wouldn't turn around to look at her. "No," he finally said oh so quietly. "I can't see you. I can't. Please, my love, let go of me, so I can remember us . . .

as I first saw you. You were so beautiful, like a young brown doe," he said, smiling, "and we were so happy, so much in love as we rode to the tall *barrancas* and played in the green meadows . . . or . . . or . . . I'll go mad!"

"But, my love, you won't go mad, *mi esposo*, I promise you. Trust in God, and we'll be fine. We just need to keep loving each other, no matter what."

"But I don't KNOW HOWWWW-WW!" he howled, he screamed, he bellowed. "Please, let me go! Let me go! Please! For the love *de Dios!*"

Hearing this, Doña Margarita now released him, opening up her hands, finger by finger, and she let go of the left leg of his new dark Levi's.

He breathed and started away, step by step, never once looking back.

The day darkened, and in came storm clouds with rain and thunder. Doña Margarita lay there on the cobblestone street, defeated, broken, dying, as she looked after her true love, *su amor de la vida,* going out of their settlement.

And in the flashes of rain and wind and lightning, she saw his hat get blown off his head and, yes, his startling red-brown hair had greyed a lot over the years, but it still had fire.

"I still love you," she said, making the sign of the cross over herself, "and always, will, *mi esposo!*"

The rain and lightning continued, and the water ran down Doña Margarita's face, gathering with her tears. The water and tears ran quickly down her body and to the street, rushing over the well-laid cobblestones.

Don Juan was now only a tiny dark form as he continued down the road from which he'd come thirty-some years before.

Jose-Luis came up behind Doña Margarita. He was holding Juan and Luisa and Emilia in his arms. They all knelt down together, hugging the old woman close. It was the son of a woman who'd been called the witch who now stood fast by them; and it was the man, who'd come from kings, who'd fled.

It rained and thundered most of that afternoon. But then the sun came out, the birds began to chirp, and Emilia got up and went out to attend to her corn. But she couldn't see very well anymore; she'd become blind. Instinctively knowing that if she could just see her child-to-be with her heart-vision and not her eye-vision, then everything would be all right and her father's terrible words wouldn't come true. For that soldier had loved her; he really had. She'd seen it in his eyes, and so they'd been married by God, if not by the Church, and so she was still pure, and her father—God forgive him—had been wrong when he'd said that she was ruined and her child-to-be was a monstrosity.

Luisa and Juan helped Emilia work out in her cornfield, and —as always after a storm of rain and wind, thunder and lightning—the wet earth now smelled as wonderful as a woman who'd just made love, and the air was as crisp and as pure as heaven. Jose-Luis stayed home in their burned-out ruins, holding their mother in his great arms as she cried and cried, mumbling to herself as she drifted in and out of sleep and dream. Yes, life, *la vida,* had finally broken her, had finally done to her what it had been unable to do to her with all these years of war, and loss of home, and dying children.

The *gran* old lady held on to her son-in-law with all her power, gaining warmth from his male fire. And Jose-Luis kept assuring Doña Margarita over and over again that she would be all right, for he'd personally hold her and spoon-feed her until she regained her strength.

For he, Jose-Luis, had fought and killed and struggled to get these supplies and food up the mountain to them, and no *pinche cabrón* little revolution was going to stop him from helping his wife and *familia* to bring his first-born into the world. He'd seen his mother—a single woman—struggling again and again without a husband, and so he knew how to see a family through without a father!

The tears ran down Jose-Luis's face. Oh, my God, there was only him and Juan left of all the males of this once-*gran familia.*

And he hadn't even been able to say goodbye to Jose—his best friend, and the greatest *hombre* the earth had ever produced.

And at this very moment, Jose was racing across a great flat with half a dozen soldiers after him. But there was no way on earth that they could catch him. It was night time; and Jose had trained all of his horses in the night, and so he and Two White Stockings were able to dodge in and out of the ravines and leap across *arroyos* in the dark where no other horses could go. Soldiers with their horses were falling all over the place, trying to catch him, but still they gave chase.

Then up ahead, cannon blasts were flashing, and an entire settlement was on fire. Jose reined in his horse. Two White Stockings was lathered white with sweat. Women and children were running past Jose, trying to hide from the *desmadre*. One young woman was all dressed up in evening clothes, and she carried a suitcase.

"Now we got him!" one soldier was heard to say as the riders closed in on Jose.

Jose whirled his horse about, trying to decide what to do.

And how all this had come to be was that seven hills back, a group of soldiers had surprised Jose at dusk as he'd been coming along, holding on to his saddle horn as best as he could. They'd seen his fine horse and weapons and they'd surrounded him, asking who was he for—Carranza or Villa?

"I'm for no one anymore," Jose had said.

"Oh, so then you're either a turncoat or a coward! You're under arrest!" said a big-faced man.

"No, I gave my word to my mother that I'd never fight again," said Jose.

Hearing this, the men all howled with laughter. And the leader spoke again. "Well, then, having given your mother your word you have no more need of that fine horse or gun, so we'll just take them from you in the name of—"

But the man never finished his words. Jose shot him through his big open mouth, blowing out the back of his skull, and dropped three others before they could move, then he lunged Two White Stockings over a fifth man, knocking the horse and rider to the ground. And he was off in the chaparral, racing before they'd even gotten one single shot off at him.

Getting over their initial shocked surprise, the seven remaining men were now after Jose with a vengeance, forgetting all about the war in their rage of wanting to kill this one incredible man.

And now here they came, shooting at Jose, who whirled his horse about and then cut off to the left away from the escaping people so they wouldn't be caught in a crossfire. The cannons were exploding just ahead of him. He saw a wide river up ahead, too. Getting to the river, he reined in, seeing that it was a good thirty-foot drop to the water. He glanced back at the men who were closing in fast, thundering hooves upon the earth, and he glanced up at the stars and the moon, said a prayer, and whirled his horse around in a spinning fury in the flashing light of the cannons and burning settlement. Then he bolted Two White Stockings at a full run over the bluff, kicking free of his great horse as they both hit the flat water with a terrible bang! But Jose didn't know how to swim. And he was in so much pain that he was drowning. But then, miracle of miracles, just as Jose thought he was breathing his last, here came Two White Stockings swimming up to him, nudging him, and he was able to get hold of the horse's powerful neck. The stars and moonlight were dancing on the water all around them. Texas was just across the river. Jose had made it. He was safe at last. Or so he thought.

And here came *la milpa,* the cornfield, gushing forth from the Mother Earth like a sea of strong, little green cocks as the *maíz* reached up for the Father Sky. And *la gente* rejoiced, and this sacred staff of all of life, *el maíz,* grew fist by fist each day before their very eyes.

Then one afternoon, a couple of the colonel's scouts came riding by and they saw the wonderful field of young green corn and one was heard to say, "But isn't this that village that we burned to *nada?*"

"Yes, I think so," said the other. "But it's hard to tell. We've burned so many to the ground in the last few years."

"Well," said the first, "we better ride back and tell the colonel that they're still going!"

And the two young soldiers turned their horses about, but they never made it out of the mountains. At the first grove of oaks, Jose-Luis was upon them, and with all his monstrous, bear-like power, he tore both men off their horses, and with nothing but his bare hands, he ripped out their throats. Then it was said that this big, gentle man cut out their hearts with their own knives, and he began to dance, to dance with all the wild abandon with which his beloved mother had danced among her treasured peach trees, giving nourishment to the earth with the blood of his kill, and it was glorious!

Two days later, Juan Salvador met Pelon down in the deep *barrancas* north of town. It was late afternoon; they only had a couple more hours of good daylight left. Rumor was the colonel had gotten word of his two scouts' deaths, and he was on his way.

"Did you tell anyone?" asked Pelon.

"No," said Juan Salvador. "I told no one."

"Not even your own mother?" asked Pelon.

"Especially not my mother!" snapped Juan Salvador. "My God, she'd be out of her head with worry if I'd told her what we were about!"

"All right, calm down," said Pelon. "I didn't mean to make

you angry. I was just checking. We can't be too careful with what we're about to do."

"Did you get the rifle?" asked Juan Salvador.

"Sure. I got it over there in those rocks, wrapped in a *serape* and covered with leaves."

"Good," said Juan, glancing over to the pile of large boulders. He could see nothing. He was glad that Pelon had hidden the weapon well. After all, they didn't want to be seen lugging a rifle around the countryside.

"Come on," said Pelon, "we'll build a little fire and eat and go over my plan once more. After all, you have Don Pio's blood in your veins, just like your brother Jose, so you should have a head for strategy. Oh, my brothers would always marvel at Jose's strategy of battle. Our brothers, they were great, eh, until —oh, my God!" Tears suddenly flooded his eyes.

Juan put his hand on his friend's shoulders, watching the tears flow down Pelon's face. They went over to the boulders and hunched down out of sight and started a little fire to warm their *taquitos*. The sun was down, and soon they'd be able to travel without being seen.

Pelon's plan was simple. He'd been watching the *Rurales* for weeks now, and the colonel and his men were coming up from the lowlands on the same trail, and every time they'd rest their horses three-fourths of the way up the mountain in a little basin where there was water and grass. The colonel had also gotten in the habit of walking a little way away from his men to take a crap over a large fallen log, from where he could keep watch on the trail above him and below him.

"So, you see," said Pelon, "all we got to do is get there tonight, and you bury me in the dirt and cover me with leaves, and then in the morning, when they come up and he pulls down his pants to crap, I'll just shoot him dead from a distance of about ten feet so I'll be sure not to miss the bastard!"

Juan nodded, figuring that this was, indeed, a good plan and it could very well work. But, also, he could see that Pelon would be a dead boy if he wasn't covered up carefully with the leaves and branches.

"Look," said Juan Salvador, "I really do think that your plan can work, but, well, it's also very dangerous. Because if the colonel gets suspicious and finds you, well, then, there's no escape 'cause you're so close."

"I know," said Pelon. "But to hell with it! I don't want an escape! If he finds me, I want to die trying to kill him. I got no one, Juan! All my family is dead!"

These terrible words drove like knives deep into Juan's chest. "Well, all right, then," said Juan, "I'll cover you up real good, but man-oh-man, you're going to have to have nerves of steel to stay there quietly all night and not panic when the colonel and his men ride up, making noise with their horses around you."

Pelon breathed. "The nerve, believe me, I've got. In fact, that's all I got left: *nada* but nerve!" And the tears streamed down his little brown face.

Juan breathed slowly. He felt exactly the same way. "But just wait," he said, "one more thing. After I bury you, how will you know when to raise up and start shooting; especially if I bury you so well that you can't be seen?"

Pelon was stumped. But not for long. "I guess I'll know to come up shooting when I hear his first farts and shits."

Both boys laughed.

"Then let's hope he eats and drinks like a pig tonight, so he'll be shitting and farting big and loud tomorrow," added Juan, laughing all the more.

And so there they went, two little boys, laughing as Pelon lugged an old *retrocarga,* homemade shotgun, in a *serape.* The old scattergun hadn't been fired in years. The sun was gone now and the western sky was painted in long streaks of pink and rose and yellow and gold. The clouds were banked up against the distant mountain called *El Cerro Gordo,* The Fat Mountain; and all the rolling little hills and valleys between that distant mountain and their own great mountain, called *El Cerro*

Grande, were green and lush, looking so beautiful and all at peace.

The two little boys began to whistle as they went. They were absolutely stout-hearted in their belief that they would succeed. Overhead, the last of the great flocks of fork-tailed blackbirds came swooping by on their way to roost in the tall grasses by the shallow mountain lakes. It had been another good day on God's sacred Mother Earth, and she, the night, was now approaching in all her splendor and magic.

That evening, no one knew where little Juan was, and Doña Margarita was very anxious. With her great coyote ears, she began to search the world, wondering if her little son's disappearance had anything to do with Pelon having come by a few nights before. She decided to tell Luisa to go and search for Juan. She just had this little, quiet, funny feeling deep inside of herself, that the two boys were up to something.

And so once more, Doña Margarita took in hand her father's once-fine handmade rosary and went outside to pray. The sun was gone and the night was coming, and soon it would be dark. Doña Margarita took off her *huaraches,* spit into her hands, massaged the soles of each of her feet with saliva, and then planted her feet well into the ground. She stood there and began to pray, swaying back and forth, as she fingered each bead, releasing her soul to God and knowing deep within herself that all would turn out for the sacred good, if only she kept faith and allowed God to do His wondrous work.

And with her eagle-soul eyes, Doña Margarita was now seeing; and with her coyote-soul ears, she was now hearing. And with her she-fox-soul cunning, she was now planning; and with her armadillo-soul powers, she was now supported from the very foundations of all the lower world—which wasn't hell, and had never been hell, until men had twisted things around in their fearful, confused minds. The lower world was the place of giving birth. The lower world was the place from where all the power of the local spirits came forth, singing and dancing in the form of little, short, happy turquoise-colored people. Doña Margarita now prayed on, calling for the help of all three worlds: the lower, the middle, the upper; and the universe listened, and the first stars of the night brightened, giving love and guidance.

Going down a steep *barranca* through the trees and boulders, the two boys dropped into the little, flat, green basin. It was dark now, and they needed to move carefully, and not leave any signs of having passed through. There was grass in the open places and leaves and broken branches under the huge, tall trees. Then, they heard a sound. They froze, not moving a muscle, and glanced around, wild-animal style—meaning that they glanced around only with their eyes, not moving their heads or bodies.

Two eyes were watching them, from over there between two mighty trees. But they couldn't quite make out what the two eyes were, until they saw the flicker of the ears; then, instantly, they knew that it was a deer. In fact, they could now make out that it was a doe and her fawn. The fawn was bedded down in front of her mother. Juan smiled. For he well-knew who this doe was; it was his very own mother who'd come in the form of a deer-soul to protect him, and she'd brought along an angel in the form of a fawn.

"*Mira, mira,*" said Pelon, blowing out with relief. "It's my mother!"

"No, mine!" said Juan.

"All right, both of ours," said Pelon, laughing. "Good God, at first I'd thought that maybe it was a jaguar, or maybe even a soldier. You know, if the colonel was smart," continued Pelon, "he would leave a group of soldiers behind to keep track of their trails. That's what I'll do when I join Villa."

"You're going to join Villa?" asked Juan.

"Of course. It's that, or continue to stay up here all alone in these God-forsaken mountains until they hunt each of us down. It's not going to stop, you know, with us killing the colonel. They'll be sending others."

"What?" said Juan. He'd assumed that once they'd gotten rid of *el coronel* it would all be over. "Then why are we even bothering to do this?" he asked.

"Because, because, the bastard—HE DESERVES TO DIE!" screamed Pelon, his eyes suddenly flooding with rage and *loco*-madness.

And just then, as Pelon spoke, the doe leaped, looking behind herself, then she was off in large, graceful bounds, and her fawn was right after her in small, tight prancing leaps. Both boys crouched down, holding deadly still. They didn't know if Pelon's scream had startled the doe, or if she'd heard something behind herself. They were terrified once again.

Pelon signaled Juan to follow him, and they moved quietly along the ground, their little hearts beating wildly. Crawling into the brush, they lay down, chests pounding against the good earth. Juan drew close to Pelon's right ear. "Look, maybe we shouldn't bury you right now," he said in a whisper. "I think that maybe we should wait until daybreak, when we can see better. That doe was really frightened."

"Maybe it was just because I raised my voice," said Pelon.

"Maybe," said Juan, "but maybe not. I think we should wait and see."

"I don't know," whispered Pelon. "They've been coming by here pretty early."

"Yes, but what if the situation doesn't look right in the morning? Once you're buried, Pelon, that's it; we can't just uncover you. I think we better wait until daylight so we can see, then I can bury you carefully and fix up the area so it doesn't look like anybody has been here. Or we might decide not to bury you and leave to come back another day."

Pelon glanced around, remembering how that Indian had caught him. "All right," he said, "I trust your judgment, Juan, but I just hope he doesn't come by too early and catch us sleeping."

"He won't," said Juan. "Remember, he's going to eat and drink a lot tonight, so he'll fart big and loud for us tomorrow!"

Both boys laughed quietly, trying hard to keep their voices down. They still didn't know what had startled the doe, so they were wary.

"You know," said Juan, glancing up at the star-studded heavens, "I think we should maybe pray."

"You still pray," asked Pelon, "after all that's happened to our *familias?*"

At first Juan was taken aback by Pelon's question, but then he recovered and said, "Yes, of course, in fact, at home we probably pray more now than ever before."

"That's stupid," said Pelon, spitting on the ground. "After my mother was killed like that, I'll never pray again."

"Pelon, now is the time for you to pray more than ever," said Juan, and he knelt down there in the brush where they were hiding, and began to pray.

Pelon watched him, and overhead the stars continued blinking, winking, giving wonderment and beauty.

"Come on," said Juan to Pelon, "join me, *amigo.* And don't worry, in the morning, we'll have plenty of time to do what we have to do, and *con el favor de Dios* everything is going to turn out for the sacred good."

"All right," said Pelon. "I hope you're right."

And so reluctantly, Pelon joined Juan, and now both boys were praying together there in the brush. The doe came back down into the grassy meadow and began to graze once again. Whatever had frightened her was gone now. Upon seeing the doe and her fawn return, the boys felt better, safer, and they finished up their prayers, feeling good and confident once again.

"And so *buenas noches,* dear God," said Juan, finishing up with his prayers, "and let us sleep in peace and keep us well throughout the night."

"And help us tomorrow," added Pelon, "that we not fail, for we are pure of heart and only wish to protect our homes and families."

Making the sign of the cross over themselves, the two boys came out from the brush and stood up in the clearing by the doe and her little fawn. It was a magnificent night, filled with thousands of bright stars and not a single cloud. The doe and her fawn watched the two small boys coming their way, but they didn't bolt. The two animals seemed very much at peace once again, also.

"I wonder," said Juan, "if animals pray, too. Look how relaxed and happy they are now."

"Animals don't pray," said Pelon, laughing. "What are you, *loco?*"

"No," said Juan, "my mother has always told us that praying calms the heart; and look how peaceful those deer are now, so maybe they do pray in their own way, too."

Pelon glanced at the deer and then back at Juan. "Tell me," he said, "did your mother really bring in the heavens and angels to tame those dogs that day?" Pelon hadn't been there the day that his mother was mauled to death by the dogs. "You know, everyone is beginning to say that your mother is really the true witch of our entire valley."

"My mother is no *bruja!*" snapped Juan. Oh, he didn't want people coming and tying his mother to a cross and burning her, as they'd done to Jose-Luis's mother.

"Look, I didn't mean to offend you," said Pelon. "It's just that, well, she brought your brother back from the dead, and she's done so many other things that, well, people talk."

"Look," said Juan, "my mother isn't a *bruja* any more than your own mother was! Damnit, we've all seen our mothers make miracles!"

"Don't call the memory of my mother a witch!" yelled Pelon.

"Well, then, don't call mine one, either!"

Pelon calmed down. "All right," he said, "my mother did do wonders, too, so I won't call your mother, well, a *bruja* anymore."

"Good," said Juan.

Pelon took a big, deep breath, glancing up at the heavens. "Just look up at all those stars. I guess we really are lucky, eh, to have so much beauty above us every night."

"Yes, we are," said Juan, rubbing his eyes. "I'm tired. I think we better find a place to bed down for the night so we can go to sleep. Look, the little fawn is coming over to smell us," added Juan, smiling and putting his hand out to the little deer.

Coming up close, the cute little fawn cautiously stretched out her neck, sniffing Juan's fingertips.

"You know, I bet animals really do pray," said Juan. "That's how they're able to live surrounded by lions and all these other dangers, but, still, live in such peace and happiness."

"Maybe you're right," said Pelon, feeling that no deer would come this close to a real witch's son, because wild animals—it was well-known—could see what lurked inside a human's heart. "Come on, I'm tired, too. Let's go over to that huge tree by the fallen log where the colonel does his *caca* and find a place to sleep."

"Good," said Juan, getting to his feet slowly. He didn't want to startle the little deer. "Let's go."

Both boys now went over to the huge tree by the fallen log where the colonel had been relieving himself the last few times he'd come up the mountain. They got down between the thick, bare roots of the tree that some pigs had uprooted, creating a little hollow. They wanted to get under the roots and down in the leaves, so that they'd be out of the wind and cold and could get a good night's rest.

The fawn, who'd been watching them, saw them disappear into the hollow and came over to see what had happened to them. The doe followed her fawn and saw that the two boys were bedding down to go to sleep. The doe took up ground, standing over the boys and her fawn like a sentry.

Juan remembered opening his eyes once and seeing the mother deer standing over them, and he just knew that his mother had come to protect them in the form of a mother deer.

High overhead, the stars were blinking, winking, by the thousands, and the Mother Moon gave her magic light, too. It had been another good day, and now it was becoming a good night. No, there were no witches or other evils on the other side; no, there was only the fear and jealousy that people carried in their hearts and souls. His mother, Doña Margarita, was just a powerful woman. And when people feared power, they called it the Devil, and when they loved it, they called it God. But it was all really just love, and nothing but love!

"Buenas noches," said Juan to the miracle of the heavens, as he burrowed under the leaves. "And thank you, Mama," he said to the mother deer.

And both boys now breathed in the breath of God and went to sleep, feeling good and safe and all at peace. They both dreamed of green meadows and happy deer.

The two boys were fast asleep when they first heard the snorts of the colonel's horses coming up the steep grade. Quickly, they opened their eyes, not knowing what to do. Oh, my God, they'd been caught with their pants down. And now they couldn't just jump up and take off running, or they'd be spotted and shot down for sure.

They glanced at each other with huge, frightened eyes, then they raised themselves up—just their heads as much as they dared—and looked between the displaced tree roots, and saw that over a hundred soldiers were already in the basin. Some were off their horses and putting them to graze. Others were taking their mounts down to the water to drink. Then, they heard the colonel's big, powerful voice directly behind them.

"Take my horse!" shouted *el coronel,* belching loudly. He sounded like a man with a bad stomach. "Over there to the water! Get the hell away from me!" he bellowed.

He sounded so sick that they almost laughed, but didn't. They could hear a soldier getting hold of the colonel's horse and quickly leading him off, coming so close to them that they could see both horses' hooves passing by as they looked from under the big roots of the huge tree. Then, here came the colonel himself, and he was passing by them even closer, step by step, his tall, black leather boots glistening in the early morning light. He was grabbing tree branches as he passed, causing leaves to fall, and belching with every step. Oh, he was in terrible shape. They could smell a sour-evil odor coming off of him.

Juan and Pelon glanced at each other, and if they hadn't been so terrified, they truly would've burst out laughing. For this was exactly what they'd wanted. They couldn't have asked for anything more. Then, there was the colonel, only fifteen feet away from them, unbuckling his gunbelt and dropping his pants. He turned away from them and barely got his big white ass over the fallen log before he began to shit with an enormous explosion of huge *pedo*-farts.

Quickly, Pelon reached under himself, bringing up the rifle, which was still wrapped in the *serape.* He tried to unwrap the weapon as quickly and quietly as he could, but he was having trouble working within the small confines of the little hollow.

Juan kept glancing at the colonel, praying to God. "Oh, please dear God," he said to himself, "let him be so full of farts and *caca* that he doesn't stop shitting and hears us!"

But they had no such worries; the big man kept farting and farting and shitting. Finally, Pelon had the weapon uncovered, but it was pointing in the wrong direction. Quickly, he tried turning it around, hitting Juan in the face with the barrel.

Seeing the huge barrel of the homemade *retrocarga*, Juan blurted out, "That's it? That's our weapon?"

"Quiet!" whispered Pelon under his breath, as he shoved the huge weapon between the roots, pointing it at the colonel's backside.

"But it won't shoot!" said Juan. "It's older than Christ Himself! I thought we had a real rifle!"

But Pelon wasn't paying any attention to Juan, and he now cocked back the two big old hammers and spoke aloud. *"¡Coronel!"* he said in a clear, good voice. "I'm the little brother of two of the men that you cut, and the son of the woman your dogs mauled. I'm going to piss on your eyes after I kill you! May you burn in hell for all eternity!"

And, as the colonel turned to see who had the audacity to come up behind him as he relieved himself, Pelon stopped his words and pulled both triggers. But nothing happened; the hammers just didn't move.

Instantly, the colonel saw the situation: two little boys with an old *retrocarga* from the days of Benito Juarez, hunched down under a bunch of big tree roots, trying to kill him. Quick as a cat, he pulled up his pants, smearing shit all over himself, and reached for his gunbelt. But at that very instant, Juan hit the two hammers with a stone. And the old weapon EXPLODED, pipe-barrel splitting in two and a fountain of rock and used-little-pieces-of-iron went shooting towards the colonel. The two boys were thrown back with the stock of the weapon, smashing Pelon against the dirt across the hollow. The colonel was thrown over backwards across the log. Instantly, his men were shouting and taking cover, returning fire.

Crawling out of the hollow with blood coming from his nose, Juan was up and trying to clear his head so they could take off running. But what he saw Pelon do next was something he'd never forget as long as he lived. His boyhood friend didn't run. No; he cleared his head and ran over to the colonel, who was squirming about in terrible pain, took the colonel's gun from his gunbelt and emptied the pistol into his naked, bloated belly, as the soldiers' bullets sang all around Pelon's head. But not once did he ever give the bullets any importance. Only when he saw that the great bad man was dead, dead, did Pelon then throw down the gun and come running toward Juan. Then they were off like deer, running down through the brush and trees, as the soldiers continued shooting at them.

"I killed him!" yelled Pelon, as they ran. "I killed him and he looked me in the eyes and knew who I was before he died! Oh, it was WONDERFUL to see his fear! May he burn in hell FOR-EVER!"

Some of the soldiers got on their horses and tried to give chase, but the two boys knew these mountains like the back of their hands and cut through the breaks, leaping from boulder to boulder, leaving the armed men far behind. Finally they were down in the deep canyons where the wild orchids grew, and they were going to start back up the mountainside through a little *arroyo* when they came upon the doe and her little fawn once again. The deer had been bedded down.

"Wait," said Juan. "Maybe this is a good place for us to hole up for the day. We don't want to get up on top and run into the soldiers or someone who might turn us in to them."

"Who'd turn us in?" asked Pelon. He was so excited that he was ready to pop. "I killed him! I killed him! Oh, my God, it was wonderful! Seeing him squirm around, I put a bullet into his fat belly for every one of my brothers! We did it, Juan! We really did it!"

"Yes, we did. But now we got to keep calm so we don't get killed, too. Come, let's get up on that ridge and bed down like the deer and keep very quiet till night time."

And they'd no more than hidden themselves, when here came five soldiers down in the bottom of the canyon with an old *indio* leading them afoot. The two boys held their breath, watching them pass by down below in the trees. Once, the Indian stopped and glanced up in their direction, but then he just went on down the canyon bottom, leading the soldiers away.

"Did you see how *el indio* looked up towards us?" asked Pelon.

"Yes," said Juan. "He knows we're up here. We better go before they circle above us and come in from behind."

"But he might not turn us in," said Pelon.

"In the hunt, the she-fox never leaves anything to chance. Let's go!"

The two boys took off up the ridge as fast as they could go, startling the doe and her fawn, who'd bedded down above them once again.

"You better run, too!" said Juan to the deer as they went racing by them.

But the deer didn't run with them; instead, they went downhill. Juan and Pelon were just coming off the top of the ridge when they heard the shooting down below.

Juan stopped. "They shot the deer!" he said, all upset.

"How do you know?" asked Pelon.

"I just know," said Juan, gripping his heart and tears bursting to his eyes. "I've got to get home!" And saying this, he took off racing for home as fast as he could go. He had to see if his beloved, dear old mother was all right or not. Good God, those two deer had given their lives for him and Pelon.

"**M**ama! Mama!" Juan was yelling as he and Pelon came racing into their burned-out settlement that morning. "The colonel is dead! The colonel is dead!"

"What?" said Jose-Luis, sitting by a little fire oven that he'd built to cook bread. His mother, Josefina, had taught him how to bake. Having been raised by a single woman, he'd come to learn many things that most men didn't know.

"Is my mama all right?" begged Juan desperately. He was all out of breath. He and Pelon had run the whole way back up the mountain. All the way, Juan had been half out of his mind, thinking that in killing those two deer, maybe the soldiers had killed his own mother.

"No, she isn't," said Luisa, coming in from the other room. "She was up all night sick with worry for you, and then she started gagging like death just a little while ago."

Then, there came Juan's mother. She'd been down at the outhouse.

"Oh, Mama! Mama!" said Juan, rushing up and hugging her. "I'm so sorry I worried you, but, well—" He stopped his words.

"What were you yelling about *el coronel* when you first came running in?" asked the old woman.

Juan swallowed. So his mother had heard him. "He's dead!" said Juan, tears of relief suddenly bursting forth from his eyes. "He's dead, Mama, and he can't bring us any more harm!"

"You saw this with your own two eyes," said Jose-Luis, completely astonished, "that this colonel himself is really dead?"

"Yes," said Pelon, "Juan and I killed him."

"Well, not really," said Juan. "We shot him together with an old *retrocarga,* but then it was Pelon who took the colonel's gun out of his own holster and emptied all the bullets into his fat belly, and I then saw his legs kicking in death—like when we butcher a pig or steer—as we both turned to run!"

"Oh, my God, *Dios mío!*" said Doña Margarita, making the sign of the cross over herself. "You two killed the colonel?! You two killed him?! But how dare you risk your lives doing that and endangering your IMMORTAL SOULS!"

And in a flash, she had Juan by the ear and twisted him down to the ground and was spanking him. "You will not go around killing people without my permission! And endangering yourself!"

Everyone was shocked. Juan was yelping in pain. Pelon was all eyes, and he started backing up so he could run.

"Oh, no, you don't!" she yelled at Pelon. "You stay here! Your mother was my friend, and she would not permit you to turn into a killer! Grab him, Jose-Luis! The boy needs to be cleansed and made pure once again!"

"But I'm a man now! *¡Un macho!*" yelled Pelon. "No one tells me what to do anymore!"

"You are a child!" yelled Doña Margarita. "A man-child with the thickest hair ever seen at birth, and that's why you've been called Pelon—'bald-headed'—all these years! You stay and get cleansed, or I'll spank you, too! We love you, and we will not permit you to become an irresponsible *hombre* because you did a little stupid killing!

"Didn't you see how sick the colonel was? A few more weeks and he would've died by himself!

"What do you think happens to all these *hombres* and their great plans who have tried to impose their empires on us for thousands of years? In the end, they all kill themselves off; and we, *la gente de la tierra*, just keep going and going as we have for untold hundreds of thousands of years!

"Do you really think that these Europeans are anything new to us? Our own people have gotten confused with the stars before, forgetting to root themselves with daily love to the Mother Earth, and have been just as bad to us as these recent arrivals from across the sea, or worse!

"You will cleanse yourself, Pelonisto, and you will honor your mother, who chose to give her life in order to make our earth Holy with her blood; and you will do it now or, I swear, I'll twist off your ear and spank you so hard that you'll be wearing diapers again!"

Pelon began to cry, becoming a little boy once again. And as he came forward to be hugged and loved by Doña Margarita, he un-aged twenty years before their very eyes.

"Oh, *Dios mío!*" said Luisa, making the sign of the cross over herself, too. "Blessed be this SACRED DAY!"

Jose-Luis started laughing as he watched the two little warriors crying and hugging the old woman, who now seemed totally well herself. "*¡Qué desmadre a todo dar!*" he said. "The colonel's worst dream came true! Fearing every Indian boy was out to kill him, and two little *indios* finally did!" And the huge, powerful man roared with *carcajadas.* "Oh, life, *la vida,* is beautiful, I tell you! Beautiful! There really are no evils here or on the other side, except for those that men carry in their own hearts and souls! And this poor damned fool colonel carried more than any *cabrón* I know!

"Congratulations!" said Jose-Luis, putting out his huge, ham-like hand to Pelon and Juan. "You two are warriors among warriors, kings among kings; but now you two do as the women tell you, or I'll spank you myself, damnit! For they're absolutely right; in killing an enemy, we don't want to lose our immortal souls!" he added, making the sign of the cross over himself. "No, in killing our enemy, we want to dance! To dance with a wild abandonment and love of life, *la vida!* Come on," he said, "let us dance, dance, dance—women and our two little *gran hombrecitos!*"

And so they began to dance, to laugh, to rejoice, and the heavens opened and the earth parted like a ripe woman, and all the universe smiled and sang with them. And all was well—who had the eyes to see and the ears to hear: life was, indeed, a living miracle, a dance up the wild steps of heaven!

AFTERWORD

The next day my father, Juan Salvador Villaseñor, and his mother and sisters and Jose-Luis, sent word for my grandfather Don Juan to accompany them, for they had to leave quickly before the colonel's men came back in force to avenge his death. But no one was able to locate Don Juan. People said that Don Juan had gone mad and had killed a burro, calling the animal Four White Stockings and saying that it was all the stallion's fault that his whole world had been destroyed.

My father told me that leaving the mountain of *El Cerro Grande* was one of the most difficult things he had to do in all his life. For the land had been made sacred with their blood and dreams, hopes and love, and no person could live for long on earth on land that wasn't sacred. He said that they each took a pinch of earth, and they spoke to the wind, the breath of God, and they ground their naked feet into the Mother Earth. They cried and cried, swearing to return once it was safe to do so.

My father told me that it was a beautiful clear day the morning they came off the mountain headed for the town of Fat Rock, where Don Pio's young widow had a little grocery store. They figured to stay with Herlinda for a few weeks until it was safe for them to travel north to the United States.

The first night out my father told me that his mother and Jose-Luis got branches and swept the ground clean of snakes and spiders and they made a little fire. They didn't have much to eat, my father told me, and they couldn't stop crying until they began telling stories to each other. Juan got to tell his story of the serpent and Chivo, when he'd tried to catch the ducks, and they laughed and laughed. Jose-Luis told the story of how he'd smuggled the supplies up the mountain and how sitting out the day in hiding could drive a man crazy-*loco*. Luisa and Emilia both told their stories, too. Then their mother closed her eyes and spoke and she wove all of their stories—including her own—into a tapestry of wonderful color, showing each of them how they had done the work of God by having survived another day. They finally went to sleep that night, my father told me, feeling good and blessed and strong and heroic, knowing that the stars above loved them and Mother Earth loved them, too.

Two months later, Jose-Luis was killed at the dinner table as they ate in the back of the little grocery store at Fat Rock by two stupid little greedy soldiers. It took all of Luisa's cunning and great powers to find a new husband to help them go north, especially since she was big with child.

Almost one year it took them to reach the Texas border, going through such hardship and starvation that what they'd experienced up in Los Altos had almost been easy. But not once did they think of giving up. Each night my grandmother told them stories of love and life, and assured my father that one day he'd find his own true love, as she had found with his father, and Jose had found with Mariposa. For learning how to love was why God had put us on earth. And my father told me that he believed my grandmother, Doña Margarita; the powers of the heavens and the earth were within her, and they were *familia*.

Victor E. Villaseñor
Rancho Villaseñor
Oceanside, CA

VICTOR VILLASEÑOR
LECTURE PRESENTATION

Victor Villaseñor shares with audiences all across
America his passion for life and his vision for
world harmony. His topics of family, pride and
global peace are told through personal stories
filled with emotion, humor and total abandon!
For current information regarding his presenta-
tion schedule or group workshops, you may contact: Victor Villaseñor, Lecture Presentations,
1302 Stewart Street, Oceanside, CA 92054.